PATHWAYS
to
CHANGE

Case Studies
of
Strategic Negotiations

Joel Cutcher-Gershenfeld
Robert B. McKersie
Richard E. Walton

*HD
6508
.C86
1995*

1995

W.E. UPJOHN INSTITUTE FOR EMPLOYMENT RESEARCH
Kalamazoo, Michigan

Library of Congress Cataloging-in-Publication Data

Cutcher-Gershenfeld, Joel.
  Pathways to change : case studies of strategic negotiations / Joel
Cutcher-Gershenfeld, Robert B. McKersie, Richard E. Walton.
    p. cm.
  Includes bibliographical references and index.
  ISBN 0–88099–156–9 (cloth : alk. paper). — ISBN 0–88099–155–0
(pbk. : alk. paper)
  1. Collective bargaining—United States—Case studies.
  2. Negotiation in business—United States—Case studies.
  I. McKersie, Robert B. II. Walton, Richard E. III. Title.
HD6508.C86 1995
331.89'0973—dc20   95-39190
                                                         CIP

The facts presented in this study and the observations and viewpoints expressed are the sole responsibility of the authors. They do not necessarily represent positions of the W. E. Upjohn Institute for Employment Research.

Cover design by J. R. Underhill
Index prepared by Shirley Kessel.
Printed in the United States of America.

This book is dedicated to Susan, Nancy, and Sharon—without whom we would have had neither the desire nor the capability to travel along the many pathways to change.

ACKNOWLEDGMENTS

We would like to give special thanks to all who have played central roles in the journey thus far. First, this project was initiated with funding from the W.E. Upjohn Institute for Employment Research and further supported by our respective institutions: Michigan State University, School of Labor and Industrial Relations; Massachusetts Institute of Technology, Sloan School; and Harvard Business School, Division of Research. We deeply appreciate the time and thoughts of the union and management leaders from the twelve sites highlighted in this book. We are also deeply appreciative of the many colleagues and practitioners who served as a sounding board—either through reading early drafts of our earlier *Strategic Negotiations* manuscript or through participation in presentations of these ideas. We want to particularly highlight the Ph.D. students at MSU, MIT, and HBS who graciously commented on our work in the context of graduate seminars and the participants in presentations to the MIT Industrial Relations Workshop, the Steel Industry Human Resources Network, the UAW/Ford Sterling Plant, the City of Winnipeg, the Work Practices Diffusion Team at MSU, and the Work In America Institute. Annette Bacon (at MSU), Michelle Kamin and Cherie Potts (at MIT), and Margo McCool (at Harvard) all processed words, faxes, and overnight packages with cheerful enthusiasm. Rod Bloedow, Chip Hunter, and Amy Andrews all provided valuable research assistance. Finally, Kathleen Rudd Scharf and Patrick McHugh played especially critical roles in the research and drafting of the cases in the paper and auto supply industries, respectively. For all this assistance we are most grateful.

PREFACE

Over six years ago we approached the W.E. Upjohn Institute for Employment Research with a simple proposal. We wanted to examine a series of cooperative and contentious labor negotiations to better understand negotiations at the extremes. Much has happened since then.

First, it became clear to us that the "extremes" were becoming the norm. The highly cooperative and highly contentious negotiations were increasingly common, while the traditional, arm's-length interactions were becoming the exception. As a result, we now see this study as speaking to the mainstream of labor-management relations.

Second, in examining these highly contrasting cases, we found ourselves building on and extending the *Behavioral Theory of Labor Negotiations,* written by Walton and McKersie in 1965. We came to see the behavioral theory as a useful framework for understanding bargaining processes. We added to the theory new thoughts about the ways that strategy and structure interact with process. Together, these insights allowed us to develop a theory of negotiated change in labor-management relations, which is presented in the book, *Strategic Negotiations: A Theory of Change in Labor-Management Relations,* published by the Harvard Business School Press (1994).

In *Strategic Negotiations,* we developed structured analysis based on a series of case studies cutting across three industries. This book features detailed presentations for twelve of the thirteen case studies of cooperative and contentious negotiations analyzed in *Strategic Negotiations.* Thus, some of the individual quotes and vignettes presented in the theory of negotiated change are now presented here in the context of the full case studies. In *Strategic Negotiations* we also explored practical implications of the theory. In this book we build on those practical implications in order to offer additional tools and guidance for strategic negotiators traveling along various pathways to change.

This book should be a valuable companion and resource for readers interested in learning more about the cases upon which the *Strategic Negotiations* thesis was developed. To the extent possible, the cases have been updated to capture the longer-term consequences of the strategies that we first encountered in our field work during the late 1980s and early 1990s.

Overview

The introductory chapter of this book addresses the threshold issue, "why change?" We conclude that major change is an almost inevitable objective for parties in traditional relationships who are wrestling with contentious issues at the same time that their common interests are growing. Further, we find that major change requires negotiations. To set the stage for presenting case studies of negotiated change, we draw on two key concepts from *Strategic Negotiations*: (1) the contrasting strategies of forcing and fostering change, and (2) the juxtaposition of substantive and relationship outcomes.

The following four chapters of the book feature our case studies. The cases are organized around distinct change strategies. Chapter 2 features three cases involving forcing strategies, while chapter 3 features three cases involving fostering strategies. Chapters 4 and 5 also have three cases each, focusing first on the sequence of forcing followed by fostering and then on concurrent forcing and fostering. At the conclusion of each of the twelve cases, we highlight salient lessons.

The final two chapters summarize lessons that extend across the cases. Chapter 6 presents general lessons about the context for negotiations over change, while chapter 7 highlights specific tools and techniques to guide the strategic negotiator.

This book completes the first cycle of work in developing a theory of negotiated change and presenting supporting materials. Yet, in many ways, the concluding thoughts to this book represent the beginning of the next round of analysis. We see the principles of strategic negotiations as generalizable to other contexts where change is the agenda. These include change initiatives in nonunion settings, as well as negotiated change in the context of strategic alliances, joint ventures, cross-functional integration initiatives, and customer-supplier relations.

Like any major research undertaking, we find that our research perspective and agenda have changed as a result of the journey we have taken. We have just begun to grasp the potential for undertaking the change process from the vantage of strategic negotiations. In presenting the theory of negotiated change in *Strategic Negotiations,* combined with the detailed cases and guidance for practitioners contained in this book, we are inviting our colleagues and strategic negotiators to join us in this new journey.

CONTENTS

PATHWAYS
to
CHANGE

Case Studies
of
Strategic Negotiations

1
Why Change?

Change is on the agenda. At negotiating tables around the world, parties are bargaining over fundamental changes. Sometimes the focus is on substantive changes—revisions in existing contracts, agreements, or understandings. Sometimes the focus is on changes in relationships—ranging from the building of more cooperative relationships to changes that threaten the other party's legitimacy and even its very existence. In most cases, changes in substantive terms and changes in relationships are concurrently on the agenda.

Why negotiate over change? Why not act unilaterally? Parties often do. Other stakeholders, however, are usually prompted to respond. At that point, negotiations—tacit or explicit—are under way. Viewed through a negotiations lens, unilateral action and reaction represent early moves in an unfolding, back-and-forth process. The process may involve escalation and collapse on the part of one or both parties. The process may involve pressure and capitulation. The process may even involve dialogue and increased understanding—reflected in joint decisions and mutual agreements. Whether or not it intends to negotiate, a party taking unilateral action to drive change that affects others as well will almost inevitably find itself on a path of negotiated change.

Why negotiate over change? Why not act on the basis of consensus? Parties often do. Rarely, however, is the consensus complete. Subtle and even glaring differences usually emerge. At that point, negotiations—tacit or explicit—are under way. Viewed through a negotiations lens, the cooperative overture is an early move in an unfolding, back-and-forth process. The process may be punctuated by the emergence of unexpected, divisive issues between the parties. And the process may surface splits within one or both parties. The process may even involve dialogue and understanding—reflected in joint decisions and mutual agreements. Whether or not the initiating party explicitly planned to negotiate, the party seeking to act on the basis of consensus and teamwork will inevitably find itself on a path of negotiated change.

Thus, where change is on the agenda, negotiations are certain to follow. This is because change involves both initiating and responding parties. Whether the initiating party is acting unilaterally or inviting cooperation, change seldom looks the same to the initiating party and to the recipient. It is the interaction between their two perspectives that places parties on various pathways of negotiated change.

This book focuses on two contrasting change strategies—forcing change and fostering change. It features a close look at a wide range of highly cooperative and highly contentious change initiatives—both of which are pathways of change that build on the strategies. Studying the back-and-forth dynamics in these cases has revealed useful insights into why change initiatives succeed or fail.

Why Study Labor-Management Negotiations?

Our particular focus is on change initiatives in the workplace. Further, we have only studied unionized workplaces. These collective bargaining relationships are important to study. They account for almost one-sixth of U.S. employment, and their influence on the U.S. and even the world economy is substantial—in both economic and social terms. Also, studying cooperative and contentious initiatives in the context of these formal, bilateral relationships has provided a rich terrain for surfacing new ideas and insights into the fundamental nature of negotiated change.

As background, it is important to understand that negotiations represent important events in labor-management relations. They present defining moments at which parties develop or revise the terms and conditions of employment. Further, it is important to recognize that, even between rounds of formal contract bargaining, negotiations over grievances and other aspects of contract administration also involve critical decisions—made either by the parties or by labor arbitrators.

During certain eras in U.S. history, negotiations occurring within the time frames of contract bargaining and contract administration have assumed great historical significance. Not only were the negotiations important events for the parties during these eras, they were also key indicators and powerful influences on social relations more generally.

For example, during the 1930s, conflicts over the representational claims of industrial unions reflected not just narrow economic struggles, but a broader set of issues involving societal adjustments to the implications of mass production industries. Similarly, negotiations over health care, pension, and other fringe benefits in the 1950s and 1960s reinforced the U.S. public policy emphasis of an employer-centered approach to extending various social benefits (in contrast to many other industrialized nations). The implications of these choices are particularly evident in current debates over health care reform and social security.

A core thesis of this book is that we are once again in an era where labor negotiations have broad social ramifications. The give and take between labor and management in the present era—in collective bargaining, grievance procedures, labor-management committees, and around various forms of worker participation—reflects a broad social process of adjustment to international competition and technological change. In studying the interactions of unions, employers, and employees in this era, we find vivid and instructive illustrations of alternative pathways to change.

Why Focus on Cooperative and Conflictual Extremes?

There are still labor-management relationships where changes take place on an incremental basis through routine, arm's-length negotiations. Recent evidence suggests, however, that these types of negotiations are in the minority. Based on one sample of collective bargaining relationships, for example, they may only account for approximately a third of labor-management negotiations—with fully two-thirds of collective bargaining tending toward the extremes (Walton, Cutcher-Gershenfeld, and McKersie 1994, pp. 31ff). Although comparable data from earlier time periods are not available, there is enough circumstantial evidence to suggest that a pattern of many relationships falling at the extremes is a recent phenomenon. To make the point differently, a majority of unions and employers find themselves negotiating on new terrain, where traditional actions can generate unexpected results. This book is targeted for leaders at all levels who find themselves engaged in these strategic negotiations. We hope to offer useful insights and guidance.

Also, when negotiations tend toward either cooperative or conflictual extremes, key elements òf the process are thrown into sharp relief. As such, we are better able to articulate general lessons about the process of negotiated change. Many of these lessons have potential applicability far beyond union-management relationships—with implications for employment relations in nonunion settings and for parties seeking change in the context of joint ventures, strategic partnerships, cross-functional integration, and customer-supplier relations.

Guiding Principles and Frameworks

Three main guiding principles or frameworks will be helpful to readers of this book. First, we make a core assumption about employment relationships—specifically, the mixed-motive nature of employment relations. Second, we utilize a particular framework for classifying change strategies into forcing and fostering, with a third strategy, escape, as a backdrop to the two primary strategies. Third, we make a key distinction around outcomes—focusing both on substantive and relationship dimensions. These guiding ideas all build on the analysis contained in *Strategic Negotiations: A Theory of Change in Labor-Management Relationships.*

A Mixture of Common and Competing Interests

We refer to labor-management relationships as "mixed-motive," reflecting the mixture of common and competing motives that parties bring to the employment relationship.[1] While the mixture of common and competing interests is most salient between labor and management representatives, there are typically multiple stakeholders with distinct concerns within labor (for example, skilled trades versus production employees) and within management (for example, line versus staff support). As well, other stakeholders (such as external customers and government) bring a mixture of common and competing interests to their interactions with labor and management.

All of our cases involve negotiations over fundamental (or potentially fundamental) changes. The first lesson that emerges from these detailed cases stems from the mixed motive assumption. We find that, for a change process to have any chance of success, negotiations must attend to both the resolution of conflict and the pursuit of common interests. The point may seem obvious, but too many practitioners and theorists downplay or ignore the need for articulation and even synthesis of these distinct elements.

The potential for labor-management relations to involve bitter, intractable conflicts is well established. In the decades of the 1980s and 1990s the experiences at A. E. Staley, Phelps-Dodge, Pittston Mines, Greyhound Bus Lines, Caterpillar, and the New York Daily News—to mention a few examples—provide ample evidence of the conflictual nature of labor-management relations. For this study, we selected several cases that typify pathways involving bitter, seemingly intractable conflicts. For example, the strikes at the International Paper mill in Jay, Maine, and at the AP Parts plant in Toledo, Ohio were both highly contentious and widely perceived as almost unavoidable, given the conflicting interests at play.

A close look at these conflictual cases, however, reveals specific points at which the negotiations changed sharply and where the various tactics employed hampered efforts to repair relations. For example, the hiring of permanent replacement workers in the Jay, Maine case marked a sharp deterioration in relations, complicated relations after the strike, and ultimately set the stage for the decertification of the union.

In contrast, other cases we selected also involved bitter strikes, but the story line evolved along a very different path. Though these cases looked just as contentious at the outset, actions taken (or avoided) during and after the strikes facilitated the restoration of constructive relations. For example, in Boise Cascade's DeRidder, Louisiana paper mill, the company forced deep concessions around work rules but did not press its advantage around wage concessions. This restraint proved instrumental to the subsequent repair of relations after the strike. Similarly, the union at Adrian Fabricators helped temper hard feelings after an acrimonious strike by using its own funds to repair broken factory windows and other physical damage incurred during the strike.

The potential for labor-management relations to be centered on cooperation and partnership is also well established historically. During the 1980s, considerable attention was paid to the key role of labor-management cooperation in the competitive resurgence at Xerox (Cutcher-Gershenfeld 1988). Similarly, the partnership structure at Saturn broke sharply with traditional adversarial and hierarchical structures (Kochan, Rubenstein, and Bennett 1994). The interest in these cases reflects a broader awareness on the parts of labor and management regarding the mutual benefits if ways can be found to increase the size of the proverbial economic pie.

We have selected several cases in this vein because they also feature initiatives designed to encourage joint planning and mutually beneficial implementation of fundamental change. A close look at these pathways reveals a complex portrait of cooperative initiatives. For example, labor and management at Packard Electric worked together to promote flexible job assignments and cost savings in the context of a lifetime job security guarantee, a multitier wage system, and an increased management capacity to utilize temporary workers. In retrospect, the Packard Electric story may seem well planned and rooted in extensive labor-management cooperation. In fact, a closer look at the case reveals several interesting features: a major internal conflict within the union, a hard confrontation by the union with management over job security, and continuing contention over the use of temporary workers. Thus, the path-breaking cooperative achievements rested on a foundation of complex, difficult, and constantly unfolding interactions—many of them conflictual.

At CSX, the parties attempted to develop a collaborative structure to address common concerns. Despite the clear advantages of working together and coordinating efforts, the decision of one key union to withdraw from the joint effort highlighted the many areas of conflict that remained between labor and management in the system.

While each case is unique, the contrasting experiences with various tactics suggest that the individual choices of unions and employers matter a great deal along these various pathways to change. Choices in negotiations sometimes led to the collapse of relations and at other times set the stage for the repair of relations. Similarly, our cases involving joint change initiatives highlight the negotiated nature of cooperation. In some instances hard confrontations were instrumental in moving in a cooperative direction, while a breakdown in internal negotiations within a party could substantially reduce the scope of a joint, cooperative initiative.

Thus, the cases illustrate: (1) that change processes are characterized by stakeholders with both common and conflicting interests, (2) that pursuit of common interests *and* the resolution of conflicts are negotiated processes, and (3) that choice of strategies and tactics in these negotiations are central to the success of the change process.

The Distinct Strategies of Forcing and Fostering

During periods of stability, bargaining outcomes are primarily shaped by tactical choices and broad external forces such as the cyclical economic swings characteristic of many industries. In the present era, however, we see the emergence of distinct change strategies that become powerful driving forces. These strategies may or may not begin as intentional change efforts, but they are identifiable after a series of patterned interactions.[2]

We will concentrate our attention on the two primary strategies—forcing and fostering—and then various combinations. Escape, a strategy of a very different sort, will also be analyzed. Before outlining the structure of the book, it is instructive to provide some guidance as to the essence of forcing and fostering.

The inherent calculus to accept change differs between the two strategies. Simply put, stakeholders who are on the receiving end of a forcing strategy agree to changes because one side (usually management in the present era) has the power to compel acceptance of the demands. The workers find themselves in an avoidance-avoidance predicament. On the one hand, they want to avoid changes or concessions, but they find themselves in a situation where the alternatives (e.g. strike or plant shutdown) are even more costly.

By contrast, a fostering process operates on the premise that solutions can be found to common problems that leave all sides better situated. However, the expectation that there will be important gains can create difficulties when it comes to the ratification phase, as will be illustrated in one of our cases where leaders of a key union expected a proportionate share of the joint gains, and when this was not forthcoming they voted against the new package.

How do the parties themselves see the differences in these two change strategies? In answering this question, one executive summarized his viewpoint as follows:

> One way to view forcing versus fostering is to distinguish when you want to assume your major risks. Under the forcing approach, your risks are all up-front. Employee attitudes will deteriorate. The politicians will beat up on you. And, if a work stoppage results, you must anticipate suffering and erosion of traffic. However, if meaningful contractual changes are implemented, your cost structure will be lowered and your productivity structure will be improved. A rebuilding process can then begin, and both the company and the employees can begin to reap benefits.
>
> In the fostering approach, your risks will come later. You certainly do not have the type of up-front risks associated with the forcing strategy. However, if the change process does not evolve beyond the talk stage, a few years down the road a company can find itself in a competitively disadvantageous position. This can be especially dangerous if your competitors already have implemented changes.

Clearly, the choice of forcing versus fostering hinges on dramatically different preferences with respect to the desired timetable and the associated risks. Under the forcing approach, management sees some degree of risk, either that the relationship will deteriorate or that the changes may not be forthcoming. On the other hand, the fostering strategy, while it involves less risk, often takes considerably more time and for an extended period may not show any benefits. As we will see in a number of our cases, the parties can improve attitudes but nothing else seems to change.

Thus, the challenge that the parties face when embarking upon the fostering approach is to translate the potential that is present with better attitudes into the realization of real changes in operating practices. Once changes are agreed upon via the fostering approach, then the implementation can be fairly straightforward, since the positive attitudes lead to some measure of joint support for the new arrangements. In fact, in some instances labor and management will establish joint implementation committees to ensure that the spirit and not just the letter of new agreements is observed.

Both the forcing and fostering strategies work with the same two variables of behavior and attitude change, but the emphases are quite different. Simply put, the forcing strategy compels behavioral changes in the short run, hoping that attitudes will not deteriorate too significantly. The presumption is that over the longer run, management will be in a position to attend to these consequences in order to derive the maximum benefit from the behavior changes realized in the short run. By contrast, the fostering approach emphasizes joint processes of problem solving and attitude change that lead to the design of new systems capable of commanding wide acceptance and new behaviors from the various stakeholders.

Organization of the Book

Three cases, which are included in chapter 2, feature strategies that unfold along a path that we have labeled "forcing." In each case, management was the moving party, and change initiatives went far beyond traditional distributive bargaining tactics. In each of the cases, labor matched management's tactics and forged its own forcing response. Sometimes the forcing initiative was part of a fully developed plan. For example, in the Guilford case, the changes sought in work rules were linked with a series of railway purchases and a restructuring of ownership, all of which required considerable planning and preparation. In other cases, the actions of the parties took on increasing intensity as the conflict escalated, leading to an emerging strategy of forced change.

In another three of the cases, which are included in chapter 3, the parties were embarked on a path characterized by what we have termed "fostering" strategies. Again, management was the moving party. Many fostering initiatives evident today are part of larger, explicit change strategies aimed at increased flexibility, improved quality, reduced cost, and enhanced organizational effectiveness. In our three fostering cases, however, the strategy was more emergent and less visible at the outset. For example, the efforts at Bidwell began with a relatively narrow focus on employee involvement, while the efforts at CSX began with a similarly specific focus on a multiunion, labor-management committee. In both cases, the initial tactical moves were cooperative in nature and suggested a larger fostering strategy, but the efforts were circumscribed by dynamics within labor and within management.

The third case—Anderson Pattern—is a robust example where the fostering proceeded without being undercut as it was in the other two cases.

In chapter 4, we present three of the cases containing multiple time periods in which the parties' path involved a sequence of distinct strategies—forcing followed by fostering. In two of the cases, Boise Cascade's DeRidder Mill and Adrian Fabricators, the forcing included a bitter strike. In the third case, Conrail, forcing occurred in the context of a governmental restructuring of the railroad. In all three cases, the initial round of forcing had important consequences for subsequent fostering initiatives.

Finally, in chapter 5 we present three cases that feature a combination of concurrent forcing and fostering strategies, the most complex path in our study. All of the cases featuring combinations of forcing and fostering initiatives are at times sequential in character and at other times truly concurrent. For example, at the Budd Company, forcing around wage concessions occurred concurrent with fostering around employee involvement. Ultimately all of these cases matured to stages of predominant fostering, but each continued to include either episodic distributive confrontations or (in one case) a subsequent forcing initiative.

Embedded in many of our cases is another strategy that has important implications for forcing and fostering, as well as mixed strategies, namely, the strategy of escape. In some of our forcing cases, such as AP Parts, Guilford, and Jay, the intensity of the forcing battle was partly fueled by labor's perception that management aimed to go down the path of escaping from the labor-management relationship. In the Anderson Pattern case, which involved extensive fostering, escape issues were part of the larger context in that most of the unionized pattern-making firms in the community had either gone out of business or experienced a decertification election. In some of the mixed cases, such as Budd and Packard Electric, management moved work out of existing unionized facilities to either southern nonunion plants or to locations in Mexico—which was perceived by labor as a strategy of partial escape from the union-management relationship.

In all of these cases, it is clear that change strategies (whether explicit or implicit) adopted by the parties interact and powerfully influence the course of the negotiations. We find clear evidence that negotiations can be classified distinctly into forcing and fostering strategies, with time periods when there is a mixture of forcing and fostering, as well as a broader context that may include a strategy of escape. The various combinations of these strategies define somewhat (but not completely) predictable paths along which negotiations unfold. We address later the dynamics that can abruptly alter the pathway taken.

*Substantive and Relationship Outcomes—Anticipating
   Unintended Consequences*

There are two broad types of outcomes in labor negotiations (and in most other negotiations). First, there are substantive outcomes. These include agreements (or disagreements) on the terms and conditions of employment, as well as agreements about specific work practices. Second, there are relationship outcomes. These include agreements (or disagreements) about the degree of joint activities, the amount of trust among the parties, and the directions desired for labor-management relations. One clear lesson from the cases is that the destination along these pathways to change includes outcomes that contain both substantive and relationship dimensions. In some cases, management was primarily seeking substantive changes and was not prepared for the degree to which relationship issues were also at stake. For example, a concessionary demand may be seen by management as a purely economic matter, while labor may view the demand as part of the larger strategy to undermine the power and legitimacy of the union.

In other cases, management primarily sought improvements in relationships and was equally unprepared for the degree to which these relationship changes necessarily were linked to substantive changes. For example, management may have initiated a joint labor-management participative process around employee involvement only to discover that continued union and worker support for the initiative depended on substantive issues such as gainsharing and job security. In all cases, labor was faced with the complex task of not only ordering its priorities on substantive matters, but also assessing its priorities around choices of whether to pursue labor-management cooperation or to view management's moves as a threat to the institutional stability of the union.

Since in the United States there is no well-established tradition legit-imatizing social compacts that affirm the status of unions and the legit-imacy of broad strategic business decisions, adding these topics to the negotiations agenda introduces a substantial measure of uncertainty and ambiguity. Not only must the parties sort out their views on mat-ters such as seniority, wages, and job classifications, but they must also assess the underlying values and intentions of each other regarding the institutional relationship itself.

As a result of these relationship issues, when unions responded with a forceful rejection of proposals for rollbacks, management in turn exhibited a reaction that was usually stronger than the union antici-pated. Management was frustrated that the union would not acknowl-edge the legitimacy of the competitive pressures facing the company. The result was often an unanticipated escalation into a protracted con-flict.

Thus, the outcomes of negotiations can be measured against the objectives of both parties, but the negotiations also produce unintended consequences, and these have the potential to overshadow the desired outcomes. These intended and unintended consequences occur with respect to substantive outcomes, as well as the nature of the relation-ship.

Conclusion

This chapter is entitled, "Why Change?"—which is often the first response of a party confronted with a change initiative. Sometimes the question is answered by an attempt to demonstrate that change is in everyone's mutual interest. At other times the question is answered with threats about the consequences of resisting the change. Most com-plicated of all, there are times when threats and mutual interests become interwoven.

We have seen in this chapter that whatever answer is provided, plac-ing change on the agenda initiates a negotiation process. To help understand this process, a set of guiding principles and frameworks has been highlighted. These ideas set the stage for the presentation and interpretation of the cases featured in this book. The principles and frameworks should also be helpful for generalizing about the role of negotiations over fundamental change in other settings.

Our main point—that change affecting multiple stakeholders inevitably involves negotiations—is deceptively simple. Change is not always seen as inherently involving negotiations. Occasionally, when one party can fully escape the relationships, prolonged negotiations may be avoided. Most typically, however, some form of negotiations is an inevitable outcome of interactions between a party desiring change and a party affected by the change.

To understand the nature of these negotiations, we make the key assumption that employment relations are inherently mixed-motive in nature. Again, this is a deceptively simple point. It might seem obvious to hold that all relationships involve a mixture of common and competing interests. In fact, however, many parties act as though employment relations are either entirely cooperative or entirely conflictual in nature.

The mixed-motive assumption sets the stage for forcing and fostering strategies. The inevitable conflicts in relations often prompt forcing strategies, while the common concerns typically underlie fostering strategies. A fundamental challenge, as we will see in the later chapters of this book, is for the parties to find means for coordinating the two strategies.

The strategies take on new and deeper meaning when we broaden the focus to include relationships as well as substantive provisions as a critical matter at stake in the negotiations. Treating relationships as a subject of bargaining is not an entirely new concept. It is rarely presented in a systematic fashion, however.

We hope that the principles and frameworks will serve as useful touchstones for understanding the cases in the following chapters. The heart of the book, of course, is the cases themselves. Today, finding detailed case descriptions of change initiatives is all too rare. Yet, it is only by tracing the twists and turns in the change process that we can fully appreciate why the pathways to change are so complex and why unintended consequences are an inevitable part of a successful journey to improved economic performance and robust labor-management relations.

NOTES

1. In contrast to the mixed-motive assumption, some scholars and practitioners operate from assumptions that employment relations are inherently and primarily conflictual in nature (with a primary focus on the economic, social, or legal implications of the conflict).   Others operate from assumptions that employment relations are essentially cooperative (with a primary focus on building consensus, shared vision, and the most effective organizational designs). An exclusive focus just on conflict or just on cooperation will bring the risk of discounting the negotiated nature of change.

2. For a more detailed discussion of these strategies, see Walton, Cutcher-Gershenfeld, and McKersie 1994.

2
Forcing

Hard Bargaining Over Fundamental Change

This chapter examines how managements in several industries have employed forcing strategies in an attempt to negotiate radical shifts in the patterns of wage and benefit settlements, as well as increasing management control over work assignments. Given a management judgment that its objectives require an attempt to force change, how does it formulate its negotiating objectives? What negotiating processes and structures does it employ to support a forcing strategy? What union and worker responses do these management actions elicit? And, finally, how does management cope with the dilemmas it encounters along the forcing path?

We explore these issues in three cases in which the initial forcing began during the 1980s: (1) an auto parts firm (AP Parts), where management's campaign to reduce costs led to a bitter strike; (2) a labor dispute at several International Paper (IP) mills, focusing on confrontations at the Jay, Maine facility during 1987 and 1988; and (3) a regional freight railroad (Guilford) that used a series of confrontations to restructure labor agreements and union representation.

Many labor-management negotiations today involve journeys down the forcing path. This chapter illustrates a variety of ways to travel down this path. Among the ways that management signaled forcing strategies in our cases are: beginning collective bargaining with demands for extensive changes, threatening and actually moving work from one location to another, emphasizing customer cost pressures, soliciting community support for its cause, utilizing replacement workers during a strike, and unilaterally imposing a contract on a union. We also find instances of uncharacteristically tight supervision on the shop floor and direct communications with workers—in effect bypassing the union. The cases illustrate the reduced effectiveness of the strike as a forcing tactic for unions, as well as the emergence of alternate responses available to unions, including not striking when it is expected, working to rule, soliciting community and government support, and mobilizing other locals and even other international unions.

The cases differ on a number of key dimensions as summarized in the following chart.

Key Aspects of Cases Featuring Forcing

	AP Parts	Jay	Guilford
Management Agenda	Reduce compensation costs	Reduce compensation costs; increase productivity	Increase productivity
Union Actions at Deadline	Work to Rule[a]	Strike	Strike
Management Actions at Deadline	Replacements[a]	Replacements	Replacements
Status of Replacement Workers at Conclusion of Negotiations	Terminated	No contract signed; replacements retained	Placed in reserve status
Substantive Changes	Minimal	Large	Large
Relationship with Union	Restored	Decertification	One union established (UTU) for all crafts[b]
Relationship with Workers	Restored	Not clear	Deteriorated

a. At the deadline, the union did not strike; however, several weeks later a strike was called and management brought in replacements.
b. Although eventually the various craft unions regained representation rights.

The three cases split on the approach taken to reducing unit labor costs, with two focusing primarily on compensation levels and one on productivity, e.g., work rules (though all of the negotiations involved some compensation and some productivity issues). At the deadline, the tactics adopted by the parties differed, though all the parties engaged in confrontation tactics that escalated to the point that relationships with the unions were severely ruptured. In the post strike period, however, the cases varied greatly in the extent to which working relations were restored.

Taken together, the forcing cases illustrate most of the hard bargaining tactics common in the present era. They also illustrate the range of possible dynamics and outcomes–suggesting some of the complexity associated with forcing strategies.

THE UNFOLDING OF A FORCING STRATEGY
AP Parts and UAW Local 14

The case of AP Parts (AP) begins in 1984 with management's initiative aimed at forcing deep substantive changes.[1] The company was apparently convinced that it needed substantial concessions to meet the economic pressures of supplying the auto industry. Anticipating strenuous resistance from the union, the company decided to recruit and train replacement workers. For its part, the union decided to throw management off balance by conducting an in-plant strategy when the contract expired. Eventually, relations became so strained that the union struck, and only after a bitter seven-month strike were the parties able to sign a new contract.

Significant Features

The AP case illustrates many dynamics common to forcing strategies.

- Each of the parties in the AP case came to believe that its organizational survival was at stake. Management's own economic analysis indicated it could not compete without concessions by labor. Labor saw threats to its survival in the ambitious and extensive nature of management's demands and the way in which they were "dropped" on labor—accompanied by handbills distributed in the plant by supervisors.

- The AP company derived bargaining power from its ability to transfer operations.

- The union's response blunted the initiatives of management and ultimately led to the rehiring of the strikers.

- The dispute in this negotiation took on broader significance for management and unions elsewhere.

- Community leaders offered their services, but their effectiveness was undercut when they came be seen by management as an ally with labor.

- AP management failed to negotiate a plan for the implementation of the work cell structure it won in formal contract negotiations.

- The acrimony associated with severe confrontational bargaining tactics continued to live on after the settlement.

- The severity of the conflict made both parties eager to negotiate the next contract early and with minimal changes.

- After the dispute the parties normalized the previous relationship, but did not embrace labor-management cooperation and worker participation.

Background

AP Parts has produced mufflers in the Toledo area since 1927. For most of its existence, the company has produced mufflers for cars and trucks in the aftermarket, as distinct from serving as a supplier to original equipment manufacturers (OEM). Although the firm was under the guidance of its founder and owner, John Goerlich, for many years, it has been bought and sold at least three times in the last decade. In addition to its home manufacturing plant in Toledo, the firm operated facilities in Michigan and North Carolina and, as of the early 1990s, was in a start-up phase for a facility in Indiana.

The stamped muffler produced by AP Parts represents an important and relatively recent technical innovation in the industry. While a conventional automobile muffler typically has as many as seventeen pieces to be individually assembled, a comparable stamped muffler has only four pieces. More than the savings in assembly cost, however, the chief virtue of the stamped process is its flexibility. The company can quickly develop dies that are custom tailored to diverse applications.

UAW Local 14, an amalgamated local, incorporated the AP Parts bargaining unit and three other units, the largest of which is a General

Motors drive-train plant. The local was established in 1938. The historical relationship between the AP Parts and the UAW was a traditional "New Deal" set of interactions—with arm's length collective bargaining and formal contract administration. The fact that the local also contained a facility owned by an original equipment manufacturer (General Motors) helped ensure that the tone for the relationship and the substantive issues in collective bargaining were closely tied to negotiations between the UAW and the OEMs.

Inability to Adjust Within a Traditional, Arm's-Length Social Contract

During the two years prior to the 1984 strike, the facility came under increasing economic pressure and made a number of adjustments—all within the rubric of a traditional, arm's-length social contract. In 1982, the firm lost a major customer—Sears—for whom it had been a supplier of replacement mufflers. Subsequently, there was a round of concession bargaining that included a 50 cents-per-hour reduction in wages. As well, a quality of worklife (QWL) process was initiated in 1982. These two contrasting responses of contending and cooperating were conceived and implemented solely as incremental adjustments within the existing labor-management relationship. They were not conceived as part of a change process leading to a new relationship with labor.

Both the wage reduction and the QWL efforts proved inadequate for the pressures facing the firm. The Toledo facility experienced further financial losses in 1983, creating pressure for yet further cost reductions. While the QWL program generated suggestions from some employees, it did not generate sufficient ideas for management to see this effort as a vehicle for addressing the competitive pressures. The union, which had mixed feelings about the QWL idea in the first place, concluded that management was not sufficiently committed to the program, and it chose not to endorse the QWL concept. Instead, it remained neutral—neither opposing nor supporting the process.

After the loss of the Sears business, management decided to move the aftermarket work to a smaller, nonunion facility in Goldsboro, North Carolina. The Toledo facility was then dedicated solely to producing for OEMs, which represented the most competitive part of the industry. This placed great pressures on cost, quality, and delivery performance. Thus, coming into the 1984 negotiations, the company was looking for broad changes in the collective bargaining agreement, while the union membership felt they had already made substantial concessions.

Dynamics of the Case

Building on the above history and context, our analysis of this case has been organized into two sections. In the first section, we examine the 1984 collective bargaining negotiations, which led to the collapse of the relationship. We trace the dynamics associated with a bitter, seven-month strike. By the end of this strike, fundamental expectations had been violated with respect to all stakeholders—management, labor, the community, and customers—and the traditional, arm's-length mode of interaction had been replaced by a form of armed warfare. Our analysis will be highly detailed in order to capture the micro process by which a contentious negotiation deteriorates. While there is, of course, a long history of contentious strikes in this country, the high profile of such strikes during the 1980s and the 1990s makes this examination pertinent.

Following the strike, the parties (with new faces on both sides of the table) entered into a process of reconstructing the relationship. For a variety of reasons, the parties ended up recreating a traditional, arm's-length mode of interaction. This set of relations provided a useful foundation for subsequently negotiating an unprecedented five-year contract and reestablishing a traditional process of give-and-take between labor and management on matters of contract administration.

As we present a prognosis in the final section, we note certain sources of tension associated with attempting to sustain a traditional arm's-length social contract in a context of severe competitive pressures. These include issues associated with the greenfield facility in North Carolina, the management philosophy regarding labor-management relations in the Toledo facility, and the turnover of leadership within the local union.

The Collapse of a Relationship

The 1984 negotiations between AP Parts and the UAW involved deep conflicts over wage, work-rule, and benefit issues. But, as we will see, the interactions were more than a ritualized haggling over specific contract language. From the outset, basic expectations of all parties about the negotiations process were violated. Further, there were deeper interests at stake for both sides. For management, it was the very survival of the plant. For the union, its very institutional legitimacy was under attack. These violations of expectations and the resulting deeper undertones of conflict are critical to understanding how a traditional relationship deteriorated to the point of armed warfare.

The Company Takes the Initiative

From the outset, management signaled to the union that this negotiation was going to be a departure from their past pattern of negotiations. Procedurally, the company broke from the familiar mode whereby the union makes most of the opening demands and the employer refrains from communicating directly with the union members. As one union leader characterized the opening of the 1984 negotiations:

> It was at the opening meeting that they dropped the entire proposal on us. We weren't expecting anything like that. At the same time they had supervisors in the plant passing out handbills stating that "we are committed to staying in Toledo."

Both the large set of initial employer demands and the active use of supervisors to communicate directly with employees violated traditional norms that had governed collective bargaining in past years. Management's ambitious proposals clearly surprised the union. According to a dismayed union official, the workers were faced with the following demands from AP Parts:

> The company requested $5.84 in wage concessions, replacement of the individual incentive system with a measured day work system, elimination of the thirty-and-out provision, freedom to subcontract, introduction of new job classifications, and the reorganization of the plant around work cells.

This opening round of bargaining in effect represented a key pivotal event, where fundamental substantive changes were placed on the table, calling into question the social contract between the parties. With respect to the substantive demands, the bargaining was explicit and the potential change deep. With respect to the labor-management relationship, the company was engaging in a tacit form of bargaining over the rules of the game. In effect, the company signaled that these interactions would have to be different from the prior negotiations that had led to concessions and the QWL initiative.

The Union's Response: Counterforcing

By departing from the usual norms of interaction, the company was signaling the depth of the changes it needed. Whether anticipated or not, the effect of such departures is usually to put the other side off balance. The union attempted to interpret or make sense of the company's shifting behaviors—as a way of reestablishing stability. Thus, every action taken by AP Parts was carefully studied by the union to assess whether the crisis was as severe as the company suggested or whether the severity had been exaggerated in order to wrest deeper concessions from the workforce and undermine the union. The fact that several other auto supply firms in other parts of the country were actively attempting to weaken or escape from collective bargaining provided a context in which this was a plausible interpretation.[2]

The union considered the company's strike preparations a critical signal of the company's intentions. As one union leader recalled:

> They erected a chain link fence around the plant on the same day that we sat down to begin negotiations. There had not been one prior to that. The company took down a sign outside the personnel office indicating there was no hiring and replaced it with a sign requesting employment applications.

> Nuckles Security [a private security firm] brought in a van load of big, ugly men in uniforms. They tried to put fear in the guys, but our men were the wrong people for that. They got a reaction— they got a lot of hate, but our people were the wrong guys for fear.

Once the union decided that its own institutional security might be at risk, it began counteracting management's initiatives. One union official characterized their strategy as follows:

> We played tit for tat. We reacted to what they did. If they sent a
> four-page letter to all employees, we would come back with a
> five-page letter.

By the contract expiration date of March 1, 1984, the drama was
well established. The company wanted the union to take their final
offer to the membership. The union refused to recommend this package. The company requested that a vote be held anyway, which
occurred on March 5th. The package was rejected by a vote of 425 to
30.

The Union's Surprise Tactic at the Deadline

When the contract expiration date arrived, the union anticipated that
the company would be expecting a strike. It came to this conclusion on
the basis of management's actions, such as installing a security fence
around the property, advertising for replacement workers, and hiring a
security firm associated with union decertification efforts in other locations. As a tactical response, then, the union instructed the workforce to
show up for work, ready to continue working under the terms of the
company's final offer.

Apparently, the union's decision caught the AP management by sur-
prise. When workers arrived for work, they reportedly found the security guards hurriedly packing up food, cots, and other supplies that
might have been used to sustain a replacement workforce confined
overnight in the factory. This time, it was the union's departure from
established norms that brought tactical advantage and that marked a
second major pivotal event in the negotiations.

At this point, both sides clearly were pursuing forcing strategies.
Each made choices at critical moments (the opening of the negotiations
for management and the expiration of the contract for the union) aimed
at gaining leverage via distributive bargaining and designed to increase
uncertainty for the other party.

Increasing Tensions Under Counterposed Forcing Strategies

Although the union members continued to work, relations were very
tense. For example, security guards regularly video-taped all activities,
and workers responded with taunts. Additionally, the workers were
paid at the rate of the company's last offer, which involved a cut in

wages and benefits of $5.84 per hour and the imposition of new shop rules giving the company more freedom in its utilization of workers. During the first month, over 150 workers were laid off (bringing plant employment to 232), and disciplinary notices were given to over 80 employees for violations of the new work rules. In all, over 200 reprimands were given to employees during the three-week period after the contract expiration.

In response to what it regarded as "surface bargaining" and other violations of the National Labor Relations Act, the union filed an unfair labor practice (ULP) charge with the National Labor Relations Board on March 22, 1984.[3] The NLRB response to the union's charge was delayed, reportedly because of the White House's failure to appoint an interim replacement for the board's general counsel. Still, on April 30, 1984, the regional director of the NLRB rejected the union's ULP charge.[4]

The third pivotal event occurred when the union indicated it was on strike after learning of the NLRB's action. The employer then began bringing in workers to maintain production. Approximately 125 picketing workers met 40 replacement workers as they arrived at the plant. After various episodes of punctured tires and broken windshields, a court order was issued limiting union picketing. At this point, the strike was fully underway—with management seeking to run the plant with replacement workers and with the union intent on disrupting such efforts.

Each side sought to weaken the other. Management put pressure on the workers, while the union responded with further unfair labor practice charges. Both sets of actions further increased tensions. Continued escalation was not, however, inevitable. For example, a different decision by the NLRB might have set the stage for a different sequence of events. If the NLRB had ruled for the union, the company might have resorted to a lockout, or it might have taken steps to resolve the negotiations without a strike.

Tactical Dynamics Contributing to the Deterioration of Social Relations

On May 12, 1984, a federal mediator brought the two sides together for the first time in two months. There was a news blackout for three days as the parties met. However, the parties did not come to agreement and this initiative collapsed.

Meanwhile, the conflicts between picketing employees, security guards, and replacement workers became even sharper. In addition to daily taunting, stone throwing, and other exchanges, the union staged a number of public demonstrations outside the facility. The largest demonstration occurred on May 22, 1984, following a company announcement on the previous day of a reward of $10,000 for any information concerning vandalism during the strike.

The demonstration involved approximately 3,000 people and turned violent when a group of demonstrators attempted to crash the plant gate with an eighteen-wheel semi truck. Tear gas canisters were used by the police to break up the protest, which in turn generated a public outcry (since some of the canisters had warnings on them that they could be deadly). One union official reflected on the experience and the overall strike as follows:

> This was a war, full of wounds. Vietnam was easy compared to this. I was over there. This was like a goddamn tour of duty in a war. Imagine months and months with no income. We had suicide, alcoholism, and divorce.

The demonstration made vivid the degree to which the relationship (and hence a shared understanding of the social contract) had deteriorated, foreclosing any substantive discussions. Formal negotiations were officially broken off and the parties settled into a war of attrition.

The Parties' Inability to Reconstruct Social Relations

In mid-June, the company proposed to the union that secret talks begin at a site away from Toledo—in Ann Arbor, Michigan. The company also changed law firms. The union agreed to the new initiative, despite its concern that the new law firm had a reputation for providing advice on union avoidance. Meetings began in Ann Arbor with a tone that was open and informal, signaled in part by the casual attire of participants on both sides.

At the same time, however, the new law firm indicated that it would not honor any existing tentative agreements; the negotiations were to start from scratch. Such an approach served to exacerbate the distributive elements already dominant in the negotiations. For example, the company brought large binders with proposed contract language changes, each reportedly containing only small word changes from earlier demands. The union expressed resentment about the extensive time devoted at the beginning of each meeting to pulling out old pages and updating the binders with new ones. In response, the union handed out its own large binders full of its own proposed changes. The fight then shifted to a debate over whose binders would be the point of reference for discussions. By mid August, this new round of talks had come to a halt. It is not clear how serious the company was in seeking resolution at this stage, but certainly the tactics with the binders and related actions blocked communications and, hence, substantive discussions.

A Competition for Community Support

The growing tensions between the parties increasingly spilled over into the community. The Toledo community had seen its share of plant closings and industrial disinvestment, and its citizens had become concerned about the deteriorating relations between AP Parts and the UAW. Each of the parties, early in the negotiations, sought ways to use community concern to its advantage in gaining leverage over the other. Thus, the company advertised in the local newspaper that it was committed to Toledo, and the union responded with full page advertisements of its own, proclaiming "The Truth About the AP Negotiations."

Prior to the strike, but after the expiration of the contract, the parties continued their competition for community support. In public statements, management representatives indicated that, without major concessions, the company might have to close the facility. In response, Toledo's mayor, Donna Owens, called for a labor-management citizens committee, but the company indicated that it would be unwilling to turn the negotiations over to such a group. It did, however, send a long editorial on April 1st to the Toledo paper explaining its position.

In this piece, the company explained that there had been a 40 percent reduction in exhaust industry production from 1973 to 1981, which drove the first round of concessions at AP Parts. AP Parts then explained the shift of its Toledo facility to production for the OEM market. It argued that this location was within 250 miles of 60 percent of all North American automobile assembly plants. Further, the company projected a loss of $10 million, which it explained as follows:

> The hourly labor costs and the restrictive collective bargaining agreement are the two items most responsible for our predica-

ment. . . . We are now faced, quite literally, with the question of whether the Toledo plant can survive. Survival is possible only after major surgery—the total and complete overhaul of the wage and benefit package and a full rewrite of our collective bargaining agreement.

The director of UAW Region 2B, which included Local 14, responded on April 8 with an editorial that attributed the economic losses to start-up problems with a new assembly process, misquotes on bids, the slow development of new process controls, and the use of unsuitable steel. Further, he stated that AP Parts was departing from a forty-year history of collective bargaining in which "gains have been made painstakingly through honest, good-faith negotiations." He stated that: "It is not concessions that AP seeks here, it is the demolition of the union contract."

In the middle of the various exchanges, AP Parts was awarded a $20 million contract to make mufflers for General Motors—the largest contract in the company's history. Production was scheduled to begin in January 1985. The company used this news in the battle for community support. It announced that its successful bid on the contract was based on the "terms of the new agreement at the Toledo plant." The company also held the GM contract up as evidence that it wanted to remain in Toledo.

In addition to serving as a potential partner on a partisan basis with one side or another, the community had its own independent interests (centering on labor peace). Highly visible violence and a festering war of attrition were directly contrary to the desired economic climate. Hence, after the mass demonstration on May 22, 1984, the mayor of Toledo appointed a five-member community committee, which included representatives from the Toledo Area Labor-Management Committee (a longstanding community organization consisting of many top local union and management leaders). In announcing the establishment of the committee, the mayor stated:in the paper:

> We've reached the point where this is no longer a labor-management dispute. We've been working hard to turn the image of the city around.

The entry of a potentially neutral third party frequently represents a pivotal event in negotiations. In the best case, the third party can be instrumental in bringing the bargaining process closer to a settlement.

It is also possible, for the third party to become another vehicle for contention, which is what took place in this case. A union official described the situation as follows:

> At one point the area labor-management group recommended a settlement. [The recommended settlement] had many of the company demands, but still was strong on cost-of-living and on the thirty-and-out pension. We instantly bought it—we would take a chance on it. The panel consisted of many prominent people from labor and management in the community. Management turned it down. That helped our image.

The union's rapid acceptance and the company's rejection served to undercut the potential for the area labor-management committee to be an effective third party. Instead, their position became a new element in the parties' contest for partners as they battled one another.

The Management of Internal Differences During the Strike

The impact of the strike also rippled through the internal ranks of both the company and the union. Although public information on this point is scarce, at least one of the principal owners of the company sold his shares as a result of the festering conflict. As well, members of the management community in Toledo increasingly separated themselves from the management of this firm. For example, management as well as union members of the area labor-management committee expressed frustration over the rejection of their proposal. This division within the management community was consistent with the union's forcing strategy—it hoped to separate AP management from others in the management community.

While management sought to similarly divide the union, the local was able to blunt such efforts by reaching beyond the region to the international union. In particular, the UAW's regional director (who was deeply involved in the negotiations) made the case to the international union and the larger labor movement that the AP Parts strike was a bellwether in the region: if the UAW won, it would temper the actions of other employers; if the employer won, it would open the way for similar strategies in other locations. In response, union members from elsewhere in the UAW and from other unions all over the United States sent food and money to help the striking workers.

Perhaps the most vivid example of the way the union sought to maintain internal solidarity took place in the late summer of 1984. In a coordinated move, UAW Vice-President Donald Ephlin and UAW Vice-President Stephen Yokich broke off their national negotiations with General Motors and the Ford Motor Company, respectively, to join the picket line in Toledo in front of the AP Parts plant. Needless to say, the move was not only instrumental in managing internal differences within the union, it was also a multilateral development in the sense that it brought the AP situation to the attention of two primary customers of AP Parts.

Resolution of the 1984 Strike

In September, the mayor again sought to bring the parties together—but she quickly denounced the company owners for refusing to meet with her and, at the same time, not empowering their representatives to come to a settlement. On September 19, 1984, the company announced that the $20 million contract with GM would go to its nonunion plant in North Carolina due to the difficulties of expanding production in Toledo. Talks did not resume until the very end of October, when the union indicated a willingness to consider the company's demand for a work-cell concept. Amnesty for striking workers then emerged as a key stumbling block.

Throughout the months of November and December, talks would begin and then break off. At one point, in mid-December, the union presented the last company offer to the membership, which included amnesty for all but twenty-one union members. This contract was rejected in a vote of 225 to 5. The company charged that the vote was "a terrible breach of faith" and again broke off negotiations.

While the plant continued to operate during the strike, inventories became depleted and customers began to question AP Parts regarding its ability to make deliveries. Ultimately, however, the event that precipitated the end of the strike was a petition filed on January 31, 1985, by the Maritime Engineers Beneficial Association for a representation election. While it is hard to assess how significant this was to the firm, shortly afterwards the company did agree to a settlement with the union that included some wage and benefit concessions, the addition of a plant productivity bonus system, a two-year freeze on the cost-of-living increase, some work-rule changes providing more flexibility for temporary job transfers, language regarding the use of a team-based work-cell structure for welding, retention of holidays and retirement benefits, and an agreement that no worker would be fired for any picket-line activity. The replacement workers were terminated at the same time. This contract was ratified by a vote of 254 to 72.

The Reconstruction of the Relationship

The resolution of the 1984 strike marked the conclusion of a sustained period of deterioration in the relationship between the UAW and AP Parts. It was, however, an ambiguous resolution. With respect to the social contract between the company and the union, there was evidence to suggest that the agreement reflected the successful application of union leverage in a context where each side had inflicted extensive harm on the other. There were no pronouncements regarding what kind of a relationship the company and the union desired—each side just agreed to sign a contract. With respect to the relationship between the company and its employees, the situation was equally ambiguous. Any company claim to mutuality with its employees was undercut by its use of replacement workers. Within the union, the management of internal differences had forged a high level of internal solidarity, though here too there were many people who had suffered financially, losing their cars and even in some cases their homes. Thus, it was unclear what future claims the union might be able to make regarding its members' commitment to concerted activity.

De-Escalation and the Arrival of New Personalities

Reportedly, shop-floor relations remained tense for more than a year after the return to work. Incidents that took place in the heat of the strike did not immediately fade from memory. Little disagreements would apparently flare up, driven by feelings not far below the surface among those who had been involved with the strike.

For some workers and most of the supervisors, this tension was too much to take. Within a few years after the strike, the lower-level management group had almost entirely turned over and many workers had left. As well, turnover occurred among some key higher-level managers, such as the plant manager and the personnel director.

Within the union, a new group of leaders was elected to office on a platform oriented around rebuilding labor-management relations. Thus, just two years after the strike, there were new faces on both sides of the table. As difficult as the strike had been, the arrival of new leaders set the stage for an affirmative step toward the reconstruction of the relationship.

A Successful, Traditional Negotiation

In 1987, the relationship between the company and the union took a significant turn. As the current personnel director recalls:

> March 1988 would have been the expiration of the contract. The plant manager and I contacted the local president to try to get early negotiations. We got together with the union and created an imaginary deadline. . . . We agreed, let's go for two weeks. If we don't reach it by then, all bets are off.

The company began the negotiations with relatively few demands, in contrast to the set of sweeping issues that it had placed on the table a few years earlier. As the personnel director commented:

> We decided not to change any of the contract language. There was nothing there that either side could not live with. Negotiations basically revolved around economics. There were some minor language changes. We spent the first week on language and the second week on economics.

Within higher management, the approach of the new personnel director and the new plant manager was greeted with skepticism. As one manager commented, "Our people downtown, who were intimately involved with the strike, did not think we could do it."

For the union, the entire tone of the negotiations stood in strong contrast to the experiences a few years earlier. One international union official recalled:

> Last June [1987] the company approached us about opening negotiations early. Ford and GM were pressuring them to have one year of inventory going into bargaining or they would pull all work. The company said, "Let's get an early agreement, with the

incentive that the wage increase could take effect early." Here it
was two years later and it was like old traditional bargaining. Each
day we accomplished something. Since the settlement, employment has been up and new work is coming in.

Despite the contentious strike, in which many traditional norms of collective bargaining were violated, both sides were apparently able to
reestablish traditional modes of interaction just two years later.
Undoubtedly, the change in the management ranks was a key factor,
but so too was the willingness of the new individuals to engage in give-
and-take.

The Elements of a Reestablished Traditional Social Contract

Even in the early 1990s, many years afterwards, the strike still cast a
shadow over the company and the union. For example, one manager
noted that:

> The media will not let us forget about the strike. If we get in the
> newspaper for something good, the last two paragraphs of the arti-
> cle will mention something about the strike.

A key question, therefore, was whether the parties had put those tensions behind them, or whether they would resurface in some new way.
Given that the parties appeared to have reverted back to a traditional,
arm's-length relationship, what would prevent them from entering into
another round of escalating conflict?

A close look suggests that certain aspects of the relationship were
different from what they had been prior to the strike. For example, a
union official reported:

> The level of information sharing is much higher now. The union
> officials will often be called in to meet with customers, and they
> all go through the plant together. Of course, Ford and GM are
> demanding it. GM and Ford want to know how AP and the UAW
> are getting along.

Clearly, this reported change was primarily externally driven. Internally, the work-cell structure, which was a key issue during the strike,
had not been fully implemented, primarily because the team-based system was not in place.

Indeed, many features of the case suggested little shift towards a new relationship. Consider, for example the way the personnel director characterized management's style:

> Our plant manager and I hold that we should be running the company, not the union. I guess you would call it a more traditional approach. I've been through all those programs like zero-defects, management by objectives, quality circles, and on and on. They are all gone.

The traditional approach taking shape within management during the early 1990s was matched by developments within the union. The union leadership elected following the strike was replaced by a slate of leaders who advocated an arm's-length relationship with the company. Many of the new leaders had served on the bargaining committee during the 1984 strike. Thus, both parties were moving more solidly into arm's-length, adversarial roles.

Analysis

An observer of the AP story would have to conclude that the yield for the parties was rather low, given all of the resources invested in the forcing campaign and the lingering resentment embedded in the social relationships. The outcomes are summarized in the following chart.

Thus, the AP Parts story affords a window into a classic deterioration and collapse of a labor-management relationship. Because each side had fundamental interests at stake, initial tactical moves took on great significance, and an escalation of conflict ensued. The escalation was fueled as each side sought to derive power by breaking from traditional norms of negotiations. The union's ultimate decision to strike, management's use of replacement workers, and the tit-for-tat tactics (e.g., around the binders), all afforded tactical advantage, but also served to erode any vestiges of a relationship upon which a settlement might be constructed.

Significant Outcomes—AP Parts

Substantive outcomes	Management-union relations	Management-employee relations	Other outcomes
Two major rounds of wage and benefit concessions	Movement from an adversarial relationship, to armed warfare, to a reestablished adversarial relationship	Limited cooperation with a QWL program Complete collapse of working relations during the strike (with the use of replacement workers) Reestablished management control system	Mutually costly strike Turnover of union leadership and management personnel

Explanation for the Standoff

The best way to characterize the above balance sheet, in terms of short-run costs and gains, is that all sides lost. Basically, the stalemate can be explained in terms of a relatively balanced power equation. Management gained leverage by its ability to transfer work to a new union facility and to hire replacements when the union struck. For its side, the union was able to mobilize pressure more generally from the union movement and the community. Quite significantly, when the settlement was finally reached the union was able to secure its demand that the strike replacements be terminated—a position that the unions in the other two forcing cases (as we will see) were not able to sustain.

The question needs to be asked as to why the parties were not able to negotiate an accommodation to the new economic realities, especially given their joint efforts during the early 1980s. It should be noted that, similar to many companies that started to experience cost pressures in the 1980s, AP Parts management set in motion several programs for closing the gap (for example, QWL and a round of wage concessions). Then, as the competitive standing of the company worsened, management unveiled its proposals for a reduction in hourly compensation costs of almost $6.00, which may or may not have been designed to precipitate a confrontation with the union.

Significantly, the earlier concessions and QWL effort at adjustment did not pave the way for the round of hard bargaining that we examined. Rather, the early adjustments apparently served to immunize the union leadership and the rank and file from accepting arguments about the need for additional changes. A response that "we have already given" often develops in labor-management relationships when management comes to the table with additional concessionary proposals. Thus, the stage was set for a showdown.

Alternate Scenarios

The question should be asked whether the parties in the AP Parts case could have arrived at a new platform for change without all of the turmoil inherent in *unrestrained* forcing. We attempt to answer this important question in terms of several key choices made by the parties.

First, should the company have presented a more modest proposal than the $5.84 reduction in compensation costs and other contractual changes as a way of easing into an adjustment program? Certainly making a credible case for such deep wage concessions would first require a justification of the company's strategic decision to shift from the aftermarket to supplying OEMs. The company saw this as an essential business decision, while the union considered it to be a power tactic. Under these circumstances, if management's business calculations were legitimate, then it must have felt that it had no choice but to open bargaining with an extreme demand. However, management did not provide the union with sufficient financial information to justify the claim, which led the union to interpret the bargaining position as a challenge to the legitimacy of the union.

Second, once the bargaining had begun, could the parties have altered their tit-for-tat sequence of tactics at any point (e.g., the battle of letters to employees, the one-upmanship of elaborate binders, the use of rallies by the union, and diversion of work by the company)? It is unlikely, given the political realities within the union and the *esprit de corps* within management that the leadership of either side could have backed away from an all-out fight.

Third, given the onset of what all sides saw as a holy war, was there a way for the parties to save face and end the hostilities? Possibly. When community leadership offered to mediate, it was probably a mistake for the company to dismiss the offer out of hand. Certainly, the company did not want to lose control or to have a settlement dictated by a third party, but it could have entered into discussions, and the agreement that eventually emerged might have been reached sooner. Similarly, there is evidence to suggest that the NLRB decision could have favored the union, which would have provided another opportunity for resolution.

Throughout the escalating conflict, each side made assumptions about the motives of the other. Due to the strained communications and low levels of trust, these assumptions were rarely checked directly. Rather, related incidents were treated as corroboration, and each then felt even more justified in its forcing strategy. Since management was the moving party seeking dramatic concessions, the burden fell on management to persuade the union of the merits of its position. Mere claims of financial necessity were not effective—a fairly dramatic *quid pro quo* involving real power sharing in exchange for concessions would have likely been required. Thus, management had two real alternatives in this case—force dramatic concessions sure to alienate the union and its members (which is what occurred) or enlist the union (and/or its members) as full partners in facing a competitive crisis.

Future Possibilities

The first point to note is that the AP Parts/UAW relationship reverted back to a traditional pattern of interaction, and this occurred with surprising speed. Instrumental in this reconstruction of the relationship was new leadership at the table as well as customer pressure for labor stability. Since the reconstruction occurred around a traditional relationship, however, it remained to be seen if this would be sufficient to meet management's long-term needs regarding cost and flexibility, as well as labor's long-term needs regarding employment security and institutional stability.

One aspect of the relationship, however, will be fundamentally different in the years to come. In the early 1990s, the company purchased and restored an auto parts facility in Indiana capable of producing mufflers. New employees were offered a benefit package and a participative system of work organization designed to maintain a nonunion status. While the company did not link this acquisition to the future of the Toledo plant, the presence of a nearby nonunion facility clearly was an ominous development for the union.

Several other factors may be sources of instability–the parties face continued customer pressures on cost, quality, and schedule; management has increased its strategic options with the above-mentioned greenfield facility; and the union has reemphasized its solidarity and willingness to confront management. Yet these same circumstances may also provide each side with the impetus to take each other seriously. The question that remains is whether they will be able to attend sufficiently to one another's interests within a traditional social contract.

Thus from a short-run perspective, the AP Parts story requires a sober recognition of the high costs. However, from a longer-run point of view, the possibility of more fundamental changes may be present. Certainly, the lesson has been learned by the parties that the process of adjustment to new economic realties has to be conducted in a manner different from their escalation saga of the 1980s.

A MUTUALLY COSTLY DISPUTE
International Paper, Jay, Maine, 1987-1988

Contract negotiations between International Paper (IP) management and the two locals of the United Paperworkers International Union (UPIU) at Jay, Maine during 1987-1988 were characterized by an unrestrained forcing campaign that was costly to both parties.[5] The negotiations involved a seventeen-month strike, which ended in November 1988 when labor abandoned its demands and accepted even less-favorable terms than it had voted down seven months earlier. In the first few months after the strike ended, only about 100 strikers returned to the Jay mill, filling only those positions opened by turnover of the permanent replacements hired by IP during the strike. The international union appeared to be weakened and divided in the aftermath of the strike. The ultimate blow for the union occurred at a subsequent decertification election in which the UPIU was defeated. As of 1994 the plant was still nonunion.

Significant Features

The Jay case illustrates a number of facets that are often present when forcing takes on an unrestrained character, specifically:

- Despite pooling and linking of separate mill negotiations by the union, the company still had only a fraction of capacity tied up at the locations affected by the various strike and lockout actions.

- The corporate campaign represented a multifaceted asset for the union.

- The company's replacement tactic led some strikers to break ranks.

- The International union was unable to expand beyond the initial pool of locals willing to support the strike.

- Community, state, and national politics become entwined in the labor dispute.

- The resulting hostility on both sides contributed to an escalation that did not serve the interests of either side.

With respect to outcomes, the Jay case can be distinguished from AP Parts in a number of respects. First, the union, UPIU, lost out completely in the Jay mill as a result of the power struggle. Second, while the AP Parts hostilities were focused on just one plant, Jay was one of four IP plants involved in this episode of protracted conflict. Third, while at AP Parts the UAW exhibited considerable internal solidarity, the Jay episode was characterized by considerable division within the union.   Our analysis will attempt to explain these contrasts as well as management's strategy, the union's strategic response, and the outcome. We also describe the implementing tactics and the process dynamics.

Background

IP's Jay mill is located on the Androscoggin River in western Maine. In 1987 the mill employed 1,200 people in a 5,000-person town. This region is not the vacation part of Maine; western Maine's economy is depressed by the industrial decline of New England and largely untouched by the high-tech boom of the early 1980s. Although some observers liked to refer to "hardy, independent" Maine workers prone to strike, the last strike at IP's Jay mill, built in 1898, had occurred in 1920.

Concerned about low profits in the late 1970s, IP management at the corporate level embarked on a belt-tightening program of familiar outline: shutdowns of unprofitable capacity and reductions in salaried workforce. IP managers also pursued two other standard avenues: they built a nonunion mill and they pushed for concessions in contract negotiations in their union mills.

The UPIU, which represented a majority of IP paperworkers, responded to early attempts to gain concessions by hiring, in 1983, corporate campaign consultant Ray Rogers. Rogers had founded Corporate Campaigns Inc. in 1981 to work with unions to pressure companies through veiled secondary boycotts and direct approaches to large customers as well as to members of their boards of directors. Before Rogers' general campaign against IP could be implemented, however, IP officers and UPIU representatives agreed to meet twice a year to discuss labor relations.

Pressures for Concessions Increase

In 1986, IP's profits were again rising, it had embarked upon a program of acquisitions, and it was pushing aggressively for contract concessions. The 550-member Natchez, Mississippi locals accepted the loss of Sunday premium pay in 1986; by December of that year the Jay locals had offered to renew their contract with neither a wage raise nor loss of Sunday premium pay. IP refused the Jay union proposal. Relations between IP and the UPIU then deteriorated rapidly.

Lockouts and Strikes

In March of 1987, a contract dispute resulted in an IP lockout of the 1,200-member UPIU local at its Mobile, Alabama mill. In April, IP delivered an eighteen-item agenda to the Jay locals, including the elimination of Sunday premium pay and 178 jobs. In June, the company made its final offer, softening the Sunday premium pay elimination into a three-year phaseout and job elimination with an attrition program. The UPIU local refused the offer, and a strike began June 16.

UPIU also initiated coordinated strikes against IP in DePere, Wisconsin (300 workers) and Lock Haven, Pennsylvania (720 workers). In effect, the several UPIU plants that were negotiating at the time had formed a "pool" to coordinate negotiations with IP.

Strike Dynamics at Jay

IP hired permanent replacement workers soon after the strike started. Although the UPIU regarded this action as a deliberate insult and threat, industry observers pointed out that the scale of the simultaneous strikes against several IP mills would have made other management strategies difficult (e.g., moving in supervisory personnel from other company mills). The mills' rural locations also made temporary hiring problematic because of high local tensions. Replacement workers were recruited throughout Maine, some of them driving several hours each way every workday.

Industry observers also suggested that the outside hires were not part of a long-term strategy, and that both IP and UPIU leaders probably developed their strike "strategies" as they went along, reacting to unfolding events in the glare of publicity. Two presidential elections--the United States and the UPIU--contributed to intraorganizational tensions as well. The Jay strike became a *cause celebre* among Democratic presidential candidates, attracting far greater public attention than might otherwise have been expected by corporate strategists anticipating a strike. It was suggested, as well, that since UPIU President Wayne Glenn was facing a contested reelection, it was harder for him to advocate restraint in the multilocation negotiations than would have been the case in a nonelection year.

A bargaining session in September, held at the request of the Maine governor, lasted only a few minutes. By October, the Jay UPIU local president had asked UPIU international president, Wayne Glenn, to support hiring Ray Rogers to coordinate a corporate campaign against IP, and Glenn had agreed—reportedly with some reluctance. Jesse Jackson appeared at a UPIU rally in Mobile in October. The Jay local also had been instrumental in instigating an investigation that led to an OSHA levy of $250,000 in fines for hazardous plant conditions, and both sides had filed unfair labor practice charges, sought injunctions, and subsequently filed charges of injunction violations. The town of Jay adopted UPIU-supported ordinances banning strikebreakers, restricting temporary housing, and appropriating funds for environmental law enforcement under Maine statutes. Workers at the Mobile and Jay plants were awarded unemployment benefits because of the lockout in Alabama and the provision of a Maine law: the replacement workers had returned the Jay plant to more than 70 percent of normal production.

The conflict continued unabated at Jay. By November of 1987, IP had implemented a "best and final offer" contract containing job reductions, Sunday premium pay reductions, and "project productivity" that eliminated jurisdictional lines between crafts. IP also announced that 988 permanent replacements had been hired, that there would be only 12 more jobs open to any returning strikers (with the additional news that 200 individuals had applied for those positions). All told, almost 3,500 UPIU workers remained on strike or lockout at the IP mills in Jay, DePere, Lock Haven, and Mobile.

The parties met for four hours in December in the Washington offices of the Federal Mediation and Conciliation Service. The IP vice-president of human resources and the UPIU president emerged to issue a joint statement:

> Despite our best efforts to explore all possible avenues to lessen the differences that exist between the two sides, nothing came from the discussions that could lead us to believe any resolution can be expected in the near future. We will obviously continue to see if other avenues exist to be explored.

Meanwhile, the corporate campaign was in full swing. Jay strikers organized themselves into caravans that traveled through Maine, and then to other New England areas, to garner support. They appeared in Boston in February of 1988, where the Democratic mayor declared "UPIU Local 14 Solidarity Day" – and also pledged to avoid buying IP products for the city. Democratic presidential candidates Michael Dukakis and Jesse Jackson vied for supportive opportunities. Rogers identified several major companies–including Coca-Cola, Avon, Anheuser-Busch, and a Boston bank–that bought paper or shared directors with IP and orchestrated picket lines, boycott lists, and letter campaigns that publicized their connections.

Rogers' goal was to demonstrate to board members that they would be treated as integral parts of IP management in every aspect of their lives. Board members encountered pickets everywhere. Political debate spread from the Maine legislature to the Democratic presidential campaign. The Maine governor drafted a bill that would keep non-Maine companies from providing strikebreakers. Each side went to great lengths to demonstrate the destructiveness, greed, and ultimate hopelessness of the other side's strategy.

Intraorganizational Activity

Every effort was made by each party to strengthen its unity and to undermine the other party's internal consensus. IP successfully sued the UPIU for injunction violations and distributed the proceeds to strikebreakers and outside contractors. The usual heckling of strikebreakers continued—answered on paydays with brandished paychecks. UPIU members attempted to enlist support from shareholders and board members on various fronts. For its side, IP tried assiduously to break the power of the corporate campaign by reaching settlements at other locations.

Ultimately, out of 1,250 UPIU members at Jay, less than 70 strikers crossed the picket line and returned to work. Although the availability of unemployment insurance for an extended period blunted the appeal of returning to work, observers suggested that, in large part, this modest hireback reflected the power of the corporate campaign in giving strikers an active focus and reinforcement for their anger at IP and their resolve not to give up the strike. In a small town in which the same family could include hourly workers and managers, the corporate campaign allowed strikers to fix upon unfamiliar faces and to engage in antagonistic encounters in other locations.

Finally, in March of 1988, at the urging of mediators—and, it can be surmised, as a result of the erosion of intraorganizational consensus in the face of months of bruising and expensive combat—three weeks of contract talks were scheduled in Knoxville, Tennessee. IP was reported to hold a "genuine desire" to reach a settlement; former Labor Undersecretary Malcolm Lovell was prepared to expand the role he had already played in scheduling negotiating sessions; and UPIU President

Glenn issued a statement at least ostensibly reflecting a new sense of optimism about the potential for bridging the company's and employees' interests:

> [The UPIU is ready] to begin developing a positive, long-term relationship dedicated to the competitiveness of the company and the welfare of the employees.

Rogers' corporate campaign also was suspended for the duration of the talks; of course IP announced that it had been "terminated," while the UPIU declared that it had merely been put "on hold."

Negotiations lasted for two and a half weeks, resulting in a proposed agreement which the UPIU insisted must be ratified by pooling votes from all strike locations. For the union, the major features of the IP proposal were provisions for early retirement and a guarantee of work within one year somewhere in the IP system for all striking workers. The contract was rejected overwhelmingly–with the UPIU refusing to reveal the locals' specific votes.

The Strike Ends

The union then went into its convention in August 1988 with strong support for continuing both the strike and the corporate campaign of Ray Rogers. It was anticipated that, as other plants came up for negotiations, they would join the "pool."

This plan came apart in November when Glenn called union presidents together from all of the IP locals for a meeting in Nashville. The national leadership tested support for the idea that plants with upcoming negotiations would "join the pool" and found that there was not much enthusiasm among delegations from these plants. In fact, some expressed concern that IP might proceed to replace all 12,000 workers. Other depressing factors for the union were a rumor at Jay that the company was planning to bring on another 200-300 workers, and growing fear on the part of local union leaders that some junior workers would break ranks and cross the picket line—quite a plausible response among the striking workers at Jay whose jobs appeared almost irretrievable after a one-year strike.

The national leadership, in conjunction with the presidents of the various locals at IP, agreed to call off the strike as of November 9. As a result, the workers were forced to accept less-favorable terms than they had rejected months earlier. The result was widely regarded as a defeat for the UPIU—strikers were not to be rehired *en masse,* and the most senior strikers who filled the handful of openings went back to positions many rungs down the job ladder.

IP's immediate fortunes suffered relatively slight setbacks: only a small percentage of its capacity had been affected; moreover, the coincidence of the strike and rising demand for paper had helped to minimize any financial strain on the company as a result of the strike.

Some costs of the dispute to IP, however, continued after the strike ended. First, important skills and experience were lost. Second, as replacement employees left the Jay mill, their positions were filled by strikers, numbering 100 by early 1990, and tensions between the strikebreakers and former employees increased. Thus, although the use of replacement workers largely insulated the mill from the antagonisms created by the bargaining tactics for a period, these antagonisms surfaced in the poststrike period.

The potential for friction can be illustrated by the "inversion" that results when a returning striker with substantial seniority finds himself working as a helper on a machine that he previously operated as the first hand. It probably had taken him fifteen to twenty years to progress through the various stations on the machine; by contrast, the replacement, now working as first hand, learned the ropes in less than a year and might be twenty years his junior.

Special animosity was directed to the strikers who decided to cross the picket line. They were referred to as "super scabs," in contrast to the replacements who were labelled "scabs"; the strikers were called "true blues."

Another development disconcerting to national leadership was the strike's temporizing effect on subsequent negotiations within the system. Some locals, especially in southern locations, conceded the Sunday premium as well as declining to engage in in-plant tactics such as work to rule and refusal of overtime. In fact, to the dismay of UPIU international officials, some of these plants actually proceeded to break production records.

But the biggest setback by far occurred in July 1992 when the workers at Jay (mostly replacements) voted by a substantial margin to decertify the UPIU and conduct their employment relations on a nonunion basis. However, the saga continued as the company proceeded to meet its legal obligation to rehire former strikers as positions opened. Thus, as openings developed, the workforce contained a growing percentage of workers who supported the union. UPIU representatives expressed hope that they would eventually be able to win a new organizing campaign.

Analysis

When IP's forcing strategy around ambitious demands at Jay was matched by the UPIU's own strong forcing efforts, institutional stakes and intergroup hostility were escalated in a way that precluded any significant integrative bargaining and trust building during or after the strike. Thus, the juxtaposition of the parties' strategic choices pushed the labor-management relationship to the breaking point.

On the substantive side of the ledger, management prevailed in negotiating the terms of employment it wanted and apparently strengthened its own confidence and power for securing concessions at its other mills. At the same time, management incurred costs: the loss of profits during the strike, the loss of the skills of experienced paperworkers, and the results of increased tension as a growing number of strikers returned to their jobs.

Management probably miscalculated the degree of union resistance. One could also argue that the union decision makers underestimated management's power and resolve. It is unclear whether either side saw itself as having alternative strategies available to it going into the negotiations. Eventually, positive employee relations may emerge, but it will take many years.

Elements of the Power Equation

The following chart summarizes the main factors that determined the outcomes in the Jay case.

Determining Factors—International Papef

Company	Union
Prepared for unrestrained forcing by lining up replacements and galvanizing management	Mounted corporate campaign
Used threats of replacement workers and other power tactics in other locations to undercut union solidarity across locations	Attempted (but failed) to create a large pool of locals willing to engage in strike action

Forcing Tactics and Related Negotiating Dynamics

The Jay negotiations illustrate the central role of hard bargaining in a forcing strategy. Each side employed tactics designed to increase its own power, regardless of their souring effects on the attitudes of the participants in the negotiations. IP's resolve to follow through with its pattern of demanding concessions in all of its mills despite the upswing in the business cycle aroused the strong opposition of union leaders and workers, not to mention their families. Its use of permanent replacements severely threatened the members as employees and the union as an institution. For its part, the union's corporate campaign, its pooled bargaining tactics, and its public relations activities reinforced IP management's antagonism toward the union as an institution.

The heightened mutual hostility in the Jay case illustrates how unbridled confrontational tactics decrease the likelihood of integrative solutions to work-rule issues and other operating problems. Similarly, the Jay case illustrates how parties try to bolster their own distributive bargaining positions by strengthening their own internal consensus and weakening that of the other side. The union's corporate campaign, for example, sought to publicly embarrass IP's directors, possibly to precipitate their resignation from the board, or at least to provide them with an incentive to urge management to resolve the dispute. At the same time, it provided a rallying activity for Jay strikers.

According to our analysis, while the interpretive frames of the two sides changed several times during this episode, they remained remarkably symmetrical. Initially, management viewed the negotiations as an economic contest over wages and other terms of employment, a contest in which it had the upper hand and which would continue the momentum of significant gains in operating practices. The union also focused on the economic contest and saw its task as drawing the line after a series of concessions elsewhere in the industry and in other IP mills.

Later, the parties interpreted their conflict as a mutual struggle for institutional power, prestige, and survival, overlaid on both sides with agendas of revenge. Two pivotal events shaped this reframing of the negotiation, serving to escalate the immediate animosity and add to its longevity. One event was the union's decision to strike the Jay mill despite the union's earlier acceptance of similar management terms at the Maine mills of two other competitors. The second event was management's decision to operate the plant with permanent replacements rather than either supervisors or temporary replacements. The choice to use permanent replacements, followed eventually by the procedure of bringing back striking employees only as job openings occurred, meant that deeply antagonistic workers would be hired into the midst of employees whom these returning strikers regarded as "scabs."

Still later, the negotiators' frames shifted again from their mutual acceptance of the no-holds-barred conflict to a mutual desire to limit the ongoing and future damage of the conflict. Mediator Malcolm Lovell played a key role in coordinating the reframing of the leaders' views, ensuring that both sides wanted to end the strike before UPIU President Glenn's upcoming campaign for reelection. The negotiations that followed confirmed that the parties' representatives could reach a compromise, but the membership's subsequent rejection of the proposed agreement suggests that at the local level the interpretive frame had not changed and was at variance with that of their representatives from union headquarters—specifically, the national leaders—who now felt the necessity of nationwide damage control, while the Jay local focused on IP's refusal to reinstate all striking workers.

Several critical events were required before the striking members would grudgingly accept their leaders' sense of resignation and agree to abandon the fight. Other IP plants with upcoming negotiations rejected the idea of joining the pool, and there was the ominous rumor that young workers might break ranks and return to work.

In retrospect, the question should be asked whether the relationship could not have been salvaged before the local union lost everything. There are a couple of options that, if pursued, might have made a difference.

Given the siege mentality within the local union, the international union leadership could have *insisted* that the settlement worked out by Lovell be endorsed by the local leadership. Stronger moves would have involved placing the local under trusteeship (similar to the action taken by a different international union in another celebrated confrontation—Hormel versus the Food and Commercial Workers at Austin, Minnesota). Further, Lovell could have been asked to serve as an arbitrator, thereby creating a forced solution and getting as many strikers back to work as possible. The alternative of arbitration probably would have been rejected by the company, since management believed it could dictate the terms of the settlement once it had demonstrated that it could operate the plant in the face of a strike.

Also, a different response by the company at the deadline might have helped the local union and workforce "come around" and be willing to accept some changes in cherished pay arrangements, especially premium pay for Sunday. By bringing in strike replacements immediately, the company shifted the negotiations from a discussion of appropriate pay and work arrangements to a struggle for institutional survival. With permanent replacements in the picture, an impossible-to-close negative range developed between the union's insistence that replacements be terminated and the company's insistence that it was honor bound to keep them because that was the pledge they had made to induce these replacements to endure the pressure of crossing a picket line and working inside a plant under a blockade.

Paper plants tend to be located in isolated communities, where a type of resolute solidarity can develop rapidly. When (in addition) militant and charismatic leaders like Ray Rogers are brought into the arena, the chances of finding common ground diminish greatly. It is possible that a delay in the use of replacement workers would have allowed time for the power realities to more fully become apparent. For example, Caterpillar, in a dispute with the UAW in 1992, followed a strategy of delayed resort to replacements. This strategy succeeded—at least to the point of getting the workers back to their jobs. Of course, the critics will point out that relationship and substantive issues "back at the plant" in Peoria have been far from resolved.

This brings us to the fundamental question of whether a company like IP sees any value in a collective bargaining relationship, and whether it attempts to roll out its forcing strategy in a way that does not severely undermine this relationship. When companies like IP and Guilford (the next case to be discussed) move quickly to hire permanent replacements, it is understandable why labor concludes that an important objective guiding employer tactics must be escape from union representation. Thus, the forcing strategy is revealed as a highly volatile option in the present economic and legal context. Power tactics prompt power responses that escalate an economic contest into a struggle for institutional and organizational survival.

THE HIGH STAKES OF A FORCING STRATEGY IN RAILROADS
The Guilford Story

The Guilford case represents the most celebrated example of unrestrained forcing to occur in the railroads during the 1980s. While it is not clear whether the parties intended at the outset to engage in unrestrained forcing, the escalation quickly occurred after impasse was reached in negotiations between the company and the Brotherhood of Maintenance of Way Employees (BMWE). This dispute was settled by intervention of the federal government; however, the company unveiled other tactics, specifically, a series of reorganizations that allowed it to drastically revise its contracts and union representation arrangements. The company gained some important changes in work rules, although working relations with labor were soured dramatically. Whether a healing process will eventually take place and the parties will be able to fashion constructive working relations is difficult to gauge as of the mid-1990s.

Significant Features

The Guilford case provides important insights into the nature of forcing in the highly regulated railroad context:

- The parties placed dramatically different interpretations on the same events, especially the strike by the BMWE to force the company to improve its final offer.

• The government played a key role in ending an escalating labor dispute.

• Even with a partial return to the *status quo ante*, the parties found themselves in a new relationship—with the unions deeply resentful over the employment of replacement workers and with the company looking for every opportunity to seize the initiative.

• Rivalries among competing craft unions were effectively exploited by management in the context of a forcing strategy.

In many respects the Guilford case falls somewhere between the AP Parts and Jay cases. The parties in this instance engaged in considerable escalation of hostilities, but the intervention of the government prevented the all-out battle of Jay. While Guilford has remained unionized, the structure of representation has changed dramatically, with one union covering all workers during an important phase of restructuring. While the outcomes are not as dramatic as the decertification of the union at Jay, they involved much more fundamental changes than occurred at AP Parts.

The Story Line

The Guilford story is complex. We will summarize only highlights and identify the key elements of the strategy as it unfolded. The Guilford saga can be divided into four phases:

1. Acquisition and anticipated expansion (1981-1985);

2. Strike by the BMWE (1986);

3. Springfield Terminal concept (1987); and

4. Work stoppage and its aftereffects (1987 and after).

Phase 1—Quest for Viability Through Controlled Forcing

The first phase, covering the early 1980s, involved a program to consolidate three railroads: one marginally profitable railroad (Maine Central), one railroad that had been in bankruptcy since 1970 (Boston and Maine), and a third railroad that was in *de facto* bankruptcy (Delaware and Hudson). The reorganization included restructuring of shops, offices, and other facilities, as well as investment in labor-saving technology, e.g., new track repair equipment.

In 1983, an agreement was reached with the BMWE reducing the number of maintenance sections from 52 to 26. In exchange, the railroad provided enhanced travel allowances. In October 1984, Guilford reached a series of agreements with the clerk's union wherein the company gained flexibility in transferring and consolidating clerical work. In exchange, the carrier agreed to various severance payments for individuals affected by these consolidations. Likewise, throughout 1985 and early 1986, Guilford attempted to negotiate a supplemental unemployment benefits (SUB) plan with the International Association of Machinists in exchange for flexibility in executing transfer and consolidation moves. In addition, numerous shop, office, and operational consolidations were implemented under the labor protection conditions imposed by the Interstate Commerce Commission in the Guilford consolidation.

While these events were transpiring, the BMWE initiated negotiations under the procedures of the Railway Labor Act seeking, among other things, lifetime protection of benefits for its members. For its part, Guilford sought to place a cap on severance pay for workers who would no longer be needed. In addition, the company sought to create one seniority district for production work at its Maine Central division rather than the then existing arrangement of four separate districts. For example, under the existing contract, if additional crews were needed outside of Portland, members of the statewide seniority district had to be utilized, subject to overtime limits, before any of the Portland personnel could be called out. Recognizing that such a composite seniority unit would reduce personnel, the company proposed a severance program of $26,000 for individuals who would be made redundant.

Mediation was initiated in September 1984, and the parties were released to "self help" by the National Mediation Board (NMB) in September 1985. The company proposed, and the BMWE accepted, a ninety-day moratorium on any unilateral action. During this ninety-day moratorium period the parties continued negotiations. In addition to the $26,000 per person protective arrangement, the company agreed to match wage increases that would emerge from national negotiations. The BMWE continued to press its demand for retroactive severance payments for employees already furloughed. When the company refused to accede to this demand, the BMWE went on strike on March 3, 1986.

Phase II—The Shift to Unrestrained Forcing

As soon as the strike began, Guilford initiated actions to continue operations, although at reduced levels. Specifically, the company hired replacement workers to supplement managerial employees. Two weeks into the strike, the BMWE approached Guilford about reaching an agreement based on the carrier's prestrike offer. From the company's point of view the onset of the strike had changed its decision-making calculus, and it responded that it was not interested in returning to its prestrike offer.

Soon thereafter (in May) the union set up picket lines at various interline points throughout the northeast (and even at selected locations as far away as the Midwest and the West Coast). Within two weeks the dispute had escalated to the point that it threatened to affect most of the operations of the nation's large freight carriers—with the result that the White House stepped in and appointed an emergency board under the provisions of the Railway Labor Act. Subsequently, the emergency board recommended a settlement along the lines of Guilford's last offer. This recommendation was rejected by Guilford. Eventually the strike was settled in September 1986 as a result of a cooling-off period imposed by Congress and creation of an advisory board that followed the terms of the emergency board report.

Phase III—Continuing the Strategy of Unrestrained Forcing

With the dispute finally settled, the labor-management relationship continued in a direction very different from the one existing prior to the strike. By fall 1986, Guilford was ready to unveil yet another piece of its forcing strategy: transferring in stages its various operations to its Springfield Terminal (ST) subsidiary.

Over the years, Guilford had maintained a small subsidiary line in Springfield, Vermont, where it had a contract with one union, the United Transportation Union (UTU), for the few workers associated with the line. In a series of reorganizations, Guilford proceeded to transfer (on paper) the Maine Central, the Boston and Maine, and the Delaware and Hudson to the jurisdiction of the Springfield Terminal.[6] Guilford maintained that as a result of these changes in organization, the ST was free to apply to the transferred operations its existing UTU agreement (that gave management substantial flexibility).

The parties to the ST agreement (management and UTU) did not reach a new agreement for the transferred operations until February 1989. Included in the new agreement were wage increases, new administrative procedures covering bidding, displacements and reductions-in-force, and most important, a mutually agreed-upon basis for dovetailing the seniority of employees across the various railroads that had been placed under the umbrella of ST. The agreement also contained a moratorium on any changes through December 31, 1994.

Phase IV—Consolidation and Union Representation Struggles

The final phase began when the UTU went on strike in November 1987, with 1,200 workers claiming that safety was not being maintained under the Springfield Terminal agreements. Again, Guilford management responded by operating the system with supervisors and replacements. The strike lasted until June 1988, when the NMB ordered the parties into arbitration.

Without detailing all of the twists and turns of the legal journey that was traveled in the aftermath of the ST reorganization, suffice it to say that the ICC, the NMB, and various arbitrators grappled with a range of issues that included seniority of transferred workers, appropriate pay levels, and protection for furloughed workers.

As of 1994, these decisions could be summarized as follows:

- Economic arrangements and work rules were restored to the terms and conditions in effect before the ST reorganization (1986) for workers then on the payroll, although wage increases that had been negotiated by the UTU in 1989 were not applicable.

- For workers employed after the ST reorganization, the revised terms and conditions of the UTU contract applied.

- Most of the craft unions ultimately regained representation rights.

Analysis

An overall assessment of the Guilford strategy is still premature. However, a number of observations can be made on both sides of the ledger.

There were positive gains from management's point of view. The break-even point for volume was reduced by approximately 30 percent. In addition, compensation costs were reduced 20 percent as a result of the implementation of contracts with lower wage scales and reduced crew sizes. For example, the run from Albany, New York to southern New Hampshire—a trip that formerly required five four-person crews—was done with two two-person crews. Overall, 90 percent of all trains operated with two-person crews as of 1994.

Management maintained that this dramatic reduction in labor costs made it possible to schedule more frequent and shorter trains, thereby providing better service to its customers. Previously, it had been forced to collect traffic into longer trains to gain economies of scale—a practice that did not provide the best service to its customers.

On the other side of the ledger is the impact of the various arbitration decisions, which eliminated a significant portion of the savings. Moreover, some of the expected benefits from the new arrangements were slow to materialize. While a major theme of the new labor agreement was flexibility and cross utilization of personnel (in fact, the signed agreement with the UTU provided for salary enhancement as workers learned other skills), little change took place, primarily because middle management did not capitalize on the new opportunities.

The bottom line for revenue and employment was also negative. Tonnage did not recover to levels existing prior to the spring of 1986, and while the railroad returned to profitability (1994), overall revenue was 25 percent lower. Employment fell from approximately 5,500 to slightly over 1,000 by 1994.

The relationship between management and the workers/unions also continued to be very acrimonious and complex, especially in light of the previously mentioned point that employees hired before the ST reorganization were returned to their former pay arrangements while new employees were held to the terms negotiated by the UTU. In addition, individual workers filed complaints with different government agencies alleging safety problems and harassment. Add to this the tension created in work groups where replacement workers found themselves alongside long-service union activists and the picture of a contentious workplace was complete.

The Power Equation

Each side possessed certain advantages that included:

Determining Factors—Guilford

Company	Unions
Closely held company with a willingness of key managers to take risks	The ability of the unions at Guilford to mobilize other unions into a secondary boycott

In the power equation above (evenly balanced), the decisive factor in determining the eventual outcome was the government's stepping in and mandating a settlement. During the second round the government again stepped in, but by this time the company had introduced simplified work rules and bargaining structures that remained in place. In effect, the function of government intervention was to get the railroad functioning again and this role could have helped either side (depending on the terms of the return-to-work agreement).

The Dynamics

The Guilford story represents a saga of "let's get even," with the company encountering the BMWE strike, then "going for broke" with the Springfield Terminal restructuring, followed by the unions striking, and finally with the company seeking to sustain its advantage through court and arbitration proceedings aimed at confirming the new operating arrangements.

These moves and countermoves can be summarized:

• Company presents a proposal that it considers fair.

• Union follows standard script: It assumes that by striking it will sweeten the package.

- Rejection of "fair" proposal by union creates "agonizing reappraisal" on management's part.
- Company "declares war" and hires replacements.
- Union is incensed by the action of the company in hiring permanent replacements and succeeds in escalating the dispute by enlisting support from other unions around the country.
- Government intervenes and mandates a settlement.
- Company uses a reorganization (Springfield Terminal) as a means for revising labor-management contracts and recognizing the UTU as sole bargaining unit for its operating employees.
- Unions strike over issue of safety.
- Craft unions other than UTU extremely resentful and form a craft council.
- Relations remain extremely tense.

Unrestrained forcing unleashes these dynamics wherein each side adopts tactics that seek to redress a power disadvantage and/or to gain a new advantage. This tit-for-tat is very characteristic of unrestrained forcing.

Why did management at Guilford undertake such drastic restructuring via the ST concept? When the emergency board made its recommendations that the dispute with the BMWE be settled on the basis of the company's last offer, "railroad buffs" would have expected that the relationship would have returned to arm's-length, i.e., to businesslike dealings that had existed for several decades. After all, the company had gained the changes that it wanted, and the workers had received a settlement matching industry levels of compensation. Why, then, was the company proceeding with additional forcing tactics by using the shell of the ST to rewrite existing labor agreements?

The campaign by Guilford to force, on a continuing basis, changes in work practices and pay levels is explained by the low value that the company placed on preserving the labor-management relationship. In most instances of change, the formal labor-management relationship remains intact, and a desire to prevent it from souring serves as some degree of restraint on the behavior of the parties. In the case of Guilford, the labor-management relationship was, for the most part, fractured when management decided to proceed with its hard forcing strategy of replacing striking BMWE workers. With nothing to lose, since it had already been labeled the "bad guy" of the industry, Guilford pressed on with other tactics—in this case, using the ST subsidiary to revise all of its labor contracts. Of course, the company was aided in its isolate behavior by the willingness of UTU, also an isolate among railroad unions, to step forward as the bargaining agent for all of the unionized workers on the railroad.

The Springfield Terminal move raises the interesting question about the circumstances that delineate the line between restrained forcing tactics and an all-out battle. In interviews, Guilford management asserted that it did not enter the negotiations with BMWE with any plan of confrontation in mind. The unions maintain otherwise. But regardless of the company's original intent, when the union rejected what the company negotiators thought was a fair package, top management shifted in their mindset.

Basically then, the strike by BMWE was evaluated from very different perspectives by the parties. For the unions it was the normal course of action to go on strike whenever the Railway Labor Act procedures were finally exhausted. For the company, the strike represented a pivotal event or, in their language, "the last straw." The rejection by the union of management's offer moved the relationship beyond the point of no return.

How could something as "routine" as the BMWE going on strike create such a shift on the part of Guilford management? The expectation of the union was that management would make some small changes in its offer, the strike would be called off, and the contract signed; or, if management insisted on holding to its position, then an emergency board would be appointed and a recommendation would come forward that would "sweeten" management's last offer. By continuing to operate, and especially by hiring replacements, management charted a very new course. What explains this pivotal development?

When management decided to "go all out," it was giving release to decades of pent-up frustration over not being able (from its point of view) to deal adequately with the "labor problem." The additional dollars that would have been required to compensate workers already on furlough were not large, but as is the case with the onset of most holy wars, a limit had been reached. This choice to move from traditional distributive bargaining to a strategy of unrestrained forcing was heavily influenced by the thinking of the CEO, Tim Mellon. The combination of a privately held company, a small regional carrier operating primarily in New England, and a strong-willed leader—all coalesced to make the strategy both feasible and desirable for management.

The Guilford strategy, to a very large extent, was dictated by economics. The 1986 BMWE strike lasted from March 3 until late May. The strike resulted in a serious loss of revenue and a permanent loss of some traffic. These facts, combined with the long-term secular decline in railroad traffic in New England, convinced Guilford management that an immediate restructuring of labor costs was necessary via the ST concept. Of primary importance was the changing of work rules (e.g., changing from five-man crews on the Maine Central and three-man crews on the Boston and Maine to two-man crews under the ST agreement). There was a real sense in 1986 that Guilford could not wait for the gradual restructuring of labor costs that may or may not have taken place on the national level. In other words, there was a sense of urgency that something had to be done in the short term.

Given this explanation it is hard to imagine ways that the parties could have reached their objectives without experiencing this debacle. One possibility would have been for the leaders on both sides to have found ways to create some type of alignment across their divergent perspectives. Such an idea sounds fine as a general proposition but becomes very difficult to operationalize in the face of a long history of arms-length dealings and the reality of bringing about changes in key assumptions within organizations characterized by many levels and factions. Nevertheless, like our speculation on the Jay case, if management at Guilford had delayed hiring replacements once the BMWE went on strike, the chances of reaching and changing the outlook of the rank and file might have increased.

Indeed, Guilford management engaged in very little direct communication with their workers. Rather, the approach appeared to be to catch the union leadership off balance by quickly hiring replacements when the BMWE struck and subsequently pushing through reorganization moves. At no point did the company put the union and members on notice that it would be forced to take action by a specific date if no agreement could be reached on the proposed program for change. Such as approach might not have worked, i.e., the company would still have been "forced to force"—but a modicum of trust across the boundary might have been preserved. As it turned out, when confronted by the various moves of the company, the unions could only conclude that they were in a fight for their survival.

The Future

In many ways 1994 stands as a key year in the history of the Guilford saga. With the recertification of the craft unions and with contracts due to expire at the end of the year, the parties embarked upon contract negotiations for the first time since the confrontations of the 1980s. All parties were committed to remaining outside of national negotiations (also scheduled to commence in late 1994).

While the company succeeded in changing key work rules as a result of its forcing strategy, and while it looked for a while like its local initiative might gain for it some advantage vis-a-vis the rest of the industry, the irony is that similar flexibility had been achieved by others. Large freight carriers like Union Pacific and Norfolk Southern, who had remained committed to national negotiations (termed "national handling"), were operating with the same reduced crews and flexibility as Guilford as a result of the 1991-92 industry settlement.

So with respect to outcomes, Guilford ended up even compared to the rest of the industry on work rules. On the relationship side of the equation, however, it had generated considerable resentment. Negotiations unfolding as this book was going to press presumably provided an opportunity for the parties to strengthen working relationships and to take advantage of a number of business opportunities in the New England region, including alliances with Canadian regional railroads, intermodal arrangements in Albany, and new warehousing at the restructured Ft. Devens in Massachusetts.

In retrospect, it is easy to be critical of the strategy chosen by Guilford. When they embarked upon their program of change in the mid-1980s, it did not appear that any substantial breakthroughs would be forthcoming from national negotiations. Significantly, virtually all of the small and medium-size railroads had found it necessary to deal locally with their respective unions. And no doubt they will continue in this vein, despite the gains realized by the National Railway Labor

Conference (the employers association) in the 1991-92 industry settlement.

The next chapter of the Guilford story will be especially important to monitor, since it will shed light on the question of whether medium-size regional carriers (as well as small, short lines) can fashion strategies that improve their viability in ways more expeditious or comparable to the change avenues available to the large national freight carriers as a result of industry-level negotiations.

OVERVIEW OF FORCING

Outcomes

In drawing up a balance sheet for our three cases of forcing, a number of patterns are evident:

- The unions involved never ended up winning. In two cases, some or all unions lost representation rights (Jay and Guilford) and in one case, they struggled to a stalemate (AP Parts).

- The workers did not fare much better, either. Some of them lost their jobs at Jay and Guilford, and in all of these cases workers suffered losses in pay during the strikes and were forced to return to work under drastically altered contracts.

- Management generally fared better. In every case they gained more favorable labor contracts. However, in varying degrees and for varying periods, the three companies experienced deteriorated labor-management relationships. Even where the company succeeded in escaping union representation, a legacy of bitterness remained within the workforce.

Lessons Learned

In reviewing the three cases, we can identify a number of best practices. They can be organized around the three time periods that often characterize a forcing effort, namely, formulation of the plan, actions at the deadline, and relations in the aftermath of the forcing episode.

Formulating and Presenting the Demands

As discussed at several points, the forcing strategies might have been executed more successfully if the companies had found ways to make their objectives more credible. In the AP Parts case, where management felt it needed to reduce compensation costs (rather than just achieve productivity gains), the task of making its position plausible became much more difficult.

Acceptance of the need for change by the union and its members at AP Parts was made especially difficult by developments that had occurred during the early 1980s. Management, in a prior negotiation, had achieved a series of concessions, leading to the conclusion on the part of many workers and union leaders that the competitive problem had been fixed. Thus, as AP management approached the 1984 negotiations it faced an even higher hurdle in making a credible case for new (and much larger) concessions.

In varying degrees, the unions felt that these companies were being unreasonable in seeking changes that could be viewed as rolling back the clock or breaking away from the patterns of the industry. Ultimately, there may not have been an elegant solution to a dilemma facing these companies, namely, how to focus attention on changes that they believed were required as a competitive necessity without being seen as abrogating the historical understandings with their unions and employees.

Thus, the best available solution in most circumstances may be for management to make its case as best it can and to deal with the inevitable escalation as effectively as possible.

From the union side of the picture, the best stance could be a course not followed by any of the unions in our forcing cases, namely, to ask for involvement in management decisions previously reserved exclusively to management. In return for concessions, the union leadership would be seeking involvement in matters essential to the competitive survival of the firm. The type of *quid pro quo* we contemplate is best illustrated by Packard Electric and Budd in the next chapter.

Actions at the Deadline

As noted in the discussion of AP Parts, if management can continue operations without resort to hiring replacements at the deadline, then more options are preserved for sustaining the labor-management relationship. Similarly, if the union avoids strike action and keeps discussions going, the chances are enhanced that some common ground can be found.

But again there may not be any alternative short of a test of resolves via a strike or lockout. Given the incompatible expectations that usually accompany any discussion aimed at securing major concessions, an outcome that all sides can live with may not emerge until the parties experience the rising costs of conflict.

Reconstruction of Labor-Management Relations

Ultimately, the best opportunity for the exercise of leadership occurs after the raw power aspects of the forcing episode have subsided. From this perspective, the escalation that characterizes a forcing regime may be inevitable, given the history of the relationship and the new direction that one of the parties (usually management) wants to pursue.

The challenge for the parties, then, is to conduct the early phase of the conflict so that the possibility for reconstruction is not precluded and to handle the poststrike period with skill and imagination.

The Key Role of Leadership

The reconstruction of relationships after a forcing episode does not happen all at once, but occurs over time as a result of a series of trust-building events. Associated with these pivotal events are critical choices centering on management and union leadership styles. In the case of AP Parts, an adherence to traditional adversarial management styles (matched in parallel by the preference of union leaders to use traditional tactics) meant that the relationship, when reestablished, would be arm's length.

Once the hostilities associated with the strike subsided in these three cases, the parties at AP Parts were able to restore relations, but at Guilford there was dramatic restructuring and at Jay the local union was mortally wounded and eventually decertified. The exact course that relationships take after the trauma of unrestrained forcing is somewhat indeterminate, as illustrated by the different journeys of these cases. Clearly, the skills and orientation of key leaders on both sides explain in large part the tone and nature of the ongoing labor-management relationships.

The Essential Nature of Forcing

These three cases vividly illustrate the dimensions that are inherent in all instances of forcing—especially the dynamics of confrontation and escalation. Although it is not inevitable that every case of forcing proceeds to the extreme stage, these three cases are representative of a much larger set of celebrated cases of intense conflict that we summarized in the opening chapter.

Rapid Deterioration of Relations

When management in these cases departed from the norms of interaction by making demands for significant concessions and hiring replacements, a sequence of events unfolded that resulted in a major deterioration of social relations. Underlying the collapse was the reality that each side perceived their own organizational or institutional survival to be at stake.

A type of siege mentality often developed during the confrontations. Management at AP Parts and Guilford, for example, believed so fervently in the rightness of their actions that they ended up isolated from large segments of the business community.

Departing from familiar rules was a tactic seen by management as a means of sending a signal of just how dire the situation had become. For the most part the response, however, was for the unions to feel institutionally threatened. What followed was a set of tit-for-tat interactions involving distributive bargaining, negative attitudinal structuring, and intraorganizational initiatives that produced progressively lower trust relations.[7]

Third Parties and the Law

A related point is that third parties often found themselves being pulled into the vortex of an escalating conflict. When the community sought to intervene in the AP Parts strike, labor and management entered into a contest for partners. Community suggestions were interpreted as supporting or threatening one side or the other, and the potential for mediation was eroded. In the case of Jay, the parties vied for support from state officials, and at Guilford the federal government found itself compelled to intervene.

The law is often intended to provide a check on destructive behavior that is not adequately regulated by market forces. In the two cases that fall under the jurisdiction of the NLRA, however, we found that the limited scope of influence and action available to the NLRB meant that the law had little impact on the escalating disputes. By contrast, the escalating tensions in the one case involving the National Railway Labor Act were moderated by the various procedures under the Act.

Prognosis

A large literature on labor-management cooperation identifies the new beginnings that often emerge after strikes. The amendment that we bring to this conventional wisdom is that the parties certainly learn some lessons as a result of unrestrained forcing, and these can have a tempering or therapeutic effect on relationships—when those relationships survive the conflict. But poststrike relations can remain turbulent for a long time, especially given the stark possibility that, for the unions involved, their very existence may be undermined. In all, unrestrained forcing in the present era has the potential to generate dramatic change, but much of the change is not necessarily what is anticipated or desired by the forcing party.

NOTES

1. Valuable research assistance was provided by Pat McHugh in the preparation of this case.

2. As of the early 1990s, long after the tensions associated with the 1984 negotiations had subsided, it was difficult to determine what private plans (e.g., getting rid of the union) were guiding management. All of the principals of management's side of the table were no longer associated with AP Parts, and the new management officials indicated that they did not really know.

3 Specifically, the union's filing with the NLRB stated that the employer had failed "to provide the data necessary for intelligent collective bargaining"; refused "to alter, except in insignificant ways, the terms of their initial proposal"; threatened to "discharge those workers who refused to accept their proposal"; made a final offer "before bargaining could narrow the issues between the parties"; "threatened and coerced its employees through the hiring of professional goons and guard dogs"; unilaterally changed the wages, hours, and working conditions of its employees without bargaining in good faith"; and engaged in "calculated mass discipline of over 300 workers because they have chosen to refrain from striking."

4 Specifically, the regional director stated that the employer's tactics did not constitute unlawful surface bargaining, that there was sufficient notice of changes in working conditions, that information regarding the employer's entry into the original equipment manufacturing market was irrelevant to the negotiations, that the employer's direct contacts with employees were lawful, and that there was insufficient evidence of concerted discipline For their part, the union representatives cited the opinion of hearing examiners that the AP Parts negotiations featured some of the worst violations of the National Labor Relations Act that they had even seen, and that the regional director's decision reflected pressure from conservative members of the NLRB in Washington.

5 Valuable research assistance was provided by Kathleen Rudd Scharf in the preparation of this case.

6 When analysts first hear the term "Springfield Terminal," they assume that the subsidiary must be based in Springfield, Massachusetts. This is not correct. In fact, the subsidiary, which in 1987 employed virtually no workers, was located in Springfield, Vermont and had served as a small switching railroad for the products of Jones and Lamson, a major machine tool company that had fallen on hard times. When one of the authors visited the property, all that could be seen was a roundhouse with rusty rails and uncut grass.

7. One illustrative feature of the resulting dynamic is important to note—in a number of our cases the managers rebuffed poststrike union offers to settle on some variation of management's final offer. Essentially the union was told that once the strike began, the cost of settlement went up. While this is not a new tactic, in the present era this tactic heightens the irreversibility of "holy wars," when the decision to strike or lock out is made.

3
Fostering
Negotiating Commitment and Cooperation

Whereas a forcing strategy is intended to enable one party to prevail over the other and relies upon coercive power, a fostering strategy attempts to advance common or complementary interests through attitude change, persuasion, and problem solving.

This chapter examines how companies have attempted to foster new relationships and new contracts with labor. Given its commitment to foster change, how does management formulate its objectives and choose its negotiating tactics? How does management deal with the anxiety in its own organization created by its efforts to negotiate employee commitment? How does the union discern the intentions of management and deal with its own ambivalence about the changes management seeks? How do employees shift from a mindset of compliance to one of commitment? We explore these and other issues via cases from the paper, auto supply, and railroad industries.

The first case, Bidwell, illustrates our broad definition of labor negotiations (not just limited to collective bargaining), and it highlights the negotiated aspects of the Quality of Worklife (QWL) genre of change efforts.

The second case, CSX, chronicles an ambitious effort by a major freight railroad to fashion a breakthrough agreement with its operating unions in advance of industrywide negotiations. The case also illustrates the complexity of pursuing a fostering strategy where there are multiple internal constituencies (represented by different unions) on the labor side.

The third case involves a small, skilled trades setting—Anderson Pattern and a craft union, the Pattern Makers Association. Distinctive issues emerged around new technology, with the parties proceeding in steps toward a productive and positive relationship.

These three cases highlight several ways of traveling down the fostering path. At the level of union-management relations, we examine the establishment of permanent labor-management steering committees, temporary (issue-specific) labor-management task forces, union involvement in business planning activities, and the utilization of problem-solving approaches in collective bargaining. At the individual level of employee relations, we trace employee involvement initiatives, quality control innovations, semi-autonomous work groups, and increased direct ties between individual employees and customers. Also, we examine issues that cut across these levels, such as information-sharing, training, and the introduction of new technologies.

Some of the fostering efforts are focused on changing attitudes—building a sense of teamwork and cooperation; others are focused more on behaviors—improving work operations and enhancing productivity through contractual changes (McKersie and Hunter 1973). For example, we will see in the Bidwell QWL effort a strong emphasis on attitude change, whereas in the case of CSX the parties focused on revising the contract (specifying changes in behavior). In the case of Anderson, both attitudinal and behavioral change processes were employed in a closely coordinated fashion.

Key Aspects of Cases Featuring Fostering

	Bidwell	CSX	Anderson
Focus of efforts	Change of attitudes	New contract language	Both attitudes and behavior
Mechanism	QWL	Early negotiations	A series of joint activities and innovative negotiations
Level of the activity	Local union officials and rank and file	Company-union representatives	All levels
Number of unions involved	4	10	1
Scope of potential change	Department by department	Systemwide	Plantwide
Substantive changes	Minimal	None as a result of these negotiations	Large
Relationship with union	Deteriorated somewhat	Improved somewhat	Improved
Relationship with workers	Little change	Little change	Improved

Against the historical backdrop, these examples of fostering are similar to the many examples of labor-management cooperation that have been fashioned throughout this century.[1] The agenda or the particular format may be different but the attitudinal and problem-solving elements are similar.

Although all three cases involve fostering, they differ from one another in many ways.

AN ABORTIVE BID TO FOSTER COOPERATION
Bidwell Mill, 1981-1984

The Bidwell case is about the initiation, development, and decline of a QWL program in a paper mill between September 1981 and early 1984.[2] It is a case of essentially pure fostering.[3]

At management's initiative, mill managers and officials of three of the four local unions negotiated an agreement to jointly sponsor a QWL program. The fourth local opposed the program but allowed QWL activities to go forward elsewhere in the mill. Participative activities took root firmly among employees and their supervisors in some parts of the mill, allowing them to renegotiate their daily work roles and responsibilities. Thus, labor and management took steps that on their face could have led to cooperative labor relationships at both the union-management and employee/shop-floor levels. However, the apparent agreement between management and the unions unraveled; and, in the absence of institutional support, employee participation activities on the mill floor declined.

The Bidwell case represents a form of fostering highly typical of the late 1970s and 1980s—one centered on employee participation. It also illustrates many typical barriers encountered by such initiatives (including changes in leadership and ownership, as well as incomplete attention to the interests of key stakeholders) and several other barriers (such as division among multiple unions) that are more characteristic of some industries than others. We will highlight many process elements in such a story. These include negotiations over the nature of the fostering, internal negotiations within labor and management, and negotiations (as well as a lack of negotiations) over various implementation decisions. Stated more succinctly, we will analyze negotiations over the timing, structure, and priority of the QWL program, as well as its eventual demise.

Significant Features

The case that follows contains a number of significant elements. Those include the following:

- Initial off-site meetings provided headway (after initial skepticism) for union and management decisions to co-sponsor QWL.
- Three of the four unions agreed to goals and a joint structure for QWL.
- The high-status hold-out union was not easily influenced, but agreed to stand aside so long as no QWL activity occurred with its members.
- Management's own underlying limited interest and/or ambivalence about more cooperative relations and more commitment was a major factor in explaining why it did not follow through.
- Eventually the hold-out union attacked management and other union officials for QWL activities.
- The use of a third-party facilitator both assisted and complicated the decision-making process.
- The process ultimately collapsed as a result of various unsuccessful negotiations within labor and management, as well as between labor and management.

Getting Underway With QWL

The Bidwell mill, started in the 1960s, employed 500 people in 1981. In a pattern typical of this industry, mill management received relatively detailed direction from corporate headquarters. Corporate staff, for example, scheduled production for the mill and negotiated local contracts.

Corporate management also provided the impetus for the QWL program at Bidwell. Executives had visited Japan and several QWL sites in the United States, including General Motors, and concluded that the company should develop a new approach to management that included QWL activities.

Several Bidwell managers attended a three day workshop sponsored by corporate staff to "encourage" mills to embark on QWL change efforts. Although Bidwell managers had little enthusiasm for the idea, they felt they had no real choice but to agree to start a QWL effort.

In September 1981, the Bidwell mill manager hired an external consultant recommended by corporate staff and began a series of meetings with local management. These early meetings surfaced the historic distrust toward "corporate folks," their doubts about the merits of the QWL effort, and their expectations that it would fail. Increasingly, these meetings and other meetings they spawned were devoted to the development of internal cohesion and consensus within management. The consultant, who facilitated team development and planning sessions of the mill manager's staff, noted that they agreed to proceed on QWL "with a cool, dispassionate resolution," without enthusiasm and without any real commitment.

Management scheduled three major activities involving salaried employees: first, all salaried employees attended a one-day QWL orientation session; second, managers participated in a series of two-day supervisory skills training sessions; and third, management staff were surveyed and feedback sessions were held on a unit-by-unit basis. Commenting on this internal management phase, the consultant observed, "this staff was approaching the process as —'taking their foul-tasting medicine'—a lot of complaining, and yet overt compliance to the plans they, as a team, developed" (Mohrman 1987).

Negotiating Union Support and Employee Involvement

The second phase was marked by the onset of joint union-management activities. The mill manager had kept the four local union presidents informed of the company's interest in QWL, the preparatory work within the management organization, and his plan to approach them formally about establishing a QWL steering committee. The union presidents reacted with a mixture of interest and skepticism.

In the spring of 1982 the mill manager decided to have preliminary discussions with the unions before summer, with the prospect of establishing a steering committee in September. On the one hand, he was feeling pressure to proceed from the consultant and from the fact that sister mills already had their unions "on board." On the other hand, he was also aware that vacation schedules in the summer made it a difficult time to hold meetings. His own staff was divided on the timing issue. Some were prepared to form the steering committee soon, others felt September was the earliest practical date.

In the preliminary meeting, the union officials asked for the same orientation workshops that managers had already attended. Management agreed and a workshop was conducted by the consultant—and attended only by union officers, who again raised questions about the seriousness of management's interest in QWL and about its intentions. At the conclusion of the workshop, officers from three of the four unions were interested and decided to proceed. Officers of the fourth union were negative, but after failing to convince their union colleagues not to proceed, they decided to participate in another meeting with management.

In this next meeting, managers and union officials agreed to establish a mill steering committee to manage a joint QWL process and to begin three-day joint training sessions. They also set up substeering committees in the three parts of the plant represented by the three interested unions. While the officers of the fourth union agreed to be on the mill committee, they did not plan any activities in their area of the mill. Significantly, the uninvolved union represented the paper machine operators, the most skilled and prestigious workers in the mill.

The decision to proceed during the summer came about at the unions' urging. Managers expressed their preference for a September start, but then agreed to go along earlier. They later expressed resentment because they felt the consultant had tilted the discussion toward the unions' preference. For her part, the consultant felt managers' inhibitions about expressing their limited support reflected the need for more management team development.

The QWL activities got off to a good start that summer (1982). The mill steering committee discussed issues in the mill and agreed to a statement of philosophy to guide the QWL process. Participants responded well to the training, and by fall problem-solving teams were active in two of the four areas of the mill. Teams tackled, among other issues, scrap rates, maintenance backlogs, and clean-up procedures. These activities produced cooperative relationships in specific departments and in some cases were self-sustaining, i.e., requiring no ongoing oversight by top mill management or local union leaders.

Internal Divisions Undermine Cooperative Work

Two factors broke the momentum of the summer's change process. First, the Bidwell mill and its sister paper mills in the company were put up for sale twice within a short period of time, deflecting management's attention and creating uncertainty about the commitment of future managements. In this context, individual managers and supervisors who had felt all along that QWL was either unwise or getting too much priority began to express their doubts more publicly. Second, officers of the paper machine operators' union withdrew from the mill steering committee and charged that the other unions' officers were being brainwashed and that QWL would undermine the unions. Although some officers of the other unions defended their involvement in QWL, the leaders of the papermakers union succeeded in raising doubts within the ranks of the other unions. These leaders also attacked management for not keeping the unions fully informed about the prospective sale and for discrepancies between its QWL rhetoric and its actions—or inaction in the case of a labor proposal to eliminate time clocks.

The QWL change effort underwent another setback in the fall when Bidwell was sold and the new corporate owners installed a new mill manager. The new executives expressed support for QWL, and the new mill manager claimed to have a natural inclination to manage participatively. However, when he realized that his own staff was internally divided on many issues, he decided that the most pressing concern was management development.

The new mill manager soon discovered that the divisions among his staff extended to their views of QWL. In February 1983, mill management staff met to review the status of QWL. The substantive reports of activities indicated that some areas were doing well but others had bogged down. In the latter areas, union members had asked for visible signs of management commitment to cooperation, such as the removal of time clocks cited earlier. The reports soon gave way to an expression of concerns: top management appeared to be preoccupied with QWL, and it was creating stress for supervisors and managers by asking for dramatic changes in behavior; too much time was spent in meetings; the unions were pressing for faster progress; and union employees were becoming increasingly emboldened to the point of criticizing supervisors.

The new mill manager's response was to redouble his attention to team development within his own staff. In the meantime, the paper-makers union also stepped up its efforts to halt the QWL effort. In the spring of 1983, two of the other three unions withdrew from the QWL effort, citing management's failure to change its ways and to support whole heartedly QWL. One union went further and said that corporate pressure was leading managers to attempt covert "work-rule changes." In these two unions only a few of the officers who were originally involved in establishing QWL were still in office; most had either lost elections or opted not to run, feeling burned out by the QWL effort and discouraged by the results. Only one local union continued the cooperative efforts in its area of the mill.

The participative processes on the mill floor had not completely ceased, but the effort by management and labor to renew their institutional relationship and to restructure the work environment of the mill was effectively dead.

Analysis

The ultimate impact of the QWL program at Bidwell is difficult to gauge. Given the limited objectives for the program, its demise probably did not have serious consequences for the parties. However, any set back, even small, can act as a deterrent to the initiation of other change efforts.

It is instructive to explore why, after getting off to a good start, the program came apart. Several explanations are possible. First, Bidwell mill management was not driven by a conviction about the need for either substantive changes or a change in the labor-management relationship. Rather, it was presented with a corporate mandate to engage in a *particular* change effort, i.e., QWL.

Underlying the QWL approach, which had become fashionable among progressive managers in many American industries by the 1980s, was an implicit assumption of the desirability of creating cooperative relations with labor. However, the original motivation of Bidwell management to foster change was not based on a clear desire to produce commitment and cooperation as much as a perceived need to conform to a corporate mandate. Because its labor relations were not marked by strong adversarialism, management assumed it would be feasible to engage the unions in the fostering process.

Another key requirement for effective problem solving and attitude change was not sustained during this QWL initiative—internal consensus within both management and labor in the mill. In fact the absence of consensus and coherence within both the management and the labor communities contributed to the failure of the parties to negotiate robust change in their relationship.

Although less significant, the parties also failed to recognize the need for distributive bargaining structures and processes. For example, when labor and management appeared to have different preferences for the timing of the start of QWL activities, they failed to caucus (or confirm in some other way their interparty differences) and decide how to resolve them. The unaddressed differences exerted a deleterious effect on the relationship and the process.

Labor responded to management's stated bid for new relationships with workers and with their representatives by making a number of requests. Management acceded to some of labor's requests, such as the accelerated start of QWL activities, but not others, such as removing time clocks and acting to correct behavior of supervisors out of tune with the QWL philosophy. These failures by management to negotiate acceptable terms for labor's commitment and cooperation probably also reflected management's own ambivalence and disunity. The omissions also underscored the need for both parties to have understood more explicitly that fostering efforts such as this QWL program were indeed a negotiation process, one in which they had to be capable of resolving contentious issues as well as engaging in problem solving.

Further, it had to be a process responsive to substantive interorganiza-
tional issues, as well as interparty attitude change.

A related limitation, often inherent in a QWL initiative, is the standard ground rule that these programs be kept separate from collective
bargaining. The often-used guideline that subjects relating to contract
negotiations will not be discussed within the participation process may
be necessary to gain support from union leaders, but unless the fostering efforts deal with fundamental work issues (governed by the contract), then the change program is likely to diminish in importance
(Cutcher-Gershenfeld, Kochan, and Verma 1991).

This necessary juxtaposition of collaboration and other negotiation
activities creates many dilemmas. When the joint activities only deal
with attitudes and the tenor of the relationship, they are dismissed
(especially by bottom-line-oriented management) as "touchy-feely"
activities that are long on rhetoric and short on results. A further issue
has to do with the deep ambivalence of unions about all attitude change
efforts. Most union leaders feel very uneasy about a process of attitude
change that may align interests of employees much more directly with
the company, thereby making it more difficult for the leaders to maintain their independent political standing.

In the case of Bidwell, one union attempted to hedge by maintaining
an adversarial stance. Such ambivalence can pose obvious difficulties
for the effective functioning of the new process. Subsequently, when
the leaders of two unions withdrew cooperation from the process after
concluding that they could not simultaneously be involved in a cooperative process and an adversarial process, the QWL effort quickly
unraveled.

Pivotal Events

Understanding "what went wrong" also involves an analysis of several critical events that influenced the course of the ongoing negotiations. The first pivotal event in the Bidwell case was the already-
mentioned perfunctory decision by mill management to undertake the
QWL effort. The follow-on steps of internal management education
and initial discussions with the union leaders were taken on the basis of
only cursory consideration of the magnitude of the changes they
implied. They were made in the absence of informed leadership com-

mitment to the change. As a consequence, management was committing the members of its organization to processes and outcomes for which it was unprepared emotionally.

A second pivotal event in the Bidwell case was the decision to move ahead on the QWL program during the summer. Managers, who resented both the outcome and the way the decision was made, were less committed to the joint effort than if they had directly and consciously negotiated their differences with the union leaders. The meaning for union leaders was different—they had successfully influenced the program and gained more sense of ownership of it than before when its terms had been shaped and initiated by management. The event also tarnished the consultant's image of neutrality in the eyes of managers.

Another pivotal event in the Bidwell case was the decision of the leaders of the union representing the paper machine operators not only to stand aside from any involvement in the QWL effort but also to actively discourage other unions from participating in the effort. This not only deepened the divisions within the local union structure, but aroused greater controversy in the mill, thereby helping to arrest the diffusion of new practices throughout the mill.

It is also important to remember that much of the fostering period was influenced by the uncertainties and changes of leadership that attended the sale of the entire mill. At the least, management and union opponents of change were handed a rational justification for their position, and key managers had to shift time and attention to sale transactions and integration of new management organization.

Revisiting the Critical Choices

If the parties had the opportunity to relive this story, what alterations in their choices might have made a significant difference in overall outcomes?

First, the arrival of new ownership and management could have been used to galvanize attention to ways of improving the performance of the mill and the role of QWL in the process. Rather than signalling uncertainty, the new leadership could have used the occasion for a renewal of commitment to the existing change program.

Second, any change program requires a certain tenacity and willingness to stick it out through the middle period of limited results. Typically, these types of programs pass through a phase of initial euphoria, waning enthusiasm, and finally (but not always) acknowledged success. Management at Bidwell may have given up too quickly.

Often in cases like Bidwell, a plateau effect develops when exaggerated expectations are not met. Specifically, management tends to view these programs as "magic bullets" that will instantly increase productivity and lower operating costs. For their part, union leaders see the projects as insuring that business and jobs will expand. When these high expectations are not met, disillusionment naturally occurs.

Third, insufficient attention was paid to creating the internal alignment within management that was required for QWL to expand and to succeed. We will see in the case of DeRidder (chapter 4) how critical it is to develop consensus and enthusiasm within management for a change program. Top management at Bidwell could not bring this about. Nor was the consultant able to help management develop the critical level of internal consensus. What was probably called for, given the fact that many managers had different interests, was a mild form of distributive bargaining. From this perspective it would have been appropriate for either management or the consultant to have allowed managers to caucus and sort out what they were prepared to endorse and then to have insisted that all managers support the concept and timetable for implementation of QWL.

In many ways, the Bidwell case may not seem very remarkable. The North American landscape is full of abandoned QWL and quality circle initiatives. However, it is important for this very reason. A close look at the case reveals a number of junctures where key issues of concern to labor or management were not engaged. The initiative was treated as a program, rather than as an ongoing process of negotiation over issues of cooperation, commitment, decision making, and leadership.

CSX: AN AMBITIOUS ATTEMPT TO REACH A
BREAKTHROUGH WITH ITS UNIONS

The CSX case is a dramatic example of fostering via integrative bargaining.[4] This joint planning project undertaken by CSX and its unions during the late 1980s stands out over the past two decades as one of the most ambitious change efforts in railroads. In this case a major carrier sought to engage in a change process with all of its operating and non-operating crafts to design a comprehensive package of new work rules, employment protection, and gainsharing.

CSX decided at the end of the 1984 negotiations to explore with its major operating unions the feasibility of joint exploration of a comprehensive change program. While management gave some attention to attitudinal change, the company moved rather expeditiously to place a proposal for substantive change in front of the unions. While this integrative bargaining effort did not produce an agreement acceptable to all of the unions, it did create a substantially improved climate and a much greater understanding of the financial realities facing the parties.

Significant Features

Among the distinctive features of the CSX case are the following:

• Management took the initiative to develop a "win-win" proposal.

• The company was willing to share considerable financial information, and the parties expended considerable effort to develop trust and to create openness.

• Within the context of an individual carrier attempting to realize a breakthrough agreement, it was important for the parties to involve all levels in the design of the new arrangements.

• A complex structure of many craft unions and many levels within the unions presented immense challenges in gaining acceptance for a negotiated plan (in fact, in an industrial relations system as integrated as railroads, opposition in just a few regions of one union stopped this change effort).

• Despite the positive attitudes engendered by the company's bold initiative, when the exercise had to be abandoned, the company was not able to capitalize effectively on the reservoir of goodwill, i.e., CSX faced the same resistance and difficulties in implementing change at the local level as other carriers.

The CSX Story

As the 1984 round of national negotiations ended in 1987, key officials from CSX asked top union leaders whether they would be interested in embarking upon a different approach to the resolution of many long-standing issues. The premise advanced by the company was that if the parties could start a planning/negotiation process before the commencement of the next round of national negotiations, then it might be possible for the parties to achieve substantial breakthroughs for the benefit of all concerned.

The concept originated with top leadership of CSX, specifically John Snow, the president who had joined the company after service with the Federal Railroad Administration and John Sweeney, vice-president of industrial relations, who had worked for Conrail during its critical period of revitalization. These two executives were convinced that a better way could be found than the arm's-length atmosphere of national negotiations and the drawn out procedures of the National Mediation Board.

The key unions responded affirmatively, and thus began a very intense and complex undertaking that spanned eighteen months and involved many, many meetings at various levels of the system. The initial meeting took place at Greenbriar, West Virginia, with the unions represented by their presidents except for the United Transportation Union (UTU), which sent a vice-president.

At this meeting, the company reviewed its financial situation and its intention to concentrate on railroading. The extent of overstaffing (from the company's perspective) was highlighted. With respect to potential solutions, the company indicated that it had several thoughts, ranging from gainsharing to some forms of employee ownership. Substantial time was allowed for the unions to ask questions of the various management representatives who were present, including those representing finance and operations, as well as labor relations.

Shortly thereafter, the executive board of the Railway Labor Executives Association (RLEA) held a meeting and invited CSX representatives to make a follow-up presentation. The president of the UTU attended this session. As an outcome of this meeting, RLEA established a task force to examine the CSX ideas that were starting to crystallize into specific proposals. RLEA hired a consultant, Brian Freeman, to represent the interests of the different railroads; and for the next several months, various meetings took place between CSX officials and Freeman, accompanied by various union representatives. It was during this period that the idea of worker ownership was dropped in favor of crystallizing a gainsharing proposal.

Finalization of the Plan

In February 1988, at a meeting of all interested parties in Florida, the company presented an expanded proposal, and the unions were asked whether they wanted to consider the proposition in a formal manner. This decision was left to each union to make on a separate basis, but the company indicated it needed participation from unions representing at least 80 percent of the workers before it could proceed with a final proposal.

The plan represented a sweeping approach to work and institutional arrangements between CSX and its unions. The deal contemplated the reduction of the CSX workforce by approximately 10,000 workers out of a base employment of 42,000, with separation pay ranging from $30,000 to $50,000 per individual. Savings from the reduction of personnel would be shared with the workers remaining in employment on a 50-50 basis after separation costs had been amortized. In most instances crew sizes would be reduced to two persons per train, and there would be substantial intercraft flexibility in the repair shops. The application of these principles would be fleshed out on a union-by-union basis.

Union Responses

The first union to step forward was the Brotherhood of Maintenance of Way Employees (BMWE). And in the discussions that took place, considerable progress was made in refining the proposal. A potential win-win arrangement involved a proposal to reduce the seasonality of work gangs—specifically, the development of additional employment opportunities within the maintenance shops during winter months.

However, the draft was rejected by the UTU general chairmen (each from a different region) toward the end of March. The meeting included a presentation by Brian Freeman, as well as by representatives from CSX. The general chairmen said, in effect: "This is the first time we have heard about this plan, and we are not convinced that it is a good deal." This response proved fatal for the plan.

Shortly after the negative vote of the UTU general chairmen, the company decided to explain the features of the proposal in a letter sent to all employees to their homes. Some local UTU leaders criticized the company for not sharing more information sooner, and others labeled the communication as an "end-run."

Basically, the opposition to the plan from the leaders of the UTU centered around the fact that almost 4,000 of the 10,000 workers who would be severed would come from the ranks of the UTU. However, the savings would be shared equally across all remaining union members. Given its proportion of the total workforce, the share going to UTU members would approximate 25 percent (compared to the 40 percent that they would comprise of the separated workers).

Another explanation for the rejection was more institutional. CSX management remarked in interviews: "If we could only have made resources available to the unions to compensate for a reduction in dues paying members, we would have been able to get over the rough spots." In essence, the parties found the task of designing a scheme to provide financial assistance to a union in decline insurmountable. By contrast, in a number of manufacturing industries, the creation of joint training and career development funds had made it possible for resources to be provided for union staff who were needed for cooperative activities. Such an approach had not emerged in railroads.

Still, it is noteworthy that the process undertaken by CSX and its unions produced tentative agreement on the part of several crafts and the development of a very innovative plan for dealing with many of the central problems of the railroad industry. A high degree of trust emerged among many key officials. Several union leaders praised management at CSX for openness and constructive efforts to deal with worker and union interests. Richard Kilroy, then chairman of the RLEA, commented that CSX made available complete financial information so that the unions could judge the "facts of the current and long-term picture." He noted that one of the striking aspects of CSX's proposal was that the company claimed no current financial crisis. Rather, the company emphasized that while it was in the black, profit levels ($400 million in 1985) were not good enough for the long term. Kilroy concluded by saying: "The first ingredient of a project of this magnitude is trust. I know there will be employment declines, whether I sit at the table or not".

The Aftermath

Subsequent to the shelving of the gainsharing proposal (as it came to be called), the company sought to reach agreements with local general chairmen on voluntary plans for reductions in staffing (in distinction to the tabled proposal that would have required junior workers to accept separation if not enough volunteers could be found). However, little if any progress was made at the local level in reaching agreement on new staffing levels despite the fact that the workers would have retained their special pay rules (usually these "arbitraries" add at least 40 percent to base compensation) and the company would not have had to share ongoing savings realized from reduced crew sizes.

Since CSX was not covered for its UTU workers by the 1991-92 national agreement, it sought in local negotiations to reach agreement on revised crew sizes. Ironically, these agreements were less favorable to the company than the arrangements that the other railroads realized as a result of national bargaining.

Yet some indication of cooperation can be cited. In 1990 the parties inaugurated an employee involvement program in the Florida region. Also, in opening a new computer subsidiary, CSX agreed to recognize the clerical union (TCU) and to train surplus workers from the other crafts for this new information center.

In general, considerable disappointment was voiced, and in some quarters there was a feeling of failure that a significant program designed by the management and union architects had not gone forward. Some of the animosity was directed at the UTU, which did not ratify the agreement and thereby forced the overall package to be put aside. The possibility that other unions interested in the proposal would put pressure on the UTU to reconsider did not materialize. In fact, the UTU distanced itself from other craft unions by stating its intention of becoming the "industry union" of railroads.

Analysis

The rejection of the package proposal illustrates a basic dynamic in large-scale fostering initiatives. From the viewpoint of CSX, it seemed logical to fashion a program to reduce the workforce rapidly, to gain more flexibility in the deployment of personnel and to share the savings with the workers who remained. But a number of key union leaders felt that it was "crass" for a union to "sell jobs" and allow those who remained (as a result of possessing sufficient seniority) to benefit handsomely from the deal. When this perceived inequity was combined with the reality that the size of the unions (especially the UTU) would be shrunk rapidly (with a corresponding diminution in dues income), then a profound difference in perspectives existed. Interestingly, if the financial crisis had been severe enough (as in the case of Conrail) and the challenge before the parties had been one of survival, then these misgivings about exchanging money for employment reductions might have been less dominant.

CSX was able to convince most of the top leadership of the unions regarding the need for change, but this conviction was not extended in the ratification process to the lower levels of the organization, especially within the UTU. This top-down approach almost worked, but in the end key leaders were not able to produce attitudinal change deep and broad enough to convince members and their respective representatives about the wisdom of accepting a dramatically different approach to industrial relations.

The CSX story also clearly underscores the difficulties in achieving internal consensus, especially on the union side. At CSX, employees were represented by thirteen different unions, with approximately 140 different general chairmen. The task of achieving majority support within each separate union, and in the case of the large unions, majority support within each region, posed a formidable challenge. Add to this the historic rivalries among the craft unions (for example, company officials were not successful in bringing representatives from several of the key unions together in the same room) and it is clear why leading negotiators were not able to use "group pressure" to ameliorate differences in outlook. In fact, after several preliminary meetings, most of the negotiations took place with subsets of the unions; and in the case of meetings with UTU representatives, other unions were not present for these critical discussions. Several strategic alternatives were available to the parties in this complex situation.

Testing the Possibilities of a More Deliberate Approach

Some union leaders criticized CSX management for moving ahead too fast and not utilizing a multiunion task force that might have achieved more buy-in both across and within the unions. In choosing its approach, the company opted for dispatch and concreteness, i.e., crystallizing a plan rather early as a way of focusing the negotiations. Significantly, it chose to meet separately with the major unions.

While the approach of a multiunion working party might have increased the chances of success, company officials point out that it was important to learn "sooner rather than later" whether its program was feasible. Basically, management wanted to determine whether an innovative package could be formulated away from the procedures of national negotiations. Key executives reasoned that they would not be worse off if discussions failed, and they might create a better set of shared understandings for proceeding with change on a more decentralized basis.

The Use of an Agent by the Craft Unions

Once the negotiations got into high gear, a professional consultant was used by the unions to represent them in discussions with the company. This choice was based on the fact that the negotiations involved fairly technical decisions about the possibility of employee ownership plans and gainsharing formulas. This arrangement did have some drawbacks, however. Specifically, it meant that there was less interaction between key company officials and key union leaders. Also, it meant that most of the interactions were happening at the top, leaving lower levels of union leadership outside the process.

The package eventually was turned down by the general chairmen from UTU, who were not involved in the process. The chances of successful ratification of the package might have been enhanced by direct involvement of such key local leaders.

Company Versus Industry Negotiations

The most important strategic choice to revisit is whether in retrospect it was better for CSX to have attempted to work out a carrier-level agreement with its unions (and failed) or whether CSX would have been better served to have remained in national handling and worked for the culmination of the 1988 round of industry bargaining. Given the fact that several other major carriers (such as Union Pacific and Norfolk Southern) chose to seek changes in work rules via national negotiations and as a result of the 1991-92 negotiations and related emergency board recommendations have fared very well (in fact better than CSX) in terms of their progress toward two-person crew sizes, the quick judgment might be that CSX gambled and lost.

However, the appraisal must be more reasoned and needs to consider other factors. First, the effort undertaken by CSX in 1988 pre-empted the attention of the entire industry. National negotiations that were due to commence that year were delayed until the outcome of the CSX deliberations was clear. For one reason, national-level union officials could not handle two sets of major negotiations. More important, many carriers wanted to see whether an individual company could achieve a breakthrough. If CSX had been successful, no doubt it would have created a pattern for other carrier-level negotiations.

Second, the effort by CSX, while it failed, did create considerable discussion and attention to schemes for achieving reduced crew sizes. In this sense, CSX must be given considerable credit for the concepts that finally were embedded in the 1991-92 national agreements.

It is not surprising that the same local resistance that prevented the gainsharing package from being approved also slowed the implementation of the 1991-92 national pattern at CSX. Only time will tell whether the improved relations that developed with several unions as a result of the gainsharing discussions can be translated into commensurate substantive gains.

Lessons Learned

The CSX case teaches a number of important lessons about large-scale systems change. First, and most important, we see that the complex network of relationships with many craft unions at both national and local levels cannot be ignored. In this case the system not only included labor-management relationships, but also cross-union relationships and dynamics within unions. Second, we see the value of an initial negotiations text (generated in this case by management) in focusing the dialogue among representatives in such a complex system. Inevitably, there is a tension between the first two lessons—building full consensus across a complex system of relationships can be an endless task, yet in this case moving ahead quickly with a concrete proposal can preempt the development of supportive relationships.

Hindsight is always 20/20. During the early and mid-1980s when it looked like the rate of change in work rules and staffing would remain slow, the effort by various carriers to work out company-level plans with their unions seemed like a winning strategy. The fact that during the early 1990s the big gains came as a result of industry level-negotiations could mean that the potential of change at this level has now been fully exploited and the future will see greater emphasis on accommodation and change at the carrier and local levels.

CUMULATIVE EFFECTS OF SUCCESSFUL
FOSTERING INITIATIVES
Anderson Pattern and the Pattern Makers Association
of Muskegon

The essence of the Anderson story is that the parties proceeded in a step-by-step fashion to implement a fostering strategy, starting with limited initiatives and eventually evolving into a broad agenda that mixed both integrative bargaining and relationship changes that benefited the company, the workers, and the union.[5]

Key factors associated with the successful sequence were the style of the CEO, who had been a pattern maker, the business decision to move away from serving original equipment manufacturers (OEMs) as a primary market and an effective linkage of technological change, revised work rules, and employment security.

Significant Features

The Anderson case represents the clearest success story in our sample of fostering strategies. In this regard it will be important to identify some of the factors that contributed to positive outcomes. Key factors include:

- In a small company situation, the style and initiative of top management had a profound impact on the process of change.

- Certain joint activities, which by themselves might seem inconsequential (e.g., a joint delegation visiting a trade show), turned out to be significant turning points for the relationship.

- Imaginative problem solving resulted in a series of packages that met the key interests of the parties.

- Innovative agreements between this employer and the union weakened areawide bargaining (involving multiple employers dealing with the same union).

- Engaging workers and the union at every step of the process of introducing new technology generated strong commitment, thereby ensuring a successful introduction of the new equipment.

- While initial pilot experiments (with new technology in this case) depended on goodwill and trust, subsequent large scale diffusion depended on substantive changes (such as language minimizing the risk of job loss).

- Despite a multiyear history of successful fostering, distributive confrontations continued to occur—sometimes even as a direct result of earlier fostering successes (such as disagreements over the use of newly acquired training skills).

While there are unique aspects to the Anderson Pattern case, such as its predominantly skilled trades workforce, there are many features of the case that are characteristic of small firms. These include the key role of the entrepreneur/owner, the informal nature of interactions, and the capacity for dramatic substantive change once a moderate degree of attitudinal change has occurred. In this regard, the case teaches lessons relevant to a large number of North American firms.

Background

Originally founded in 1931, Anderson Pattern is a leading North American firm in what it calls the "shape" industry, which includes the manufacture of permanent molds, dies, patterns and related design and machining operations. The firm's specialties include wheel molds, engine castings, and other design-and-build work for the automobile industry. This is a small firm with 110 employees and annual sales of $12 million, though it is the flagship plant for a company that includes two pattern-making operations in Michigan and one each in Ohio, Arizona, and Ontario. The larger company has a total of 200 employees and sales of $20 million. It also has international production arrangements with shops in Mexico.

The president and chief executive officer of Anderson Pattern, John McIntyre, was at one time a journeyman pattern maker. He came to Anderson Pattern as general manager in 1980 and purchased the firm in 1982 along with a partner, Thomas Lerowx, the current vice-president. In this small-firm context, McIntyre's values and personality have played a critical role in negotiations over fundamental changes. His commitment to implementing the best practices has built on his voracious appetite for popular business literature. Hence, McIntyre sought to make this an "excellent" firm, orientated towards total quality, and he has coined the following motto or overall goal for the firm: "We will be leaders, innovators and masters of the shape industry . . . competitive worldwide."

At the time of this study, about 85 employees were highly skilled and members of the Pattern Makers Association of Muskegon, an affiliate of the Pattern Makers League of North America. The balance of the employees were supervisors, managers, and sales and office staff. Pattern makers, once they achieve journeyman status, were paid the same wage (in the early 1990s, just over $20 per hour).

Historically, the pattern-making industry was entirely unionized, with uniform wages across all shops. Workers were highly mobile, often leaving one shop for another to get more overtime or more interesting work. However, by the early 1990s, workers tended to stay with the same employer for longer periods of time due to the rise of non-union operations. For example, in Muskegon, only half of the pattern making industry shops (four out of eight) remained unionized. As one pattern maker who was working as a supervisor expressed it:

> Pattern makers are kind of independent. It was always: "If I don't like it here, I can go down the street." There is less moving now because there is less down the street.

Jim Howard, the business manager of the Pattern Makers Association of Muskegon, also worked at Anderson Pattern. The workforce at the other three unionized operations in Muskegon also belonged to the Association, with collective bargaining traditionally negotiated on an areawide basis. Given that certain aspects of employment relations were governed on an areawide basis (such as wage levels and benefits administration), a key challenge to the union was the desire by Anderson Pattern for increasingly distinctive contract provisions.

Our focus will be on fundamental changes that occurred with respect to several substantive outcomes, specifically the addition of profit sharing to the compensation package, increased flexibility in the utilization of new technology, increased job security, expanded worker training, and greater worker autonomy on the shop floor.

A Managerial Initiative to Offer Profit Sharing

In 1984, approximately two years after McIntyre became co-owner of Anderson Pattern, the collective bargaining agreement expired between Anderson Pattern, the three other unionized pattern-making firms, and the Pattern Makers Association of Muskegon. Although most of the negotiations were conducted on an areawide basis, a proposal to establish a profit-sharing plan, raised by John McIntyre, was of no interest to the other employers. As a result, discussions proceeded bilaterally between the union and Anderson Pattern.

The union's initial response to the proposal was negative for two reasons. First, the union had higher priorities and did not see this subject as highly valued by its members. Second, the union was concerned about breaking from the single areawide compensation package. However, McIntyre felt that a profit-sharing plan would more tightly align the interests of the employees with those of the firm. As a result, he indicated that he was prepared to "give" the union profit sharing without seeking anything in return. In this case, the union saw little reason to say no. As the union's then business manager and lead negotiator put it:

> At the time, we told John McIntyre that the people didn't give a damn about profit sharing. He insisted. There was nothing to lose, so we took it.

By including the profit-sharing provision in the contract, the parties departed from traditional practices in a number of aspects. First, it was unusual for management to raise such an issue. Second, this was not a case of traditional hard bargaining. Instead, as a most simple form of fostering, management gave the employees the chance to earn additional income via profit sharing without asking for anything in return. Third, this was a decentralization of bargaining over compensation, which was previously handled on a centralized multiemployer basis.

Finally, the provision represented an explicit attempt by management to move toward a social contract based on employee commitment.

Over the first five years, the profit-sharing plan paid out $260,000 in benefits. The annual distribution of a profit-sharing check took place at a special dinner in August, for which printed invitations were sent to all employees and their spouses. Featured speakers were invited. For example, the speaker in 1989 was Martin Devries of Grand Valley State University, who discussed: "Can the U.S. Sustain its World Economic Position?" In addition, door prizes were awarded and the two owners distributed the year's profit-sharing checks. Over 120 employees and spouses attended the 1989 dinner.

Profit sharing posed dilemmas and opportunities for both parties. One minor issue was that some employees would have preferred larger checks to having a ceremonial dinner, while others enjoyed the event. A larger issue was illustrated by the following union member's comment: "I have become a believer. The concept has merit, though there are still some problems with the way it is designed and administered." As the statement suggested, the profit-sharing plan posed continual administrative challenges for management if it was to serve as a motivator. For the union, it posed a deeper challenge—should the union take on a more active role in this aspect of compensation (e.g., sharing credit for its successes and blame for any shortfalls)?

Bargaining Over the Introduction of New Technology

Approximately one year after the profit-sharing language was negotiated, a second major managerial initiative unfolded—this time in the area of new technology. Historically, Anderson Pattern had regularly upgraded equipment, for example, replacing lathes and drill presses and adding computer numerical controls (CNC). Machine tolerances and consistency improved, but the organization of work did not fundamentally change. In 1985, however, the president of Anderson Pattern approached the union with a unique proposal.

A Proposed Quid Pro Quo

McIntyre indicated that he would be willing to spend a few million dollars to purchase a state-of-the-art center containing a coordinate measuring machine. He noted as a *quid pro quo*, however, that increased flexibility would be required in order to run the equipment with fewer workers (and with each worker running multiple operations).

At issue was a restrictive contract provision (Article XIX) that only allowed operators to run more than one "automatic" machine if no workers were laid off and, even then, only for certain combinations of machines.[6] Under this arrangement, the firm was constrained in bidding on certain contracts since the only safe assumption in making a bid was to plan on one operator for each machine. The importance of the contract language to the union was evidenced by a two-year strike against another firm in the Muskegon area over "one man running more than one machine." This strike ultimately ended in the decertification of the union at that location—creating an object lesson of forcing and escape for the parties at Anderson Pattern.

Management's approach to the subject of new technology was a departure from the traditional modes of interaction in a number of respects. First, the proposal was made outside of the areawide bargaining structure. Second, it was made on an informal basis, while the existing collective bargaining agreement was still in force. Third, the proposal asked for a sharp departure from the highly specific provisions in the existing collective bargaining agreement. Finally, management wanted dialogue with the union regarding capital resource allocations—usually a carefully protected strategic right of management. The proposal was pivotal both with respect to the process (representing a potential shift toward decentralized and more informal interactions) and the substance (as a potential change in the contract regarding machine operations and management rights).

A series of meetings followed. The subject was hotly debated among all employees. The second pivotal event involved a form of attitudinal structuring directly aimed at resolving the internal differences within the workforce. The president of Anderson Pattern offered to make arrangements for any interested employees to travel to Chicago to see the proposed equipment at a trade show that was then under way.

Although only twenty-five machine shop employees would be directly affected by this new technology, almost the entire workforce chose to go to the trade show. According the union's business manager, the workers returned with a vivid understanding of how computer-controlled equipment could operate feasibly with fewer workers. Moreover, he reported that most workers were persuaded that the equipment could "make us competitive enough to increase volume so that we wouldn't have to eliminate people."

Management's initial overture embodied a fostering approach—it was a proposal, not a demand. The decision to subsidize the education of the entire workforce on the issue (via the trip to Chicago) served to reinforce the initial fostering strategy. Still, the union was concerned just how far to depart from existing practice.

In retrospect, the negotiations were distinguished as a special case in two ways. First, management did not push for the complete elimination of the contract language on machine operation—it only asked for an exception for the two proposed pieces of equipment. Second, the proposed exception was only to be in effect until the expiration of the existing collective bargaining agreement. An additional issue of importance to the union concerned the new work associated with programming and maintaining the equipment, which it wanted to keep in the bargaining unit. Management agreed to this proposal.

This fostering approach proved successful. On May 10, 1985, the parties signed two letters of understanding: one for a programmable coordinate measuring machine and one for a vertical CNC milling machine. The wording of the letters was similar, with each waiving the "one employee, one machine" rule and guaranteeing that programming and other such work would remain in the bargaining unit. For example, the text of the CNC milling machine letter was as follows:

Agreement

It is herein agreed that until May 31, 1987, the following letter is in addition to the current contract between Anderson Pattern and the Pattern Makers Association of Muskegon and vicinity.

Anderson Pattern, Inc. will purchase a Mazak V-20 Vertical CNC milling machine with toolcharger and a pallet system. This machine will have functions allowing it to run unattended.

This machine will have an assigned operator at all times who, under the guidelines of safety and common sense, may be assigned to operate another machine at any time it is feasible to allow the Mazak V-20 to run unattended.

All work done on this machine will be considered bargaining unit work.

The one man/one machine provision of the Article XIX does not apply to this machine.

All programming for this machine will be done by bargaining unit employees, except a program provided by the customer may be used or it may be translated into the V-20's language from an out-source.

The agreement itself marked a third pivotal event, taking the parties a step further down a fostering path. They had agreed to conduct a two-year experiment that represented a fundamental departure from established machine operation procedures.

In reflecting on the agreement, the union's then business manager (who negotiated the agreement) commented:

Until recently, pattern making was 99 percent unionized. Restrictive work rules didn't matter because we all worked under the same rules. That changed in the 1980s. Now an employer will only spend a half-million dollars on a new machine if that machine can be fully used. What do we gain if, instead, that investment goes to a nonunion shop? The best thing to do was to negotiate training arrangements so that our people learn the latest technology.

It is important to note that the parties did not depart fully from a traditional frame of reference emphasizing contractual specificity. Even in allowing for increased flexibility, they were very precise about the scope (two machines), the time frame (two years), and the additional conditions (programming being done by bargaining unit employees). Thus, while the substance of the contract had been dramatically altered and the parties had departed from the areawide bargaining structure, some key norms governing the labor-management relationship had not changed.

Making Flexibility the Rule, Rather than the Exception

In 1987, the collective bargaining agreement expired, along with the letters of understanding regarding the new equipment. This set the stage for a fourth pivotal event. The parties were faced with the question of whether to abandon or continue to expand their experiment.

Management again took the lead. It proposed the elimination of the entire contract provision on machine operations (Article XIX). Further, management proposed establishing a new form of work organization around work cells where the work of each operator would be defined relative to multiple machines.

Management's proposals were highly controversial within the union. Although the union membership had been correct in their assessment that the two new pieces of equipment—as a special case—would generate a sufficient increase in volume to maintain the existing workforce, it was much harder to assess the potential impact of completely eliminating the contact language. It was very possible that the increased flexibility would contribute to increased business, but it was also possible that severe consequences would be triggered by a sharp downturn. Further heightening this concern was the fact that within the pattern-making profession layoffs had not been made on the basis of seniority, but rather on the basis of work requirements and worker skills. As a result, management's proposal provoked deep job security concerns among the entire workforce.

As a small auto supply firm, job security was a difficult issue to address. The industry had been cyclical and small firms generally did not have the slack resources nor alternative work that was available in large firms. Nevertheless, the union took a strong bargaining stance and indicated that unless management addressed job security, it would not agree to the work cells or to the elimination of Article XIX.

While Anderson Pattern could not provide a blanket no-layoff pledge, the parties found a way to ensure that no individuals would disproportionately suffer the consequences of the increased flexibility. Specifically, in the event of a downturn, the parties agreed that a worker could not be laid off for longer than two months, unless 75 percent of the workers in that work area had been laid off for more than two months. Management also requested the elimination of the union's midterm right to strike under the contract.

The midterm right to strike, historically an emotional issue, was less important to the members given the outcomes of strikes they observed in other area firms. At the same time, the promised new investment in the business and the language on job security were viewed as important gains. The workers thus agreed to eliminate Article XIX. Summing up the union's justification in eliminating the contract language on machine use, the current union business manager stated:

> Do we want to protect jobs and skills that are becoming noncompetitive or do we want to provide the opportunity for our members to learn new and more competitive skills?

He also noted that highly skilled pattern makers "would go nuts if their only job was to program a machine and watch it operate."

In eliminating Article XIX and the midterm right to strike, while introducing job security language and a promise of new investment, the parties were not only making significant substantive changes, but they were also moving away from the traditional regulatory approach to issues. Stated differently, they were moving away from positional bargaining (how many machines could one person operate) and toward more of a problem-solving approach centered on underlying interests (flexibility and job security). It is important to note, however, that management's fostering overtures on flexibility occurred in a context where the union had lost the ability to keep work rules out of contention, and where forcing and escape were realistic alternatives. Equally, the union had to take a distributive stance on job security to establish this interest as a legitimate part of the discussion.

Further Pivotal Events in Training and Health Care

The training programs at Anderson Pattern illustrate the evolving nature of the relationship following the introduction of new technology and the expansion of job security. The first pivotal event occurred when training was expanded to the entire existing workforce, once the agreements were reached on new technology. The initial actions on training occurred on a unilateral basis by the employer. Management created educational opportunities for all employees by forging partnerships with external institutions (a local community college and a four-year college). First, a series of training courses were established with the community college that were just focused on the new technology. Then, additional courses were added so that employees could earn a two-year degree. Ultimately, an arrangement was established with a local four-year college that would accept the two-year coursework towards a four-year degree—all paid for by the company.

Initially, the expanding educational options played a pivotal role by reinforcing the fostering between the employer and the employees. The course offerings propelled employee-employer relations in a direction that emphasized increased commitment, as evidenced by the high number of employees that chose to pursue the additional training. The educational choices, however, did not involve the union and hence did not reinforce the growing focus on labor-management cooperation.

A subsequent pivotal event did involve the union. This was associated with the emerging equity issues around utilizing the new skills. As the union business manager described the situation:

> The training program is popular. Many members have taken advantage of it. But, it has caused some hard feelings for people who have taken classes and who are not able to now use the skills. Realistically, it isn't practical to have everyone run every machine. It would be great to allow people to run the center for a length of time, but there are still only 4-6 CNC positions and 25 guys who have now been trained to operate the equipment.

Issues such as these could inevitably undermine management relations with individual workers and union leadership—simply because employee commitment might be reduced for those who cannot use the new skills, and union-management cooperation might be weakened since the union would be saddled with the task of managing complex internal differences. It remains to be seen how these issues will be resolved, but it is clear that there is more at stake than merely the interests of a few workers being able to use their skills more fully.

A separate set of pivotal events also took place with respect to health care, involving the union, Anderson Pattern, and other area pattern-making shops. In 1984, the union had pressed the employers to move from a set contribution for health care to a situation where the employer bore the full cost—a pivotal shift in the structure of the system. When the employers responded by focusing on cutting costs, the union came back in the 1987 negotiations to request a return to the old situation, which the employers rejected—a second pivotal event. Then, by 1990 the continued escalation in health care costs led the employers to indicate that they would indeed be willing to return to making a set, defined contribution rather then covering the full cost of health care. This time, the union rejected the idea—a third pivotal event.

This sequence of events teaches important lessons about strategic negotiations. Under the original arrangement, there were both common and competing interests between the union and the employers, but the structure emphasized the common interests. When the structure shifted to total costs, the parties interests diverged. Subsequently, events that led one or the other party to want to return to the original arrangement did not produce the desired change. While maintaining the original structure would not have eliminated the inevitable tensions associated with rising health care costs, the parties would have at least faced this challenge from the vantage point of a cooperative structure for joint governance—rather than in the context of an already contested set of relations on this issue. Changing the "rules of the game" is a powerful tool, but it can produce unwanted as well as beneficial outcomes.

Analysis

The Anderson Pattern case represents a long-term unfolding story with numerous fostering initiatives.

On the substantive side, the main accomplishments were the implementation of profit sharing and the introduction of advanced technology, with more flexible staffing patterns. In summarizing their experience with new technology at the 1989 Michigan Governor's

Conference on Labor-Management Relations, the union business manager identified the following positive results from a union perspective:

- The workers who are involved in operating these machines feel a sense of accomplishment in both their ability to master the machine and also the type of work they can produce from this equipment. They are glad they can go on to something else while the machine is operating in the automatic mode.

- The machines allowed us to be competitive in types of work that are nontraditional for pattern shops.

- No one lost his or her job because of the changes.

Among the significant outcomes were the following:

Significant Outcomes—Anderson Pattern

Substantive outcomes	Management-employee relations	Management-union relations	Other outcomes
Investment in new technology	Increased worker autonomy	Increased informal dialogue and midterm negotiations	Increasing departure from area pattern bargaining structure
Flexible work rules	Increased information sharing with employees		
Profit sharing		Management investment a subject of negotiations	Dramatic business growth
Limitations on layoffs	Frustrations over use of new CAM skills		New institutional arrangements with a community college and a four-year college
Health care formula restructured		Gradual movement toward cooperation, but with few formal institutions	
Elimination of midterm right to strike	Gradual movement toward high commitment, building on the base of a highly skilled workforce		

The union business manager also noted the following negative consequences from a union perspective, which focus on equity issues:

Because of the high utilization of the machines, men in the traditional machining area are at the bottom of the overtime list and at the top of the list for layoffs. They also feel left out because they have not had the opportunity to be trained on the new equipment.

At the same panel session, the president of Anderson Pattern pointed to five years of new technology investment totaling over $3 million, which had been possible as a result of the agreements with the union. During the same period, sales tripled to over $11 million (including $1.5 million in exports).

On balance, the relationship between Anderson Pattern and the union shifted from arm's length toward cooperation. As well, the relations between management and employees shifted from one of moderate control toward one increasingly characterized by employee commitment.

However, unresolved issues still remained. For example, the initial profit-sharing plan strengthened ties between the employer and the employees, but created a new area of ambiguity for the union. The accord linking new technology with job security served to reinforce relations between the company and the union as well as between the company and its employees. Yet, unresolved issues remained regarding training for the new technology.

To explain the successes at Anderson Pattern it is important to look at both internal and external factors. Internally, the values and background of the primary owner/entrepreneur (including his ability to speak the workers' language and his commitment to sharing information) were critical. Equally critical was the union's willingness to break from traditional areawide collective bargaining and to engage in mid-contract negotiations. The tradition of autonomy among skilled trades workers was also important, including a desire to return to "the way things used to be" regarding self-directed work. In the larger context, the small size of the firm was a key factor. For example, it was feasible to educate the entire workforce about proposed changes in technology. A backdrop of escape and forcing in the broader community and area industry was also a key factor—management did not have to articulate forcing threats since the forcing alternative was readily apparent to all parties involved.

Taken together, the experiences of Anderson Pattern and the Pattern Makers Association of Muskegon illustrate the iterative process by which a cooperative labor-management arrangement was constructed. At the time of our study, the parties were fashioning, on a piecemeal basis, elements of what appeared to be a very different labor-management relationship. It remains to be seen whether they will choose to explicitly discuss the nature of the social contracts that the major stakeholders (management, the union, and the employees) would prefer. One thing is certain, however—as a small firm the process is informal and highly pragmatic. As the union business manager commented: "There is no formal setting to work out problems, we just tell each other our problems and we work them out." The president of Anderson Pattern expressed the same point even more bluntly: "With about 100 people you can eliminate the B.S. factor and deal with reality."

OVERVIEW OF THE FOSTERING CASES

Our three fostering cases fall across a wide spectrum in terms of results. One case, Bidwell, barely got started with a QWL program only to have it abandoned. A second case, CSX, embarked upon an ambitious integrative bargaining exercise that did not come to fruition. The third, Anderson, succeeded admirably in a multiyear iterative process of negotiating dramatic substantive and relationship changes.

Like all strategies, fostering contains risks—not just that the goals might fail to be realized. There is a deeper risk that relationships might be worsened as a result of the venture down a path of change. Bidwell, for example, ended up without a QWL program, with increased discord within management, and with slightly increased distrust between labor and management. Even though CSX did not end up worse off when the gainsharing approach had to be shelved, the setback affected the overall momentum for change.

At Anderson Pattern, we saw that the small size of the firm, leadership, risk-taking on both sides, a skilled trades workforce, and a backdrop involving forcing and escape were all keys to success. By contrast, at Bidwell and CSX, where multiple unions were present, the complexity of the change process increased considerably, and the parties were not able to solve issues of internal consensus. Bidwell illustrates that this task is often as difficult on the management side as on the union side of the equation.

In terms of the important choice of starting with attitude change versus substantive integrative bargaining, clearly an emphasis on both dimensions was ultimately necessary. Anderson Pattern illustrated the need to deal with both the relationship and substance.

It is helpful to abstract several themes in terms of best practice for executing a fostering strategy. First is the development of initial levels of trust. Some of this occurs as a result of the time spent together in joint activities by key players who previously may have interacted only in an adversarial atmosphere. Credibility and good faith are particularly important ingredients. Often the process starts out slowly because one party, usually the worker/union side, is skeptical of whether the other (management) really wants to conduct its affairs with input from other stakeholders. Thus, some token or symbolic action is required early on in the process to convince all concerned that management is serious and open minded. This requirement can be realized when management moves quickly to handle worker/union concerns, e.g., dealing with long-standing safety problems.

A second feature of the process is what theorists have referred to as an unfreezing event and the creation of a superordinate goal that provides a rallying point to bring parties together on a common basis. In some cases, threatened bankruptcy of the firm has produced the crisis. As well, improving quality of service or products has become a similar catalyst in a number of attitude change programs. Increased business opportunities (and hence jobs) can be another catalyst.

A third ingredient of a successful process is the ultimate "bottom line" that there be concrete benefits for all parties. For management, concrete benefits may include demonstrated gains on cost, quality, and delivery outcomes, as well as increased flexibility in operations and fewer daily hassles in managing operations. For union leaders and members the benefits may come in terms of job security, increased skills, the sharing of financial gains, greater institutional stability for the union, and also fewer daily hassles on the job. In other words, outcomes must be present that meet the respective interests of workers, union representatives, and management in order to reinforce and extend fostering strategies.

If these guidelines had been employed at Bidwell and CSX, would they have helped move these two cases into the success column? We have already made some comments along these lines respectively in the analysis at the end of these two cases. Clearly there was unrealized potential for increased joint gains in both cases. But fostering, by itself, usually is not a sufficient strategy. It must be well executed in a context where there is sufficient time for the unfolding sequence of relationship building and substantive change. In the absence of these circumstances, some forcing may also be required—as the next two chapters demonstrate.

NOTES

1. This history dates back at least to the turn of the century, when joint labor-management committees were established to address safety issues in the mining industry. It includes a variety of labor-management committees established during the 1920s and 1930s in the railroad and textile industries, as well as over 5,000 such committees established to improve production during the second world war. During the 1950s, the Armour Automation Committee, the Modernization and Mechanization Agreement in the West Coast longshoring industry, cooperative efforts in the steel industry, and numerous early experiments with gainsharing were well known. The joint initiatives described in this chapter are part of this larger historical story.

2. Valuable research assistance was provided by Kathleen Rudd Scharf in the preparation of this case.

3. This account is based on Mohrman (1987).

4. In addition to field interviews with key participants, we have benefitted from the availability of a report by Goldberg (1990).

5. Valuable research assistance was provided by Pat McHugh in the preparation of this case.

6. Specifically, the language in the 1984 contract reads as follows:

Article XIX Machine Operations

Section 19.1 Machines must be attended at all times, but this is coupled with the understanding that there be a limit of (2) machines assigned to a man, the first be an automatic stylus machine designed for duplicating. That machine shall not have more than (2) operating heads in use while being used as a second machine. The operator, when he attends an automatic machine, does not leave the other machine cutting stock. When the machine department is regularly scheduled for a reduced number of hours, then the automatic machines will run for the same reduced number of hours. Any employee laid off in the machine department will trigger one employee, one machine.

4
Managing the Dynamics
Sequences Of Forcing And Fostering

Even though there are many complexities that arise in the implementation of either forcing or fostering strategies, the challenges are even greater when forcing and fostering strategies are employed in sequence. Of the two possible sequences, the most common is forcing followed by fostering. All three of the cases in this chapter feature this sequence.

The cases begin with periods of sustained forcing around substantive concessions and, in two instances, with strikes during the forcing periods. Subsequently, all three cases feature repaired relations and substantial fostering initiatives centering, in two cases, on joint labor-management committees. A third case features fostering primarily aimed at individual employee involvement. The parties in all three cases were faced with the challenge of being effective during the forcing initiative, while mindful of the subsequent need to foster. During the subsequent fostering it was necessary to move past the anger and mistrust built up during the forcing period.

Of course, a reverse sequence is also possible. In the AP Parts case presented in chapter 2, for example, there were some limited cooperative efforts around employee involvement that preceded the forcing initiative. Similarly, in a case covered in the next chapter—the Pensacola case—we will examine forcing that follows a period of sustained fostering. When the sequence is reversed, with forcing following fostering, the challenges center on the degree to which trust built up during the fostering period will be undercut by the subsequent forcing.

There are few historical parallels to these sequences of sustained forcing and sustained fostering observed during the 1980s and 1990s. One notable case occurred in 1960 in the West Coast longshoring industry, where Harry Bridges departed from a highly adversarial approach and agreed to the Mechanization and Modernization Agreement.[1] For the most part, however, the historical cases of hard forcing have been followed by the complete collapse of relations or by the resumption of arm's length relations. Similarly, most historical cases of far-reaching fostering are built on histories of relatively positive relations. Thus, this look at several instances of forcing and fostering sequences involves the exploration of new territory.

It is the purpose of this chapter to better understand how the parties have been able to combine the best elements of the distinct forcing and fostering strategies into a coherent program for change. We present three cases that cover a wide range of experience on this path of sequential change.

The first case involves sequences of negotiations occurring during the period from 1983 to 1990 in the Boise Cascade Mill at DeRidder, Louisiana. This story begins with a bitter strike over work rules and management's imposition of greater flexibility in assignments. Following the strike, management rebuilt relations with the workforce in order to effectively implement the new work system.

Adrian Fabricators, our second case, is a small auto parts company that moved through several phases, characterized by the introduction of an ESOP as a response to bankruptcy, then a bitter strike arising out of unmet expectations on the part of the workforce. This conflict was followed by mutual efforts to repair relations and finally a period of intense fostering on issues that ranged from daily safety matters to the overall business strategy.

The Conrail story is our third case. It also involves a struggle back from bankruptcy. In this case, the hard forcing occurred while the company was under the protection of the federal government. After its return to stock ownership, the parties continued a relationship marked by some contention but also by a range of joint activities.

Before presenting the separate stories, it is useful to profile some of the key attributes of these three examples of sequential forcing and fostering.

As the table indicates, the forcing in all three cases occurred in the context of contractual negotiations, while the fostering primarily occurred during the subsequent period of contract administration. The cases focus on the immediate periods following the forcing, through the fostering initiatives persisted in all three cases through subsequent rounds of collective bargaining.

Key Aspects of Cases Featuring Sequences of Forcing and Fostering

	DeRidder	Adrian	Conrail
Background factors	Cumbersome work rules and low productivity	Bankruptcy and creation of ESOP	Bankruptcy and federal government intervention
Locus of negotiations	Plant	Plant	Company
Time frame for forcing	Contract negotiations	Contract negotiations	Government-imposed reopening of contracts
Time frame for fostering	Contract administration	Contract administration	Contract administration
Pivotal events	Strike; new management team	Strike, union abandoned and reestablished; new CEO	Stock privatization
Substantive outcomes	Reduced job classifications

Elimination of most work rules

Elimination of Sunday premium pay

Substantial wage increases

Increased job security

Improved plant safety, maintenance, and training practices | ESOP with employee majority ownership

Wage and benefit concessions

Flexible work practices

New direction in business strategy | Major changes in work rules and staffing levels

Reinvestment in the business |
| **Relationship outcomes** | Increased worker commitment

After a long delay initial steps toward improved union-management relations | Increased worker commitment

High levels of union-management communications and trust | Some increase in worker commitment

Increased levels of union-management communications |

During the rounds of forcing in all three cases there were important substantive changes made in collective bargaining agreements. During the subsequent periods of fostering, important improvements in relationships occurred. Thus, the cases featured in this chapter are notable in that they all feature major changes along both substantive and relationship dimensions.

MANAGEMENT SUCCESS IN FORCING
FOLLOWED BY FOSTERING
Boise Cascade (Deridder), 1983 to 1990

Boise Cascade Corporation succeeded in forcing major change in the way its workforce functioned in its DeRidder, Louisiana, mill during 1983 and 1984, and then succeeded in fostering related changes over the rest of the decade.[2]

Management won a two and one-half-month strike that targeted work-rule changes, but *not* economic concessions. Management's subsequent fostering achieved an impressive move toward mutual commitment with workers, but did *not* involve any revision in union-management relations over the next six years. Then, in late 1990, Boise Cascade management initiated an effort to build a new cooperative relationship with the international union and the locals at the mill level. The union responded positively to the overture.

By 1990, the DeRidder mill had risen from one of Boise Cascade's poorest to one of its top performers. The workers had become the highest-paid papermill workers in America, according to the company.

Significant Features

The DeRidder case represents a management success story, first on the forcing side of the ledger and then on the fostering side as well. The following are significant dimensions of this case:

• Management conducted a forcing campaign in contract negotiations with the union leadership and then made the transition to a fostering strategy aimed at rank-and-file employees.

• The company shaped the agenda by focusing on productivity improvements (new work rules and management rights) and in return offered higher pay and enhanced job security.

• The company prepared for a strike but refrained from using replacements (that had been trained and were standing by).

• After the strike, management took direct responsibility for getting workers on the same wave length by an elaborate program of communications and related actions.

• After the strike, the new mill management made a concerted effort to listen to employee concerns (especially those regarding safety, maintenance, and training) and then took action on these issues.

• Pay increased to the best in the industry (by combining and moving people "upward" into a reduced number of job classifications), and people-oriented policies and practices were emphasized.

• Mill managers used selective rewards and punishments to get managers on board with the new program.

• Management avoided antagonizing union officials, but at the same time did not offer them additional power, status, or information.

• Eventually the parties entered into early negotiations, and this mill became the first in the company to take Sunday premium pay out of the contract.

• International union representatives and local leaders eventually were favorably impressed with the people policies espoused and practiced by management.

Within the labor movement this type of case is, of course, controversial. In the pure forcing cases—such as the International Paper negotiations at Jay, Maine—the battle lines are clearly drawn. Here, the sequential strategies made this case much more challenging to union leaders. Management was in the driver's seat and able to achieve many of its long-sought goals (such as simplified work rules, reduced job classifications, and elimination of Sunday premium pay), while concurrently paying workers well and responding promptly to many of the issues they raised. In fact, high levels of worker commitment to the firm were evident at the time of our study. As a result, the union faced the complex task of redefining its role in a new work system.

If the union succeeds in redefining its role and a union-management partnership unfolds, then this case will represent a complete transformation of an industrial relations system. As of the mid-1990s, it already stands as a clear example of a hard forcing strategy executed in such a way as to facilitate subsequent fostering—meeting management's dual objectives of rapid, far reaching substantive change along with high levels of employee commitment.

The Forcing Campaign

The forcing phase of this change effort began during preparations for (and the subsequent collapse of) the 1983 negotiations, intensified during a bitter two and one-half-month strike, and continued into the first year of the new contract.

Management had become progressively dissatisfied with the performance of the DeRidder mill. Built in 1969, it was the company's newest and largest mill, but it had generally failed to meet management's performance expectations. As an index of the mill's poor performance, hourly employment increased steadily between 1976 and 1980, rising from 385 in January 1976 to 490 in January 1980, without commensurate increases in productivity; in fact, during this period DeRidder's return on total capital employed declined both absolutely and relative to other comparable Boise Cascade mills. The addition of a new paper machine at DeRidder in 1980 helped improve the mill's overall returns, but the size of the increase itself was disappointing.

The performance of the DeRidder mill also fared poorly when judged against three other indicators: its accident rate was among Boise Cascade's highest, its grievance rate was high compared to other company mills, and its management turnover rate was also high—there had been seven mill managers in the previous fourteen years.

Management attributed the mill's poor efficiency and disappointing returns to adverse labor relations and the increasingly restrictive rules governing work assignments negotiated during the 1970s. The work rules constrained operational flexibility, DeRidder managers felt, and generated an endless stream of disputes that absorbed time and energy and helped to sustain an adversarial climate.

The mill had been organized by the UPIU shortly after it opened. Employees were represented by two locals, one for maintenance workers and the other for production workers. Contract negotiations in 1971 and 1974 produced bitter strikes of over two months' duration. In 1977 and 1980, management avoided strikes, but in the process accepted what it came to regard as an increasingly unmanageable labor contract. The restrictive aspects were contained not only in contract provisions, but also in a proliferation of work practices recorded in memoranda of understanding between supervisors and workers.

Ichniowski (1986a) analyzed the relationship between grievance activity and productivity in Boise Cascade's eleven mills and found that grievance rates had a significant inverse relationship with mill productivity. For example, the mills experiencing grievance rates at the average were more than 10 percent more productive than the two mills with the highest grievance rates—and DeRidder was one of these two mills.

In 1982, Boise Cascade management reflected on how labor matters had come to their current state at DeRidder. It identified factors that went beyond the union's relative power advantage in the 1977 and 1980 contract negotiations just cited. The union's daily pursuit of these protective work rules was both systematic and effective, and upper-level mill management provided little oversight. As a result, department foremen and supervisors had wide latitude in making agreements with employees and union representatives on the mill floor—agreeing to local practices that were inconsistent with each other. The union also kept better records of agreements than did management, and their officers generally had longer tenure than management.

Introduction of the Team Concept

Management decided to force change during 1983 contract negotiations—to eliminate the system of rules it found restrictive and to install what it called the "team concept." In particular, it sought to eliminate all side-bar agreements, to establish greater management discretion over work assignments, and to win contractual authority to make decisions based on business needs. Boise Cascade also sought a containment of health care costs, but chose *not* to seek wage concessions.

Management's interest in the new team concept was based on the reportedly favorable experiences at IP and Crown-Zellerbach mills. Because management anticipated strong union and employee resistance to these changes, it planned carefully for negotiations, a possible strike, and unilateral implementation of the new contract.

To enhance the company's bargaining power, a management group arranged for continuation of the inflow of raw materials and outflow of finished products with the following contingencies: staffing the mill during a strike with managers from other Boise mills, training of managers in skills not readily available, provision of temporary housing, and the development of an extensive security plan. The group also constructed a new access road to the plant and, in doing so, bypassed the union hall which was located on the regular access road. Another management group planned for communications within management, to the workforce, and to the community.

DeRidder managers apparently had relatively little contact with UPIU Local and International officers ahead of the formal contract talks. Once negotiating agendas were exchanged, the union's reaction to management proposals was so negative that the union committee never really engaged management negotiators over the proposed changes. Neither side was prepared to make significant concessions to the other. A strike began in September of 1983 and only ended two and one-half-months later in November, when the union agreed to call off the strike and accept the already implemented conditions. During the strike, the mill operated at about two-thirds capacity, using management personnel and temporary contracted workers. While management had threatened to hire permanent replacements for the striking workers, it never did so. The lost production resulted in significant reductions in profits for 1983 and 1984.

New Contract Language

Returning workers found themselves facing a company-implemented contract containing the changes management originally had proposed. Annual wage increases (that had not been at issue) consisting of 6 percent, 6 percent, and 5 percent were implemented—in line with other industry settlements that year. The important changes were the introduction of team concept and the insertion of a "zipper clause" explicitly overturning all previous side agreements. The 1983 contract also included a ground-breaking employment security provision.

The zipper clause represented a thorough elimination of the agreements and practices DeRidder managers believed had hampered their ability to manage successfully:

> The elements of team concept supersede all conflicting limitations on management rights provided in the labor agreement, and all preexisting rules, commitments, understandings, work practices, past practices, grievance settlements, arbitrations, or side agreements written or unwritten.

The intent of the Team Concept language was straightforwardly introduced in the new contract as well:

> Team concept simply means the company has flexibility in how it assigns employees.

The ninety-four separate job classifications—and the progressions that applied—contained in the 1980 contract were telescoped into a small number of "clusters," i.e., groups of related jobs to be performed interchangeably. For example, in the paper machine area, workers formerly known as fourth, fifth, sixth, and seventh hands, paper tester, refiner hand, and utility hand were now all included in the "C Operator" cluster. Significantly, workers received the rate of pay for the highest-ranked jobs in the clusters. As a result, DeRidder's hourly employees received increases in base rates—in addition to the 6 percent across-the-board adjustment.

The contract expanded management's right to contract work out and to decide whether and how temporary vacancies would be filled. Within-shift seniority replaced across-shift seniority in determining bumping rights in layoffs of less than thirty days. The contract also provided for a new performance evaluation system, the results of which would be taken into account in filling permanent vacancies. This tilted the balance between merit and seniority clearly toward merit.

The contract also offered an employment security provision that for 1983 was unusual in the paper industry:

> No current employee will lose his employment or suffer a reduction in wage rate due to the implementation of team concept or as a result of the company's contracting out work.

Distributive bargaining, which had dominated the 1983 contract negotiations, continued to be a major factor during the first year of implementing the team concept. For example, top management made sure that the organization complied with the overall plan, specifically that the new job structures and appraisal systems were developed and introduced, that supervisors were trained to play their roles in negotiating the day-to-day operation of the system with workers, and that a monitoring system was developed to help ensure that units were following the provisions of the new work system and to measure the advantages of flexibility.

A Phased Transition to Fostering

For represented employees, the first day back on the job in November of 1983 consisted of an eight-hour orientation session that included three hours of safety instruction and five hours on team concept contract language and "new rules of order and discipline" to be implemented.

Managers had already attended extensive contract implementation training during the strike, and management training continued. This training—and the fact that the union had not been in a position to make its usual request for hundreds of pocket-size copies of the new contract for its members—put managers in clear command of the contract and its interpretation. As a manager later described the average DeRidder supervisor's new position, "He could just eat a shop steward alive." Top management's determination to exercise the supervisory discretion spelled out in the new contract was made clear in many ways.

New Mill Management

Soon after workers returned, a new mill manager was appointed. Although this individual had filled several managerial positions in the mill in earlier years, he had been away from DeRidder for a time and so was not associated with the events of the strike. He arrived prepared to be firm in implementing the 1983 contract, but also to change management practices that hurt employee morale. Shortly before his arrival, a new human resources manager was hired, as well.

The new mill manager acted quickly to demonstrate attention to quality and productivity, safety, and hourly workers' concerns. He recalled later:

> I started right away emphasizing safety, quality, productivity, and management on the people side. Then we just tried to sell it. [The mill human resources manager] and I had meetings with all the natural work groups and their supervision, and they really unloaded on us. . . . Our whole thrust has been that the people are going to make the difference. . . . We put our whole emphasis on people. They had the feeling we would sacrifice one of them for a ton of paper [in the past], and sometimes they were right.

The meetings with work groups, known locally as "listening sessions," were a key part of direct negotiations with the rank and file. Meetings were scheduled so that all shifts in all departments eventually met with the mill manager and human resource manager. Without any formal union involvement, DeRidder employees had an opportunity to express their feelings, perceptions, and complaints. Mill managers either addressed the problems brought up in the listening session or explained any delays to the departmental groups.

The new mill manager also used other tools to foster—and force—change in the management organization. He established a Management-By-Objectives system in which safety performance was a genuine criterion, along with the more usual productivity and quality goals. Supervisors who used poor judgement in safety matters were disciplined, to the point of "severance arrangements" in some extreme cases. Management merit increases, essentially automatic in previous years, were now reduced by poor safety performance. The human resources manager said later:

> The safety issue was a thing they could grasp. People knew safety was bad there, and a lot of supervisors would just say, "It's dangerous making paper." Supervisors would say that all accidents arose from "unsafe acts."

The plant and human resource managers understood that the actions they took toward supervisory staff would at once affect two negotiation subprocesses. First, they would promote managerial consensus around changed priorities. Second, the emphasis on safety would help unfreeze the negative and skeptical outlook of the workforce. Several other actions were taken:

• An Employee Assistance Program was set up, with the assistance of a specialist from the UPIU's national headquarters, but without formal local union participation.

• The Bridge Committee, a peer contact point for referral for substance abuse and other problems, was launched.

• Hourly employees were asked to join in customer visits, which provided independent evidence of quality issues and market factors.

• Significant and visible expenditures on maintenance to address productivity, safety, and quality of worklife issues were instituted.

By the time top managers made a second circuit of the mill for department listening sessions, the tenor of these meetings had changed. The initial wave of anger and frustration had begun to recede, and some promised changes could be seen.

DeRidder managers realized also that training would be critical to their efforts to implement the team concept. Although there was some objection from upper levels of management during a period of depressed profits, the new manager built a training center—once again seeing it both as a practical site for necessary activity and as a symbol of management commitment to training and to change. Training was also visibly supported when fifteen additional operators were hired in 1985 so fifteen others could rotate off the floor to analyze training needs and to develop training materials. This was part of a large and ongoing effort to involve hourly employees in codifying operating practice and writing standard procedures, training materials, and skills tests.

By the end of the new manager's first year, many supervisors had left the mill, reportedly in reaction to reduced merit raises and new performance demands. They were largely replaced from within DeRidder. Again, these appointments moved the composition of the managerial corps in directions supportive of change, rewarded supervisory flexibility, and demonstrated the depth of top management's commitment to change. During this period hourly turnover was negligible.

Union-Management Relationship

The change effort at DeRidder was targeted on managers' relationships with hourly employees. For the first two years of the new contract, the officers of the two UPIU locals refused to sit on joint committees, and mill managers did not extend any public gestures of support or rapport for union leadership. By the end of 1984, there had been a complete change of union leadership. One manager said later:

> It was a reaction against the strike. They were saying, "We were as misled by the union as we were ever mistreated by the company."

As of the early 1990s, the maintenance local president first elected in 1984 had remained in office, but the production local was on its third president. Mill managers explained this in terms of the union's changing posture and significance at DeRidder, since the old mechanisms of grievances, arbitrations, contract demands, and strikes looked far less central to employee well-being, but at the same time the union had not taken on any new modes of interaction with management. The human resources manager left his door open to the union officers, and he gradually built personal relationships with them, but he continued to emphasize direct contacts with employees:

> Throughout this entire period my group and I have dealt with the union officers on anything they want to deal about. We've negotiated a third extension [of the 1983 contract, with few changes] until 1995. By the time they come to me I've usually heard everything at the listening sessions.

Even contract negotiations became very different events from the earlier patterns. The company firmly declined to renegotiate issues other than wages and benefits, and negotiations were conducted in an integrative rather than distributive mode.

The first contract extension, negotiated in 1985, embodied an important change in team concept language and practices. It had been difficult under the 1983 language to persuade workers to move into positions in higher paid clusters because increased pay came only with permanent promotion, and managers were not required to fill vacancies. The 1985 contract changed this, providing pay at the higher cluster's rate for fully qualified workers if a vacancy had been declared, even if they had not been permanently promoted into the new cluster.

This agreement reportedly was worked out during informal discussions between union officers and the human resources manager in response to complaints raised during the listening sessions.

Team Concept Effects

Ichniowski (1986b) analyzed various indexes of performance under the new contract to determine whether the team concept was actually making a difference. He compared average monthly performance for three periods:

- January-June 1983, which he called "1983" or "prestrike";

- April 1984-March 1985, called "1984" or "year 1" of team concept; and

- April 1985-March 1986, called "1985" or "year 2" of team concept.

His analysis confirmed that by early 1986 management was achieving the advantages it desired from the changes. Management had contracted out much of a large backlog of maintenance projects during 1984. Controllable overtime hours for production workers were cut from 7.2 percent of all hours worked in 1983 to 3.5 percent during 1984 and 1985, reflecting the fact that management had exercised its new contractual right to leave vacancies unfilled and to transfer workers temporarily across departments. Maintenance overtime hours also had declined. However, total straight-time pay for both production and maintenance employees had increased substantially in both 1984 and 1985 as a result of the general increases of 6 percent and 5 percent plus pay-for-knowledge increases.

Total employment remained stable. The agreement's employment security assurance to "current employees" and the low rate of turnover in the mill precluded significant workforce reductions. Moreover, the major amount of cross-training required to make the team concept work required a buffer of extra employees.

Given a stable level of employment, productivity increases, if any, would be reflected in increased production volumes, due mainly to an avoidance of disruptions to the continuous flow process of paper manufacturing. Productivity did not increase in year 1 of team concept but did increase in year 2. The average tons per day in 1983, 1984, and

1985 were 1744, 1703, and 1830, respectfully. The increase of 86 tons per day from 1983 to 1985 generated an increase in monthly revenue of about $800,000, which more than offset the increase in total monthly labor costs of about $500,000.

By early 1990, DeRidder's managers were able to report further changes in performance and labor relations indicators:

- Tons per person-hour had risen steadily, from .44 in 1983 to .54 in 1990; this reflected some technical improvements but no additions of capacity. Most of the 24 percent productivity increase was attributed to improved working practices.

- Significant improvements in yield resulted from closer attention to the usage of materials.

- Grievance filings had declined still further and were now almost completely limited to disciplinary matters.

- The mill—which had been one of the most dangerous in the company—received an industry association safety award in 1989.

- The labor agreement had been extended again, this time until 1995, without Sunday premium pay. DeRidder thus became the first Boise Cascade mill to eliminate entirely the Sunday premium, since the contract did not entail a gradual phase-out.

In 1990, DeRidder managers reported that their workers averaged the highest straight-time pay in the paper industry, due to annual increases and the effects of clustered pay. While labor costs had continued to rise, productivity had continued to more than match this rise. DeRidder made a $98 million profit for 1989, on 800,000 tons of production.

DeRidder and Boise Cascade

As of the early 1990s, developments at DeRidder had exerted limited influence on the overall Boise Cascade/UPIU relationship. Boise Cascade continued to be thought of as "the scoundrels of the South" by UPIU activists as a result of strikes in the DeRidder and Rumford, Maine mills and because of the company's reputation for aggressiveness. Nevertheless, the UPIU International officers had begun to soften their stance, based on reports of the "people-oriented" management at the DeRidder mill. While the UPIU representative for the southern

Boise mills had not become deeply involved, neither had he been openly critical of the DeRidder change process.

Analysis

Several factors help explain the ability of DeRidder management to first force substantive change and then foster new relations. It is particularly instructive to contrast DeRidder with Jay, our pure forcing example from the paper industry.

- The ambitiousness of demands: DeRidder focused just on work-rule changes, whereas Jay included both economic and work-rule concessions.

- Power tactics: the use of temporary but not permanent replacements at DeRidder avoided the ultimate threat to institutional and job survival. Permanent replacements were used at Jay, which led to both job loss and the decertification of the union.

- Power perceptions: DeRidder management clearly appeared to have the advantage and therefore the ability to prevail; labor did not have any tactical advantages at their disposal. By contrast, the coordinated bargaining at IP and the use of the corporate campaign seemed to offer labor a chance to defeat IP.

- Regional attitudes: DeRidder is located in the South and Jay in the North—consequently, cultural differences in these regions probably explained much of the contrast regarding resolve and power perceptions.

- Time frame: DeRidder's proposals were made at a different point in time from Jay—1983 versus 1987. UPIU had been forced to accept several contracts it saw as concessionary in the intervening period, and by 1987 it had decided to draw the line. Several IP/UPIU contracts came up during a short period, presenting the union with an opportunity to "pool" several mills in order to increase its bargaining power—an opportunity it did not posses in 1983 at DeRidder.

In addition, DeRidder's managers invested in communication mechanisms (including a daily newspaper and team meetings) designed to support the messages conveyed symbolically by maintenance expenditures, management behavior, training, and customer visits. Management essentially bypassed a problematic relationship with the UPIU by dealing directly with employees in permissible ways. In so doing, they avoided the intraorganizational consensus problems they perceived within the union, and they kept local officers from having to confront the possibility of a disjunction between the desires of some local officials for open cooperation with management and the more anticooperation and generally anti-Boise Cascade stance of the national as well as many local officials of the UPIU.

Could the union have played a more central role in the change program at DeRidder? Clearly, the union decided it was wise to neither support nor oppose DeRidder management's initiatives aimed at its members. While the union officials were concerned about what management was doing, they perceived the mill manager to be gaining so much support from workers that they feared a test of wills over the new program. One practical reason for the stance: it was not invited to be a party. A crucial question is whether the local union leadership could have insisted on some type of partner role in fostering the new regime, thereby deriving some credit for the improvements that emerged. The answer to this question is at the heart of the dilemma faced by all union leaders in today's economic environment: If they remain aloof to avoid being co-opted (and in so doing ensure their independence), they run the risk of being marginalized. On the other hand, if they seek to play a leadership role in the new initiatives, they may encounter opposition from management, as well as from a vocal minority within their membership.

As of the early 1990s, it looks like local union leadership at DeRidder had made the right choice. The company's program was viewed favorably by most members and as such was generating positive economic returns. And DeRidder management had started the process of involving local union leadership in decisions regarding the team concept. However, the success of their strategy depended on two factors that are not always present. First, it depended on management choosing not to press its power advantage and undercut the union. Second, it depended on management being effective on its own in implementing the team-based work system and then being willing to bring the union back in as a partner. Since these circumstances are not always present, the DeRidder story may not be a model for union leaders confronted with a fostering initiative on the heels of a period of sustained forcing.

RECONCILING FRAMES OF REFERENCE
The Case of Adrian Fabricators and UAW Local 963

The starting point for the Adrian story began with an ownership transition—the conversion of a private stock company to a majority employee stock ownership plan (ESOP).[3] This transition modified employee assumptions about the existing employment relationship. Labor saw itself as new owners and held high participatory and monetary expectations. In contrast, management adhered to a traditional view of employee-employer relations and pursued an autocratic style of management.

In the midst of this set of incongruent frames, management responded to competitive pressures by adopting a forcing change strategy that ultimately provoked a strike—an unusual event since the employees were literally striking against themselves. The resolution of tensions occurred with a change in top-level management, an expanded role for the union, and the emergence of a fostering strategy more consistent with the employee ownership structure.

Significant Features

Adrian Fabricators is an independent manufacturer of wire mesh industrial containers used in warehouse operations of manufacturing facilities. Located in Adrian, Michigan, the company serves many automotive production facilities. With total employment of 141 in 1989, it has been a relatively small supplier.

The Adrian Fabricators case is unique in many respects, including the following:

• The ESOP emerged out of a common commitment to avoid a plant closing, but with relatively little attention to the structure and meaning of the plan, thereby creating the potential for future conflict.

• The employees abandoned their union as unnecessary following the establishment of the ESOP, only to reestablish it as a vehicle for collective voice.

• Initial wage and benefit concessions were made in the spirit of the ESOP, but subsequent demands for further concessions by management were seen by workers as negating their standing as owners.

• Despite violence on the picket line, the parties settled the strike (in part because some worker-owners continued to operate the plant, and management did not hire replacements for striking worker-owners).

• After the strike, the relationship shifted rather quickly to robust cooperation—with help from state government; with a new CEO opening the books, sending letters to homes, and initiating an open door policy; with symbolic union gestures (such as replacing broken windows in the factory); with the parties renegotiating the profit-sharing formula; and with the establishment of a labor-management committee.

The Adrian Fabricators case teaches many lessons about the specific challenges of an ESOP structure, but the case also has broader applicability. In particular, it illustrates the important roles of leaders in managing the shift from a forcing period to the implementation of a fostering strategy.

The case is notable in that the sequencing of forcing and fostering was not part of a larger intentional strategy (which was the case in DeRidder). The forcing occurred in the context of an unexpected escalating dispute. The subsequent fostering reflected a desire on the part of all parties to build a constructive relationship. Thus, the case illustrates the way sequences of strategies (as well as particular strategies) can emerge in a relationship.

Employee Ownership Within a Traditional Frame of Reference

The history of Adrian Fabricators began in 1966 when the Adrian facility started fabricating operations under the ownership and operation of the Tri-State Engineering Corporation. The facility was organized that same year by the UAW. For the next twenty-five years, the success of the company was tied to the cyclical movements of the automobile industry, since well over 80 percent of its business came from the automotive industry. Collective bargaining arrangements mirrored those throughout the automotive sector. During this period, the established pattern of bad times followed by prosperous periods contributed to complacency on the part of management when faced with a downturn in business. Thus, management was not well prepared for the deep financial exigencies that emerged in the early 1980s —especially with a backdrop of near-record sales of $26 million in 1979.

Management's inadequate financial foresight in terms of cash flow planning and capital planning, coupled with the recession of the early 1980s (which was especially severe in the automotive sector) led to sales levels falling to $6 million by 1982. During this downturn, intermittent layoffs left only the most senior employees in the workforce. At one point, the collective bargaining agreement was virtually discarded as several employees voluntarily worked without pay in the hopes of keeping the operation afloat. By February 1983, the company had filed for bankruptcy.

The ESOP Plan

At the request of several senior employees, a team of state government agencies and private consultants helped formulate an employee stock ownership plan. By the fall of 1983, Adrian Fabricators was reconstituted as a majority employee-owned company. With the creation of the ESOP, the workforce chose to discontinue its relationship with the UAW. This decision was difficult for the international representative to accept since he had led the initial organizing effort of Tri-State in 1966 and had been a strong proponent of the ESOP revival effort. The employees' desire to disassociate from the union exemplified a shift in the frame of reference of the workforce. In essence, the workers believed that employee-owners did not require representation.

As one worker put it: "Management will be by committee . . . there will be no foremen here."

Ultimately, the "employee ownership" expectations of the workforce conflicted with the principles and assumptions about the employment relationship held by management. For example, the first president of the company after reorganization was described by some members of the firm as a "benevolent dictator" with a nonparticipative management style.

Tensions arising from contradictory assumptions about the character of employment relations were heightened by the day-to-day reality of trying to salvage an underfinanced operation. Specifically, management announced that financial constraints would make wage increases difficult. Many workers found this hard to accept, not just because they needed wage adjustments, but because they had envisioned that stock ownership would mean a less arduous work pace and eventual wealth.

By 1985, the tensions had precipitated a reorganizing drive by the UAW within the facility. Management's subsequent approach toward the resurrected union was characterized by a member of the union's bargaining committee as "a resistance to recognize, never mind bargain with, the union." Managers felt that the union would only intensify the financial problems faced by the company because the leadership of the union would make "irrational demands." This attitudinal orientation (with overtones of escape) further polarized management and labor.

Workers Striking Against Themselves

On February 5, 1986, after management fired the chair of the bargaining committee for leaving work early to attend a union meeting, over half the workforce walked off the job with the statement that, "If you fire him, then you have fired all of us." Consistent with their escape/forcing strategy, management attempted to continue operations during the strike using employees—a minority of the workforce who were willing to cross the picket line. The worker-owners who did not cross the picket lines were, in effect, striking against their own firm. Sometimes brothers or relatives were split, with one working and the other on the picket line. As one worker who chose to cross the picket lines commented:

> I crossed because of the ESOP. I felt like it was our plant and that
> we would lose our jobs and everything we had worked so hard for.

In terms of the negotiations themselves, one member of the bargaining committee stated:

> It was pure hell. They brought in some lawyer and he presented us
> with a dinosaur contract. It was an old-style contract that those at
> the international level hadn't seen in twenty-five years.

After three months of extremely tense negotiations, punctuated by occasionally violent confrontations between striking and nonstriking employees, management and the union finally reached agreement in May 1986 on a three-year package that included a one and one-half year freeze on wages, recognition of union stewards, creation of a union shop, implementation of a grievance procedure, and a seniority system. Labor and management agreed that economic pressure felt by both parties provided impetus for the accord.

Construction of a New Frame of Reference

Following the strike, labor-management relations remained tense. The union helped soften some of the tension by assuming the cost of repairing windows and other property broken during the strike. Still, it was a traditional, arm's-length set of relations between labor and management. The precarious financial situation served as a continuing source of tension.

A Change in Management

In the fall of 1987, the president of the company left for another job and, on his recommendation, the chief financial officer of the company became president. With this change in top leadership, labor-management relations slowly began to change. Although the new president was at first skeptical of the value the union would have for the plant, his management style was more participatory than his predecessor. Over time, he concluded:

> The union gives more benefits than costs, by providing a more
> acceptable voice to employees . . . the union has been the method

that they have chosen to voice their concerns. Having union representation is a very stabilizing factor.

Thus, a major shift began to take place as management came to recognize the legitimacy of the union and the full range of employee concerns. This change in management was a pivotal event—though its pivotal nature only became clear over time.

Establishing a Labor-Management Committee

Coinciding with the managerial transition at Adrian Fabricators, state officials from the Michigan Governor's Office for Job Training provided consultation assistance to both labor and management and recommended the initiation of a joint labor-management problem-solving committee—a second key pivotal event following the strike. Both parties signed a letter of understanding acknowledging commitment to the creation of the committee where:

> The purpose of the committee is to enhance communication and understanding between and among labor and management. Through formal participation in this decision-making process, it is the intent that labor will gain a greater appreciation for the necessity of the profit motive, and management will gain insights that may promote this motive.

This committee addressed substantive issues, such as the absenteeism policy, production problems, and safety concerns. Subsequently, the parties also agreed to use the committee as an additional step in the grievance procedure, indicating that the labor-management committee was seen by the parties as a valuable forum and marking a movement away from the formal arm's-length model of labor-management relations.

Revision of the Profit-Sharing Formula

The next major development involved a revision of the profit-sharing component of the ESOP plan. Under the original plan, the first year payment of profit-sharing checks was perceived by the workforce as substantially more favorable to the managers in the firm. In fact, workers received payments earlier as part of their wage package, but the differential in the checks surfaced deep equity issues arising from the workers-as-owners frame of reference. The resolution of this situation involved agreement on uniform profit-sharing payments. In this situation, the ESOP arrangement served as a vehicle by which the workers were able to force equity (or the perception of equity)—an example of union forcing within a fostering context.

Additional Developments

Several developments emerged, not from internal forces, but from external prompts. In 1989, state MIOSHA inspectors cited the plant for a number of safety violations. In response, the president of the firm met with the union leadership, and the parties each appointed representatives to a joint safety committee, established outside of the formal structure of collective bargaining.

A subsequent development, also outside of the formal collective bargaining process, involved the establishment of what the parties termed the "equipment committee." This was established at the initiation of the firm's president, after consultation with the union. The equipment committee oversees the installation and training needs for major capital investments projected to eventually increase productivity by at least 300 percent.

Although this case began with harsh forcing, the increasing use of joint committees created a form of governance consistent with a fostering approach to change. A further step in the fostering direction likely to have implications for the daily work experiences of all workers was the exploration of the team concept.

The shift in frames of reference can be seen in the startling contrast between the two negotiations. In the 1986 negotiations, management would not recognize the legitimacy of the union, whereas in the 1989 negotiations the company's books were open. As the president of Adrian Fabricators put it, "We wanted to have as much mutual trust as possible, so we invited the UAW economists to look at our books." In essence, a dramatic change took place in the assumptions underlying the employment relationship.

Economic Stability and a New Social Contract

Clearly, the financial success that the company began to experience in the fall of 1988 had been a necessary condition for the widespread changes in trust that occurred. After the strike, the value of shares increased 247 percent, employment rose 145 percent, and in 1989 profit sharing became a reality. For the hourly workforce, financial success was best seen in the fact that wages increased by over 25 percent. While causality is always hard to attribute, most managers and union officials gave the improved labor-management relationship significant credit for the improved economic performance.

The parties viewed the emerging social contract as vital to corporate strategy. First, financial success was not just seen as an end in itself, but as a foundation for building trust between labor and management. Second, small auto supply firms such as Adrian Fabricators needed to "guarantee" creditors and customers that "there would be no problems" in terms of labor-management relations.

In addition to moving toward a fostering strategy in labor-management relations, management at Adrian Fabricators worked jointly with the union in developing a business strategy that would insulate the company from the cyclical automotive supply industry. One aspect of this strategy included efforts by the company to garner long-term contracts with large customers. Adrian Fabricators was somewhat successful with this approach. While the company was locked in on prices, one management representative noted: "if there is a downturn, we will have some security with our foot in the door with a huge company." A second and more important component of Adrian's strategy was to remove the company from the auto supply industry by actively seeking to diversify its mix of customers. For example, in 1986 over 75 percent of the company's business was with customers in the automotive industry, whereas by 1990 that figure had fallen to below 15 percent.

In short, there was a conscious strategy to remove the labor-management relationship from the volatile context associated with the automotive supply industry. It is significant that this case began as an example of forcing within the auto supply industry and it continued as a case of fostering that took the parties increasingly outside of the industry.

Analysis

The Adrian Fabricators story features a series of shifts in the labor-management relationship that occurred over a period of hard forcing, followed by a period of sustained fostering. The multifaceted nature of the outcomes that characterized the Adrian story can be summarized in chart form:

Significant Outcomes—Adrian Fabricators

Substantive outcomes	Management-employee relationship	Management-union relationship	Other outcomes
Early economic concessions	Movement from control	Movement from adversarial	Major performance improvements
Contingent compensation	to expectations of mutuality	to a form of escape (since employees no	Mutually costly strike
Work-rule flexibility	to disillusion and strike	longer saw the union as necessary)	Strategic business plan to seek business
Employee stock ownership	to sustained movement toward commitment	to arm's-length involving a strike to sustained movement toward cooperation	outside the auto supply industry

The Adrian Fabricators story contains many elements of the classic sequence wherein a severe crisis occurred, the parties reached for a quick solution (ESOP), matters become more complicated, and only after a second crisis was the situation ripe for a breakthrough. In this case a new CEO and a skilled international union representative provided the leadership necessary for the parties to move into a constructive relationship.

At the time of the first crisis, several divergent interests were at work. Most members of management and some employees saw the ESOP as a means for emphasizing the employee *qua* owner status and de-emphasizing the role of the union and collective bargaining in matters of governance.

When management came on strong and took a very traditional approach to the next negotiations, any semblance of cooperation that had been engendered by the ESOP was shattered. With matters worsening, new leadership (both the CEO and government officials), coupled with a series of constructive, fostering steps, moved the relationship decisively in the cooperative direction.

Several questions can be asked about critical junctures in this story. Was a second crisis necessary—i.e., would it have been possible for the parties in the throes of bankruptcy to have moved directly to a positive relationship in a manner similar to Conrail (a case soon to be considered)? The answer has to be yes. But such a changeover would have required a thorough reorientation of all stakeholders regarding the opportunities and limitations of an ESOP. It also would have been necessary for the parties to have initiated earlier the cluster of fostering activities that eventually were implemented after the strike.

If, on the other hand, management had wanted to escape from the union, what steps could have been taken to this end? (This is a question not normally asked by industrial relations researchers, and it surfaces some uncomfortable issues, but it is important for both union and management leaders to consider.) A skillful management, intent on escape, would have shared power, used the ESOP as a communication channel, and strengthened the axis of management to employee communication—all at the expense of the union. Moreover, at the next negotiation, management would not have come on strong but would have laid out the problems to the employee-owners, with the possibility that attentive supervision could have successfully marginalized the union leadership. Eventually, the union might have been decertified—not as a result of confrontation but as a result of the workers asking: "What is the need for a union?"

The lesson in all of this is that a crisis prompts management to take the initiative. If done properly and in a way that creates credibility, then what starts out as forcing can be transformed into a fostering regime. However, if the crisis induces management to act precipitously or induces the workers to lock on a solution on the basis of unrealistic expectations, then matters become more complicated. Eventually, management, the union, and the workforce at Adrian arrived at a constructive stage, but only after several painful episodes.

The case illustrates the degree to which a structural change such as the establishment of an ESOP did not guarantee success for a firm and its workforce. The new ESOP structure merely provided a platform for negotiations, which brought both new opportunities and new dilemmas. Initially, the interactions were dominated by the dilemmas, such as inflated employee expectations, an ambiguous role for the union, and the persistence of autocratic management styles. In time, and after the painful episodes, the opportunities became more apparent, including high levels of employee motivation, complete information sharing, and extensive union-management dialogue.

Three factors are most important in accounting for the successful realization of the opportunities. These same factors, in their absence, account for the initial difficulties. First, leadership on both sides was key—initially it was absent or contradictory with the ESOP concept and a key factor later on. Second, employee knowledge and expectations were critical—when they were out of line, relations suffered and when there was alignment, motivation was high. Third, government officials played a key role as a source of training and third-party facilitation, which was not present initially, but was subsequently very helpful. Thus we see that the same forces that, in their absence, drive an escalating forcing contest, can also serve, by virtue of their presence, to support a robust fostering initiative.

FOSTERING AT THE SYSTEM LEVEL
The Conrail Story

The experience of Conrail illustrates a unique combination of forcing and fostering. Dire economic circumstances created a need for forcing, while the skill and values of management established the rationale and feasibility for fostering.

Conrail faced bankruptcy. As a result, the federal government stepped in with a revival program. The carrier dropped out of national bargaining and renegotiated its labor agreements. Extensive communication occurred with employees and with the various unions. With the return to profitability, Conrail rejoined national handling, and the parties implemented a series of joint activities.

Significant Features

The Conrail story features the most active role of government across our cases and has the following distinctive features:

- Management prepared the rescue plan in conjunction with federal agencies and in consultation with the unions.
- The CEO and top management dealt with all parties in an open fashion.
- Considerable information was made available to all unions and rank-and-file employees.
- The government provided a powerful and face-saving framework for initial forcing on substantive issues.
- Reinvestment in the business concurrent with the concessionary requests reduced opposition to changes in work rules.
- Subsequent fostering produced positive economic gains and lessened the extent of catastrophic job loss.

There are many features of the Conrail story that are unique to regulated industries in general and to the railroad industry in particular. It is instructive to see how intervention by government can exert such a positive influence on labor-management relations and economic performance.

Highlights

Conrail was formed as a result of the Regional Rail Reorganization Act of 1973 (3R), combining railroads formerly known as the Penn Central, Erie Lackawanna, Central Railroad of New Jersey, and several other smaller lines. The new organization did not begin operating until early 1976.

The next several years saw big losses, and by 1981, with Conrail still losing money, management moved to develop a plan to place the railroad back on a profitable basis. After substantial analysis, a plan that management felt was realistic was brought forward and, at compensation levels then existing, a gap of $200 million remained. To deal with this gap the concept of a wage freeze emerged that would defer national wage increases up to 12.5 percent.

At about the same time, management also developed a plan for reducing crew size on trains from the customary complement of five (engineer, fireman, conductor, and two brakemen) to three (dropping the fireman and one brakeman). This plan called for a separation payment of $25,000 per individual and required federal funding.

A number of structural changes also were implemented. As part of the continuing consolidation, many duplicate facilities were eliminated. For example, the number of maintenance shops for diesel locomotives was reduced from fifty to nine. The remaining shops went to three-shift operations in order to better use the plant and equipment.

As a result of the Northeast Rail Service Act of 1981 that transferred ownership to the federal sector, Conrail was able to expedite procedures for abandoning unprofitable lines. In addition, the number of local labor agreements was reduced, and virtually all of the arbitraries (special payment provisions) were eliminated. For example, when Conrail commenced operations in 1976, there were 285 separate agreements; by the early 1980s, the number had been reduced to 23.

Results

Due to these changes, Conrail gradually returned to profitability and was spun out from under government ownership and placed in the private sector in 1987. In the process, staffing levels had dropped from 90,000 to approximately 25,000 by the early 1990s. With the reduction in crew size, most trains were able to operate with three-person crews—93 percent for through freight, 84 percent for local, and 96 percent for yard operations. By 1994, labor costs stood at 36 percent of total costs compared to 62 percent prior to restructuring. While compensation increases had been deferred for several years, eventually these wage deferrals were restored in lump-sum payments, averaging approximately $6,000 per employee. Most workers who remained with Conrail more than recouped their losses, taking into account that they received stock when Conrail went public.

Analysis

Conrail succeeded in reducing crew size and realizing other changes in work rules almost a decade ahead of other carriers, and it achieved these major improvements while maintaining positive relations with most of its unions. In fact, labor leaders place Conrail at the top of the "good guy" list for the railroad industry. What explains these favorable outcomes?

In terms of our framework, the Conrail story possesses certain elements of forcing, but with special characteristics. The key driver, of course, was the economic crisis: Conrail was losing large amounts of money and it was clear that the federal government would be forced to do something drastic (like selling pieces of the system to other carriers) if the corporation were not returned to profitability in the early 1980s.

A second significant factor was the role of legislation and administrative directives establishing procedures that enabled management to reduce the size of the workforce rather directly—something that other railroads have not been able to do as easily. Specifically, when workers who had been hired after 1969 were offered a $25,000 buyout (and large numbers of them accepted), the company was able to shrink employment by eliminating these positions—unlike other railroads who (until the mid-1990s) had been required to bring back furloughed workers, i.e., allowing them to exercise seniority rights to fill vacated positions.

A third factor (and in some ways pivotal) was the federal bailout; Uncle Sam "footed the bill." Summing up the various pieces of the overall program, namely, the massive physical rehabilitation of the system and the labor protection costs and financial settlements with the various predecessors of Conrail, the total price tag for the federal government came to over $8 billion (unadjusted for inflation). Labor protection (primarily the buyouts) alone amounted to $630 million in direct federal grants.

Unlike other carriers that attempted (unsuccessfully) to convince their union leaders and workers that change was necessary to improve profitability, management at Conrail did not have to engage in such rhetoric. The situation spoke for itself: Agree to changes or face the uncertainty associated with splitting up and reorganizing the Conrail system.

When the compulsion for change comes from objective circumstances rather than a one-sided initiative (often coupled with a contract expiration), it is easier for the parties to maintain and even improve their social relations. Thus, in the case of Conrail, management emphasized the importance of developing strong rapport with key union leaders and handling the change process in an open and participative manner. These elements of fostering were facilitated by the values and style of the CEO and other key executives.

Extensive communication programs also were instituted to inform all employees about the challenges being faced and the progress being made during the early 1980s. Wherever possible, management looked for ways to continue the employment of workers who were no longer needed. For example, when a shortage developed of skilled signal personnel to staff a range of new electronic technologies, Conrail recruited approximately 300 individuals from other crafts and instituted both classroom and on-the-job training in keeping with the company's policy of affording employment opportunities to employees who had been furloughed from other lines of work.

The fostering process also benefitted from the services of facilitators such as William Usery, former Secretary of Labor, who played a key role during the 1980s in bringing about consensus on the major pieces of the labor relations program involving severance payments, reduction in crew sizes, and consolidation of local agreements, as well as encouraging the parties to approach change in a constructive manner.

Significantly, the industrial relations function was a part of the top management team within Conrail. The vice-president for labor relations played a key role in the formulation of business strategy, and top management placed the highest priority on achieving constructive labor-management relations.

The best term to describe the tenor of labor-management relations would be "accommodation." The CEO met regularly with top union leaders, and a number of them sat on what is referred to as the Conrail Subcommittee that was made up of top executives and presidents of most of the major railroad brotherhoods. However, the approach was not one of jointness. Management's objective was to keep the unions informed, but not to bring them into co-management. In the example of retraining craft workers to become signal operators, Conrail initiated the training and only notified the union as a matter of information.

The main conclusion of the Conrail story is that by taking an ailing railroad and placing it under the shelter of government support, the parties were able to restructure operations and to streamline the work-force to the end that economic viability was restored. In effect, management took advantage of the federal clout to force through the necessary changes, but at the same time strove to maintain positive relationships with its employees and unions.

The question needs to be asked whether the working accommodation forged in the throes of bankruptcy would continue. Several pieces of evidence suggest an affirmative answer. During the late 1980s and early 1990s, the parties instituted a joint labor-management safety program, and a labor-management cooperation program was expanded substantially. The chairs of the various subcommittees alternated each year between management and labor representatives. These programs were guided by an overall Joint Labor-Management Committee. Significantly, union representatives on this latter committee were full-time Conrail employees.

Frequently, these joint labor-management teams worked with customers in designing procedures for better service. For example, a cross-functional team from Conrail interfaced with a team from Bethlehem Steel to reduce billing errors from 14 percent to 3 percent, with an eventual target of zero defects.

Compelling circumstances and a well-managed process combined to produce the favorable outcomes at Conrail. We have seen in other cases that neither a compelling context nor an effective process alone is sufficient. Adrian Fabricators, for example, experienced the focusing effect of bankruptcy, but the parties did not emerge from bankruptcy with a jointly understood and viable plan for recovery—so economic crisis alone was not sufficient. In the CSX case, the parties handled the process reasonably well, but the absence of a crisis allowed the local chairmen of the United Transportation Union (UTU) to opt for the status quo—indicating that a collaborative process alone was not sufficient.

By dropping out of national handling and by focusing the attention of union leaders and workers on the tough realities facing the company, management was able to gain acceptance for fundamental changes that would not have been possible within the traditional structure of multi-employer, multiunion, collective bargaining. The fact that ownership was (for an important period) in the hands of the federal government also lent credibility to the need for fundamental restructuring.

This case teaches, therefore, that the use of compelling economic arguments is most effective when accompanied by a positive relationship between labor and management. Conrail found itself in a situation where the economic situation (impending bankruptcy) created considerable credibility for change. However, even with these objective circumstances, the union leaders and rank and file could have easily concluded that they were being coerced by circumstances or that management was using bankruptcy to extract undue concessions.

The challenge is the following: How does management present an accurate picture without the union reacting in a negative fashion—thereby setting in motion an escalation towards unrestrained forcing. In the case of Conrail, the strong positive relationship that had developed between top officials (building on the commitment of top management to proceed in an open way) made it possible for the forcing elements that were present to be viewed in a constructive fashion. In essence, labor had no other choice than to accept major concessions, and full information sharing made the concessions more attractive than the alternative scenarios (such as the collapse and breakup of the entire railroad).

In certain circumstances the role of third parties, especially the government, can be crucially important for the change process. In the instance of Conrail, the federal government brought resources and its good offices—all of which provided considerable impetus to the fashioning and implementing of a recovery plan. By contrast, in the case of AP Parts, the role of governmental officials remained limited—they were local (lacking the authority of federal agencies) and, most important, they lacked resources to bring to the table. Indeed, from this perspective, some analysts criticized the Conrail rescue as an overly generous bailout that cost the taxpayers dearly.

Holding aside the taxpayer issue, another lesson that then emerges is that union concessions are more palatable when they are accompanied by reinvestment in the business. From this point of view, sufficient resources make it possible to overcome a good deal of what would have been resistance to the large-scale change.

Significantly, Conrail did *not* revert to the typical arm's-length relationship (characteristic of railroads) when it was spun out from under governmental ownership. Basically, the explanation is that once a positive relationship had developed and the parties had realized benefits as a result of this relationship, it was unlikely, short of major changes in personnel or the environment, that the strategic approach being followed by the parties would be modified. Thus, like the DeRidder case, key choices made during the initial period (with heavy elements of forcing) laid the foundation for a subsequent period of constructive fostering.

COORDINATING STRATEGIES
Strengths and Challenges

Ultimately, all three of the cases featuring a sequence of forcing and fostering strategies met with success—of course, in varying degrees and after different journeys.

In two cases (Adrian Fabricators and Conrail) bankruptcy provided the forcing impetus; however, in the case of Adrian, a second crisis was required before the parties turned the corner and embraced a robust fostering strategy. In any event, in both of these instances the positive results were realized relatively quickly. In the DeRidder case, the crisis was not externally imposed, and the reconstruction of relations took longer. In that case, however, the sustained fostering initiatives ultimately transformed the mill into one of the company's most productive, safest, and best-paying paper mills.

The significant difference between these three cases, on the one hand, and the cases discussed in the preceding two chapters, on the other, is that here the parties avoided the destabilizing tendencies inherent in an exclusive reliance on either of the two distinct strategies. The parties engaged in such integrative arrangements as extensive information sharing, problem solving, and consensus decision making, yet they found ways to surface and to handle serious conflicts.

All of the cases were characterized by the emergence of a new set of norms governing relations on an ongoing basis. Significantly, the exercise of power became more subtle and certain distributive tactics were foreclosed. Basically, the new norms were integrative in nature.

On the other side of the ledger, when the parties engaged in forcing, they did so without letting it escalate into an out-of-control confrontation. Management at DeRidder picked its issues carefully—focusing on work rules rather than the economic package. Similarly, Conrail sought major contractual concessions, but demonstrated continuing commitment to the business (made possible by the federal bailout funds).

Lessons Learned

The experience of these three cases suggests a number of important lessons regarding the effective sequencing of forcing and fostering strategies.

The important role of key leaders cannot be overstated. DeRidder, Adrian, and Conrail all were eventually characterized by a consultative style of top management and illustrate the dominant influence of key individuals on the process. Management leaders in the DeRidder and Conrail cases ensured that the forcing remained restrained, and in all three cases management ensured that the fostering proceeded in a focused fashion. Union leaders in the Adrian and Conrail cases played key reciprocal roles in the reconstruction of relations after the forcing.

Objective standards were critical as justifications for forcing and for moving past the forcing. The speed with which Adrian and Conrail tackled their problems was in large part due to the credibility of the stories presented by management.

The importance of persistence and a steady approach is also underscored by these cases. In these three success stories the parties kept their eye on realizing both substantive gains and improved relations. In several cases these results were slow to materialize, but the parties kept their attention on the long run and did not veer towards escape, unrestrained forcing, or "soft" fostering.

The ability of the parties to learn was key as they proceeded to grapple with the many challenges. In all of these cases organizational learning occurred as crises were addressed and solutions developed—often generating new problems. For example, it took the stakeholders at Adrian some time to sort out the complex interrelationships between management initiative, employee ownership, gainsharing, and collective bargaining. Similarly, at DeRidder management first focused on building employee commitment and ignored the union. Eventually corporate management revised its approach and decided to build positive union-management relations. The DeRidder mill management joined in the new corporate policy.

Taken together, the sequence of forcing followed by fostering has the potential to address the key limitations of strategies that are exclusively oriented around one or the other pure strategy. An exclusive focus on forcing may yield fast change, but the benefits may prove elusive due to soured relations, while an exclusive focus on fostering may improve relations, but may not yield substantive change quickly enough. Properly sequencing the strategies both tempers the forcing and creates sufficient change to create a strong economic foundation for fostering initiatives. The appeal for management of such sequencing should be clear. The sequence is much more problematic for unions, which face a double loss—they may lose the forcing battle, and then they may also lose again in the fostering period if a program of employee commitment weakens the union. Thus, the sequenced approach depends on management's power and skill during both the forcing and fostering phases. Where labor is strong or the tactical moves poorly executed, a different combination of forcing and fostering may be required—which is the focus of the next chapter.

NOTES

1. Signed in 1960 for the West Coast longshoring industry, the Mechanization and Modernization Agreement established a $5 million productivity fund, wage and employment guarantees and incentives for early retirement in return for the union giving up work rules that required multiple people to handle goods, extra workers to be employed and that facilitated containerization facilitation (see Kochan 1980, pp. 351ff for a discussion of this and other early instances of far-reaching fostering preceded by some degree of forcing).

2. We rely heavily on published and unpublished materials from Casey Ichniowski (1986a, 1986b) for a description of DeRidder change processes and analysis of selected performance results through 1985. Our own discussions with mill and corporate managers provided us with

additional details of the period before 1985, as well as with the data to construct our account of subsequent events. Valuable research assistance was provided by Kathleen Rudd Scharf in the preparation of this case.

3. Valuable research assistance was provided by Pat McHugh in the preparation of this case.

5
Combined Strategies
The Interweaving of Forcing and Fostering

Negotiation strategies can become quite complex. We have already seen that travel down the forcing or fostering paths is complicated in itself and even more complicated when the pathways are traveled in sequence. Most complex of all, however, is the simultaneous travel down both forcing and fostering paths or multiple sequences of forcing and fostering strategies. When skillfully executed, elements of the two strategies that would normally be at cross purposes instead can lead to positive synergies.

Two of the cases presented in this chapter, Budd and Packard Electric, feature periods of simultaneous forcing and fostering, followed by extended fostering periods (each also featuring some distributive confrontations). The other case, Pensacola, involved a sequence of forcing, followed by fostering, followed by a combined period involving both forcing and fostering.

There are no obvious historical parallels for these complex strategies. In part, this reflects management's ascendancy in power. In the past, labor was primarily setting the tone in negotiations, and its strategies relied primarily on forcing in combination with periods of arm's-length accommodation. This reflected labor's dual desire for increased economic gains combined with the stability of equitable and well-defined work rules. Now, with management primarily setting the tone, complex combinations of forcing and fostering reflect management's dual desire in many cases for rapid change and for high levels of worker commitment.

Interestingly, only one of the cases, Pensacola, features a period in which forcing and fostering were intentionally combined in order to achieve certain benefits associated with each. This occurred in the context of a collective bargaining negotiation that was designed to roll back certain economic benefits while still sustaining existing fostering initiatives. In the other two cases, the combined periods reflected simultaneous but independent management initiatives. Both at Budd and at Packard Electric, the combined periods featured forcing around the relocation of work into lower wage locations that occurred at the same time that quality of worklife efforts focused on shop-floor employee involvement were being implemented. Even though these forcing and fostering initiatives were not tightly coupled, each had important implications for the other.

The following chart features salient elements of all three cases. The complexity of these cases is evident in the time frames for forcing, fostering, and combined strategies. In all of these cases, the various strategies were executed both during the contractual negotiations and (in between) during contract administration.

Key Aspects of Cases Featuring Concurrent Forcing and Fostering

	Pensacola	Budd	Packard Electric
Background factors	Declining market for primary product; sale of the mill to a new owner	Fierce competition in industry; new capacity in southern nonunion plants	Fierce competition in industry; new capacity in southern nonunion plants and Mexican operations
Locus of negotiations	Plant	Company and plant	Company and plant
Time frame for forcing	Contract negotiations	Contract negotiations and administration	Contract negotiations and administration
Time frame for fostering	Contract administration	Contract administration	Contract negotiations and administration
Time frame for combined strategy	Contract negotiations	Contract negotiations and administration	Contract negotiations and administration
Pivotal events	Arrival of new owners	Massive layoffs in early 1980s	Threatened loss of work to Mexico
Substantive outcomes	Work-rule flexibility Team-based work system	Wage and benefit concessions Special issue joint task forces at national (health care) and plant (die transition) levels	Lifetime job secutiry Multitier wage system Flexible work practices
Relationship outcomes	Increased worker commitment Strong working relationship between union and management	Some increase in worker commitment Strong working relationship between union and management	Increased worker commitment Strong working relationship between union and management

As we saw with the three sequential cases, strong substantive and relationship outcomes occurred in all three of the combined cases. The relationship gains were particularly strong between management and the union in these cases, reflecting extensive joint problem solving on many issues. While the stories also featured increases in worker commitment, this was tempered by strong feelings around the concurrent forcing.

ALTERNATING AND COMBINED EPISODES OF FORCING AND FOSTERING
Pensacola Mill, 1985-1990

By the end of the 1980s, many companies in the paper industry had concluded that to stay competitive they must be prepared to bargain forcefully for substantive changes and also employee commitment and union cooperation.[1] The efforts of management at the Pensacola mill of Champion Paper Company over the period 1985 to 1990 provide us with a rich illustration of this combination of objectives.

Specifically, management at the Pensacola mill forced major changes during the 1985 contract negotiations. It then developed and fostered high levels of employee commitment and union-management cooperation over the next several years. Management returned to the 1988 negotiations, however, with a major wage provision objective it knew it could not sell by persuasion and would need to force.

Pensacola management forced concessions in contract negotiations in 1985 (as well as in 1988) without precipitating a strike. In 1985, it took advantage of the vulnerability labor felt about the future of the mill and employment at the mill and exploited this power factor to rewrite the contract in its favor. It was not constrained in 1985 by concerns about souring employee or union relations.

In 1988, the situation at Pensacola was different. Management was in a bind. Corporate management insisted upon the elimination of Sunday premium pay, a demand strongly resisted by the workforce. But mill management wanted a contract and a negotiation process that would not disrupt worker commitment and union-management cooperation generated during the preceding three years.

Accordingly, Pensacola management moderated its demands and its tactics in an effort to put the best possible face on its position. The fact that relationships had become more constructive during the preceding three years helped the parties through this difficult negotiation without a breakdown in their relationship. While the corporate agenda to eliminate premium pay for Sunday throughout all plants required company negotiations to force this bitter pill on labor, management sweetened the overall settlement with an unrequested 401K plan and employed tactics that were as nonprovocative as possible.

Significant Features

This is a complex case with many dimensions, including the following:

• In the 1985 negotiations, management assessed its business needs and used the opportunity presented by its new ownership to engage in fairly aggressive forcing.

• During the time period between contracts, management engaged in an intensive program of education, involving off-site conferences attended by both management and union officials, visits to a non-union mill, and considerable attention to the reorientation of the workforce.

• During this same period management initiated a series of fostering tactics that: (1) used sociotechnical system (STS) techniques to redesign work; (2) introduced the team concept and other forms of participation; (3) used pilots where units were ready; (4) worked on jointness, e.g., a trip to an Ecology of Work conference where joint union-management teams shared experiences and best practice; and (5) shared both power and responsibility with workers and union leaders, e.g., the creation of a millwide stakeholders' committee.

• Management approached the 1988 contract negotiations with the necessity of securing some significant changes in contractual language, especially the elimination of Sunday premium pay, while at the same time holding the objective of preserving the good working relations that had developed during the preceding period of contract administration.

- Management achieved these seemingly incompatible bargaining objectives by: (1) placing the blame for the elimination of Sunday premium pay on the corporation; (2) not attempting to justify its Sunday premium pay demand as reasonable from the union's point of view; (3) minimizing the influence of the UPIU national bargaining council; (4) urging that both sides communicate their positions as widely as possible; (5) agreeing that language about participation and cooperation be treated as a *quid pro quo* to assist internal alignment within the union; and (6) facilitating the elimination of a Sunday premium pay with a 401K plan.

The initial periods of forcing and fostering in the Pensacola case parallel the three cases presented in the previous chapter. That is, the exercise of restraint during the initial forcing period set the stage for subsequent, far-reaching fostering. Implementing these bargaining strategies required all of the care and subtlety we noted in our discussion of sequential strategies. This case became even more complex, however, when management was faced with the prospect of having to seek a controversial give-back—after three years of joint fostering.

Background

Although the Pensacola mill was established in the 1940s, it became a part of Champion through a merger with St. Regis Paper in 1984. After a long career as St. Regis' most profitable mill, Pensacola had begun to decline as shifts in the supply and demand for kraft paper products made them less profitable in the 1970s.

In 1979, St. Regis began a $250 million capital project at Pensacola whose centerpiece was P5, a huge new kraft machine designed to produce a 350" wide web at the rate of 750 tons of paper per day. In the ensuing years, management bargained several major human resource developments related to P5. First, St. Regis managers hand-selected the new P5 crew from among the crews working on other paper machines—a procedure agreed to by the affected unions only under threat of wholesale outside hiring. This episode created an isolated, elite crew for P5 and angered machine tenders who were not chosen.

Second, St. Regis and the four union locals—three from UPIU and one IBEW—signed a memorandum of agreement in 1979 to explore "team maintenance" for the huge new computerized machine. The parties agreed it would require new and more efficient procedures so that machine operators, for example, would not have to wait for a maintenance crew to repair their machine. The union saw an opportunity to obtain labor rates established elsewhere in the South for multicraft positions, and management was willing to reverse several years of resistance to higher rates in exchange for more efficient use of personnel—and of its large capital investment in P5.

Third, the terms of a further subsequent agreement also created smaller maintenance crews and fewer classifications for the P5 machine. While premium pay for operating extra pieces of equipment was eliminated, maintenance workers gained a 10 percent wage increase. Then in 1981 the "crew concept" was negotiated for production workers in departmental side agreements—deliberately discussed long enough before the 1982 negotiations to insulate it from the contentiousness surrounding formal contract negotiations.

Both team maintenance and crew concept experienced unplanned and uneven implementation, ranging from little to extensive acceptance in various parts of the mill. At the very least, "crew" and "team" language was familiar terminology to Pensacola employees by 1981, as it had permitted managers to streamline certain lines of progression, albeit with compensating wage rates.

Machine shutdowns and personnel layoffs occurred at an accelerating rate, however, as one pulp mill and three paper machines were shut down and one paper machine was converted to bleached kraft during the 1981-1985 period. By 1984, St. Regis' sinking return on investment was attracting unwelcome suitors. After some narrow escapes, the company agreed in 1984 to be acquired by the "white knight" Champion, a smaller paper company also invested in related forest products.

The Pensacola mill was clearly a money-losing proposition in its 1984 condition, a place of silent, outmoded machinery, peeling paint, and a new, high-tech behemoth reeling out a product whose time apparently had passed. The P5 was by now a great technical success, but a strategic blunder. By the time P5 was running at full capacity, the market could not absorb its enormous output of a superior grade of high-strength kraft paper aimed at multiwall bag manufacturers.

Even before the merger was financially complete, officers of the two corporations began stock-taking and planning efforts with many consequences for the mill. Champion already had embarked on a program of acquisitions and sales that emphasized the growing white paper market and had all but withdrawn from low-profit kraft manufacturing and converting operations.

Early in 1985, another of Pensacola's kraft machines and the entire paper bag plant were closed down. Many at Pensacola had understood Champion to be a company without interest in kraft operations, and these shutdowns reinforced that belief. In mid-1985, Champion began to assemble a team to explore the feasibility of converting P5 to uncoated white paper. Many engineers and managers came from other Champion mills, to join this team and to replace other Pensacola mill personnel.

With the three-year labor agreement (negotiated by the previous owner, St. Regis, in 1982) due to expire, Champion mill and corporate management met periodically early in 1985 to analyze the effect of the existing contract on the staffing flexibility and economies they deemed necessary to achieve profitable mill operations. The company saw these negotiations as a unique opportunity to regain control over staffing patterns and work rules, capitalizing on local fears regarding the fate of the entire mill. The final company agenda reflected both local management's desire for far greater flexibility and control over labor relations, and a corporate focus on containment of medical care costs, the elimination of cold (shutdown) holidays, and elimination of a large accumulation of restrictive work rules and side agreements. The corporation was also prepared to insist on a "zipper clause" explicitly overturning all previous side agreements and past practices.

In addition to Pensacola's own unique history, general labor relations patterns in the paper industry also conditioned the unfolding picture in the mill. Traditionally, little contact had occurred between company and unions at the industry or company tiers. There had never been an industrywide contract, although many companies had followed the lead of International Paper. And on the union side, the national offices of the UPIU had begun to convene councils of representatives from all of its locals at a particular company.

1985 Negotiations—Hard Bargaining

While the 1985 negotiations, the first under Pensacola's new owners, were traditional in both structure and process, the company's proposals violated union expectations. Champion was prepared to press the advantages inherent in the mill's sense of having been snatched from the jaws of death, whereas the union was still accustomed to annual wage increases. Management surprised the union committee with its forty-nine-item agenda, which was longer than any company agenda in the history either of the Pensacola mill or, for that matter, Champion. The union agenda was a far shorter and less formalized "wish list," and this disparity coupled with the general sense that the corporation had the fate of the mill in its hands permitted the company team to dominate the negotiations. One company participant recalls:

> We knew going in that this was going to be a flabbergasting experience for the union—they were frustrated, irritated, and felt we were taking advantage of them. Correctly, I might add.

The company argued that the substantial investment that would be needed to return the mill to profitability required significant union concessions in return. For its part, the union committee argued that language such as the management rights clause was unnecessary in view of a local tradition of accommodative labor relations, that the staffing flexibility envisioned by management would lead to the very kinds of abuse that unions and work rules were in place to prevent, and that the long company agenda represented an attempt to do too much too soon.

As the negotiations progressed, the union negotiators avoided discussion of flexibility language while the company repeatedly insisted upon discussing the subject. The UPIU International representative expressed philosophical agreement with flexible staffing and participative management, but opined that some of the Pensacola managers with whom he had worked would be incapable of adhering either to the spirit or the letter of the company's new language. The union team continued to refuse either to embrace flexible staffing or to propose language modifications or substitutions. In the face of this resistance, the company negotiators insisted that flexible staffing language be included in the proposed contract to be presented to union members so that it would be voted up or down with the rest of the contract provisions.

Finally, in September of 1985, after twenty-seven days of bargaining, the union committee "nonrecommended" a contract embodying nearly all of the company's agenda items, including both economic concessions and work-rule changes. Not surprisingly, it was rejected by the locals. The parties returned to the table, a federal mediator was called in, and further discussions yielded a few minor economic gains for the union, but no substantive changes in language on flexible staffing or in other noneconomic areas. In November, the only slightly changed contract was recommended by the union committee and ratified by the membership.

The atmosphere at the final negotiating session, traditionally reflective of a mutual desire to move from the adversarial posturings of the bargaining table to the more congenial relationships characteristic of contract administration, was in this instance clouded by the union team's sense that the company had taken advantage of the mill's economic crisis in order to take an unexpected and aggressive step toward gaining substantial control over labor deployment in the mill. While company negotiators expected that employees' elation over the large capital investment that Champion had made at Pensacola would overshadow negative union reactions to the strategy of forcing change in contract negotiations, the union team felt that it had been required without notice to play an old game by new rules. A member of the company negotiating team recalls:

> They felt really used at that time. I can recall the final session that they had. . . . it was a very depressing situation. Typically, final sessions--there's handshakes, congratulations on a job well done. This one was very tense, cloudy, you could cut the air with a knife. Union people made comments to me to the effect that we just raped them. . . . It was pretty bitter, that we had in essence shoved it down their throats.

Company negotiators had written provision for a joint union-management steering committee into the new contract, but fear of the potential for vocal opposition in such a forum led managers to exclude union representatives from early discussions about implementation of the new agreement.

Meanwhile, in December of 1985, a corporate decision was made to move the Pensacola mill toward a "participative" or "commitment" model of management practices, in addition to the other contract implementation efforts already in motion. Consultants and corporate officers reasoned that the time had come to move their mills away from traditional tight supervisory control over hourly workers and their work and toward a more participative model that would encourage workers' commitment to productivity, quality, full utilization of workers' time and knowledge, and the success of the corporation. Corporate officials reasoned that Pensacola presented them with an excellent opportunity to pioneer these changes with the hope that they would spread to the corporation's other unionized mills.

New Cooperative Initiatives

During 1986, a tension developed between the contract provisions designed to increase line supervisors' flexibility and control in utilizing labor resources (later called "Team Concept" or "Operations Efficiency Language" in some Champion mills) and "Participative Management," a management initiative aimed at the gradual development of a committed, involved, and innovative workforce. The contradictions inherent in the hard bargaining required to introduce new management controls, the subsequent unilateral promulgation of the participation program, and the company's desire to roll these two initiatives into a single process were quickly perceived by many employees.

There was also some difference of approach to new work systems and philosophies among unionists. Although the international union's stance toward such innovations at the time was generally negative, the International Representative for the region had experienced similar changes in other paper mills and found himself in philosophical agreement with many of its features, as long as traditional union-protected safeguards against managerial abuse were maintained.

Contract implementation efforts were headed by the assistant manager of human resources, who had been part of the company negotiating team. This provided some continuity between formal negotiations and the many informal negotiations entailed in implementing a contract with many new provisions.

Management also decided that the new system had to be driven by line management to be successful, and that Sociotechnical Systems (STS) analysis introduced to promote participative management could also be used to implement the goals of team concept in an intelligible way, particularly in a context of rapid technological change. Several meetings were held early in 1986 to explain the new contract to supervisors, to enlist the support of line management for fewer rules and more participation, and to assist department managers in presenting relevant information to their own departments.

During this period, consensus and integration of interests within the respective union and management organizations were achieved by management trips to mills with strong participation programs (including a new Champion nonunion greenfield mill) as well as by attendance by joint union-management teams at a series of labor management conferences. One conference that brought union officers from Pensacola and another Champion mill together under company sponsorship was unprecedented. (Indeed, the company previously had carefully avoided bringing leaders from different mill locals together with company personnel.) This conference featured the international union president, Wayne Glenn, as one of the presenters. The four union presidents from Pensacola returned to the mill enthusiastic about the prospects of labor-management cooperation. One local president (who eventually opposed company efforts to implement new contract language and cooperative programs) remarked at the time that union-management cooperation sounded good "as long as it wasn't an excuse for the company to screw the people."

The meeting that most mill managers at Pensacola regard as the start of the fundamental reorientation was held off-site in March of 1986. While many leaders in the mill already understood the nature of participative management because of numerous in-mill explanatory and planning meetings, this meeting reflected a recognition of the need to enlist the support of key managers at all organizational levels. The gathering convened forty Pensacola managers and supervisors. The lead corporate negotiator from the 1985 contract round and other personnel from headquarters were invited in recognition of the need for corporate support for such efforts. Discussions explained the concept of participative management and attempted to enlist the enthusiasm and informed support of the mill's managerial corps. Those attending received reading material contrasting traditional "control" management with the desired "participative" style, as well as reading and discussing case descriptions of participative programs at other companies.

The attendees were encouraged to keep their discussions centered on specific plans for the Pensacola mill. At one point, the conferees broke into department groups to discuss action plans. The two managers from the converting, finishing and shipping, and technical departments immediately saw an opportunity to achieve reorganization along lines they each had long contemplated. At the same time, other departments favored a more limited application of the new philosophy. The papermill managers, for example, already in the throes of wholesale technical change, decided to postpone the initiation of participative management, although they agreed in principle with the long-term objectives.

A consultant who was present suggested that some managers might volunteer their own departments to be "pioneer departments" by redesigning their departments and encouraging all members to contribute more of their knowledge and experience. Six departments—converting, finishing and shipping, technical, the power house, accounting, and production control—volunteered, and a group was formed to write a "Pensacola philosophy" consistent with the newly articulated goals for the mill as a whole. Managers from other departments apparently decided that they were already overburdened with the enormous technical demands of the conversion. Those present also resolved that the next major meeting on participative management should include union officials if the effort was to succeed. In retrospect, the philosophical demands for wholehearted participation weighed more heavily than the mill's need for *successful* leaders, and the "pioneer department" designation merely represented their managers' desire to move ahead with STS redesigns and other participative mechanisms.

The need to take a concrete step toward a new union-management relationship also was addressed. Management and union officials, with consultants in attendance, met (again off-site) in April of 1986. The agenda was similar to the off-site management meeting, adjusted to include a bid for union support. Significantly, the UPIU International representative spoke in support of participative management. Other union officials in attendance also expressed support for the plan to gradually move toward participative management.

The Emergence of New Structures and Process Norms

Once the joint steering committees and department-level redesign teams were instituted, many aspects of Pensacola's traditional industrial relations system—formal, bilateral, periodic, power-bargained contract negotiations followed by informal, bilateral, continuous, more accommodative mid-contract problem solving—no longer seemed appropriate. The management and joint union-management off-site meetings had been designed to bridge the traditional gaps between contract language and daily operations, between formal and informal negotiations, between industrial relations professionals and line managers, between union local committees and managers, and between corporate and mill managers.

Process norms needed to change as well, and the off-site meetings modeled these changes. Facilitators urged participants at both meetings to adopt a problem-solving orientation as they worked on mutual goals and shared plans.

Of the six departments that had volunteered as pioneer departments, three were directly involved in the technical changes to the mill associated with the conversion of P5 to white paper. The technical department was in the throes of gearing up to test the new white paper processes and products. The finishing and shipping department needed to be substantially reorganized to deal with new products and to operate new automated equipment, and converting was an entirely new department whose hourly force had yet to be hired. Mill managers decided to postpone organizational redesign work in accounting, technical control, and the powerhouse.

In each of the pioneer departments, joint union-management design teams were formed utilizing the STS approach to redesign work and the associated compensation systems. The greatest successes were achieved where job tasks happened to be discrete, departmental culture was cohesive and positive, managers and union representatives genuinely desired a more participative and logical work system, and factors bearing on task assignment and pay were treated in a timely and sensitive manner. In general, outcomes were mixed, however, because of several factors only visible with hindsight. Team selection processes were not standardized; some managers exerted excessive control; hourly workers in some cases floundered in their efforts, and major sources of anxiety, such as job-skill certification processes, remained unresolved. Preexisting disputes over jurisdictional and seniority issues were only magnified by the pressures and scrutiny inherent in the STS design process.

Many at Pensacola later observed that departments should not have been allowed to self-select, since unresolved issues in these already-contentious departments had thrown the entire participation program into question early in the implementation. There also was widespread recognition that enthusiasm and the desire to sell participation had led managers and facilitators to imply that wages would go up in every redesigned department, and these high expectations could not be fulfilled.

The focus on STS as the *sine qua non* of progress toward participation also came to be seen as having limitations. Some departments, such as technical, adapted well to STS and achieved significant successes. The P5 crew, with its sense of isolation and elite status, refused to embrace a process that implied that its efficiency and coordination were below par.

As the Pensacola plant community moved through the challenges of 1986, events led many local observers to decide that norms about interactive process had to shift, from continuous mill-level negotiations of contract implementation issues punctuated by formal contract negotiations (dominated by higher-level corporate and union representatives) toward more continuous negotiations processes, over both implementation issues and desired changes in contract language.

Negotiating the STS Arrangements

The mid-contract wage adjustments required in the redesigned departments became the chief arena in which the need for new negotiating structures and processes became evident. Finishing and shipping came up first, and the corporate regional negotiator and his counterpart, the union International representative, rolled into traditional wage negotiating routines as a reflex. After many rounds of high demands and low offers, the parties came within 25 cents of each other for a key job classification and hit an impasse: department members had come to expect higher wages as a *quid pro quo* for acceptance of the uncertainties of the new work system, and the corporate negotiator had insisted on adhering to 1985 contract language that required rates to rise only when new tasks were added—which in this case resulted in a zero adjustment to the top shipping job, according to the company's analysis. The embittered local president took the wage package back to his membership as a nonrecommended proposal, and it was unanimously rejected by department members—including the design team.

Management demonstrated quick reflexes. Despite contract language that would have permitted unilateral establishment of new lines of progression for finishing and shipping, area managers quietly installed just those changes absolutely required for the upcoming start-up of the rebuilt P5. Managers, both on the human resource and operating sides, also decided to change the format for upcoming wage negotiations in the technical department. Talks began with an emphasis on integrative problem solving, moving into economics only on the second day. The shop steward in this case was committed to the plan, and the existing wage schedule was clearly below industry norms. The UPIU International representative also drew on his experience in other companies to press for an agreement on composition of a joint certification group, which met immediately and developed a workable plan that codified the new work system and posited higher wages.

Later, when the power house area was ready to begin work on its STS redesign, team members were accorded more time to work, more technical and facilitator assistance, and periodic meetings with the regional negotiator to discuss contract-related issues before they reached the more formal and distributively oriented wage negotiations table.

Thus, despite the cooperative gains, the negotiations over change surfaced many differences within and between the parties. All agreed that they had underestimated the planning, training, and overall time their ambitious change agenda would require. The local president involved in the finishing and shipping imbroglio remained an implacable foe of redesign, joint committees, and participation in any form despite the International representative's efforts to move ahead. Philosophical differences between mill-level and corporate-level human resource managers, first highlighted by the midterm wage negotiations, continued to be evident as preparations began for the 1988 negotiations at Pensacola and other Champion mills.

1988 Contract Negotiations—Mixed Bargaining

The 1988 contract negotiations demonstrated that hard distributive bargaining continued to be the dominant mode for formal, periodic contract negotiations, even if it looked inappropriate to many actors for periodic mid-contract wage negotiations, and to others for any and all negotiations.

Many company actions during the 1988 negotiations, however, reflected new attention to preserving the relationship, and new sensitivity to the intraorganizational consensus and ideological issues faced by union negotiators. Although company negotiators continued to depend upon the dominant and moderating presence of the UPIU International representative, they also (as we describe below) took local union politics into account in many of their proposals and reactions.

Pensacola had enjoyed a sense of independent and pioneering spirit since 1985, but emerging corporate and international union agendas created a major challenge to the lead negotiators: the human resources manager and the UPIU International representative. Each saw potential for a shift away from the absolute sway of hard, distributive bargaining in the approaching negotiations, but each had reason to be uneasy about this prospect.

The corporation had declared itself, both in word and deed, committed to eliminating premium pay for scheduled Sunday work. In an earlier time, this might have been a difficult issue, but the negotiating norms would have been obvious. It would have seemed clearly appropriate for corporate officers to press for this rollback across the company, and mill-level negotiators would have followed this lead; debate would have been joined at the formal negotiating table in terms of relative power and *quids pro quo*.

In 1988, in a context at Pensacola of emerging joint experimentation, union members were infuriated by early corporate statements and actions about the Sunday premium. Corporate attempts to explain its position in an integrative bargaining mode—by carefully crafted reference to mutual goals, the reasonableness of company negotiators, and the ostensible lack of an absolute company position—caused even greater anger. Key leaders within both parties, both before and during the 1988 Pensacola talks, agreed that the Sunday premium was one issue that would in fact have to be presented and discussed in a fairly traditional, distributive bargaining spirit.

Corporate labor relations strategists also realized that many mill-level managers, both human resource and operating, perceived a contradiction between the new stated methods of participative management and what they feared was an inflexible corporate commitment to elimination of the Sunday premium—regardless of whether or not equivalent, alternative reductions in labor costs could be developed by local union-management groups.

Company negotiators also realized that many earlier statements to Pensacola employees and their unions could be taken as a promise that their cooperation with management change efforts would eventually be rewarded with "a bigger piece of the pie." The paradox for some managers was that the efforts to enlist employees' "sense of ownership" through shared information about company and mill performance had now borne fruit. As one manager put it:

> *Everyone* knows that things have been going very well in the mill
> and in the company. May's production figures were *very* good.

Other issues affecting intraorganizational consensus were addressed in novel ways at Pensacola in 1988. Once the parties exchanged agendas, the union made an unprecedented distribution of both negotiating agendas to its entire membership. This action surprised company negotiators, but the mill human resources manager also had moved quickly to acquaint foremen and department supervisors with the content of both agendas. Several operating managers formed part of the company negotiating team in an attempt to address intraorganizational consensus issues critical to successful implementation of new joint ways of managing, and to bring technical operating expertise to the table. By corporate policy, the mill manager himself was not a member of the company committee. The unions also named an unusually large committee.

Talks began in May of 1988. After rapid consideration of "housekeeping" issues such as contract dates, the committees moved to major noneconomic issues. These discussions can be characterized as a mixture, on both sides, of "traditional" distributive and "new" integrative modes.

Discussions of one set of issues related to filling vacancies indicate the tenor of the 1988 talks. Under previous contracts, managers were required to fill vacancies in lines of progression as they occurred, by calling in off-shift workers in temporary circumstances. As part of the 1985 drive to secure greater management control over labor use, the company had negotiated the right to use a setup from *within a shift* to fill a temporary vacancy. In 1988, the company proposed language that would permit managers to move people *between departments* located above the bottom of their lines of progression. At the same time, the union proposed reversion to pre-1985 contract language.

Company negotiators argued in favor of their proposal in terms of operating efficiencies, citing cases where workers known to have specific skills needed in their former departments had to remain in new assignments, while employees with needed skills were called in--with extra costs and delays--to replace absent workers. The UPIU International representative replied that "the company has more flexibility than they know how to use intelligently now," and he and other members of the union committee cited examples of abuses observed and grievances filed under post-1985 company vacancy practices.

The parties reached an integrative resolution of their differences. They agreed to language that allowed for department-specific solutions to be worked out on their merits rather than attempting to specify a new set of millwide rules.

During these early discussions, as both sides tried to sense the tenor of the relationship, the corporate negotiator was pleased to note a change from attitudes he had seen during the 1985 negotiations. He realized that the trend toward sharing business information, begun under the 1985 contract, could be a double-edged sword in negotiations now that performance was rising rapidly, but he also thought he could see growing satisfaction in the success of the mill.

> Generally people are pleased with the situation here in the mill. They like being involved, and the mill's making good profits. But the union is saying, "We've got more knowledge and you should pay us for that knowledge—share the pie with us." But that in itself is very different from previous years. There's no more talk of "compensation for this terrible job."

After the end of the first week of negotiations an external event signalled the extent of change at Pensacola. By earlier arrangement, and despite fears that the negotiations would cause union participants to renege, a Pensacola union-management group attended an Ecology of Work conference in Louisville, Kentucky. Three effects could be discerned. Foremost in some minds was the fact that a joint group could attend a conference during the negotiating season—indicating that an improved relationship was undamaged by the strains of formal negotiations. Second, Pensacola managers and unionists alike were able to gauge their real progress against the struggles recounted by other participants, and to share the pride felt by members of the converting department who were told that they should be presenting rather than just listening to others' achievements. Third, UPIU members from Pensacola were questioned closely by their union brethren from other Champion mills, wanting to know how the Pensacola group intended to react to company demands for an end to the Sunday premium. In this regard, members of the Pensacola group were reminded of company-wide interest in their progress, which extended not only to the efforts toward participation and commitment for which they had been congratulated, but to the outcome of their pending contract negotiations as well.

After the conference, negotiations continued in mixed bargaining style. Management evinced more consciousness of union officers' needs in achieving intraorganizational consensus by agreeing:

- to notify the union before outside contractors performed in-plant work, in order that union officials would be informed when asked about unfamiliar workers and vehicles; and

• to postpone discussion of a controversial drug-screening program until after a labor agreement had been signed.

Company negotiators also took care not to undermine the UPIU International representative's direction of the union negotiating committee:

> These negotiations are pretty much following the standard format, but the approach is different because we're coming to a resolution much more quickly than other locations I've negotiated. Things are tested maybe once, and then we'll get off of it. It's been pretty traditional. . . . because it *is* negotiations, and because [the UPIU International representative's] control would be lost if things were more participative, and this would not help the company at all.

Company labor strategists took the multitiered nature of labor-management relations into account in other ways. They delayed presenting their economic proposals until after a scheduled meeting of the UPIU Champion Council (comprising all Champion mill locals). No one from Pensacola had planned to attend, and the union committee did not request that negotiations be postponed. At the same time, the realization developed that any show of corporate force could threaten a delicate local negotiating balance.

Company negotiators dealt with several different compensation issues within a single new concept: the continuous process allowance. The Sunday premium originally had been established as an inducement to workers to abandon the traditional inviolability of Sunday as a day of rest in order to run the mills seven days a week. Meal allowances and shift differentials also had been established over time as compensation for the demands of continuous process manufacturing.

By 1988, some nonunion paper mills had established "continuous process allowances" in lieu of the mechanisms described above. Champion proposed to install such an allowance at Pensacola in order to streamline its compensation system. The company's precise construction of this proposal was intended to do several things at once: avoid enumerating the pay practices to be replaced and avoid adding the continuous process pay to the regular paycheck to which many other benefits were indexed. The union accepted the concept without major objection, but demanded, in traditional fashion, a far larger hourly increment (initially 70 cents per hour compared to management's offer of 17 cents per hour).

Union spokesmen also persisted in treating participation language as a rather undesirable company demand, rather than the mutually embraced declaration of philosophy that company negotiators hoped to achieve. As economic proposals appeared on the table, the union committee reiterated its opening position: Pensacola workers had taken wage cuts and had ceded areas of job control in order to save the mill in 1985, and now the mill was profitable. Not only was it time to restore wages, in the union view, but those wages had already been promised in exchange for cooperation with both a corporate and plant change agenda of participation and union-management cooperation.

Negotiators on both sides proceeded to move between distributive and integrative modes in new ways, especially in recognition of their opponents' intraorganizational political needs and in view of the evolutionary nature of the changes underway, and they tacitly evolved guidelines to assign issues to appropriate negotiating processes: integrative bargaining for participative and cooperative programs and distributive bargaining for wages, work rules, and other work-related policies. However, the distinction broke down somewhat when the union continued to insist that management itself had linked participatory programs with financial rewards and was trying to separate the two. Toward the end of negotiations, when the union announced that it did intend to propose participation language, it insisted that agreement in this area be linked to company movement on other issues, although by this time it was not specifying which issues these might be.

As the parties tackled the sensitive issue of Sunday premium pay, the process came close to reverting to the very traditional adversarial mode. The chief corporate negotiator had made the company's adamant position clear in his opening remarks, but once he commenced negotiating the status of Sunday premium pay, he unfurled the company's major argument—that the economic context of the paper industry and competitor companies' reactions to that context had resulted in a trend toward elimination of Sunday and other premium pay. He argued that Pensacola had to follow the pattern, and he buttressed his arguments carefully with a host of statistics, as if he were relying upon *persuading* the union committee of the merits of the company's position.

Union reaction to this presentation reflected the perils of transitional relationships and processes. As the mill human resource manager recalled later:

> As the week wore on, the more we talked about justifications for the Sunday premium, the madder the guys got.

The UPIU International representative charged that the company was disingenuous in using other paper companies' actions as a justification for its own, in view of the fact that the company had accepted compromise arrangements in earlier negotiations at several other mills. It was also becoming clear that the union negotiators saw political advantages in being *forced* to accede to an unpopular and symbolically controversial change. The Sunday premium had become an explosive issue among some Pensacola workers, and UPIU locals at other Champion mills anxiously awaited results at Pensacola as they prepared for their own negotiations in 1989. In this arena, an overt forcing strategy might work more to the advantage of both parties than would the difficult realignments and intraorganizational negotiations required to achieve the result by any other process. In fact, the corporate negotiator finally said, during a late session, "Let's not try to justify it, let's just work out ways to deal with it." The International representative, for his part, informed the company that the union had no intention of "just giving up" on the Sunday premium, and issued a barely veiled threat: He would hate to have the hard work it had taken to maintain this relationship wasted, only to deteriorate into implemented contracts and lockouts.

At the same time, leaders of both committees acknowledged changed expectations for negotiations. They no longer saw formal contract and informal mid-contract negotiations as different species. The international representative said later: "The point was not just getting a contract, it was getting a contract *and* maintaining a relationship."

A management observer pointed to the disposition of one union agenda item as an illustration of a new approach. The union had proposed one day at a time (ODAAT) use of vacation time, which management resisted on grounds of administrative difficulties with scheduling. The union finally proposed a side agreement which would permit a one-year experiment with ODAAT vacations—and an assessment of its performance after one year. The company committee accepted the union proposal, at once as a reasonable compromise and as a way of reinforcing the union's problem-solving approach that led to integrative language sensitive to both union and management concerns.

The union's participation language, finally placed on the table during the last week of negotiations, delighted company proponents of union-management cooperation. The proposal's significant clauses were: a strongly worded endorsement of the importance to the mill of commitment and participation; a call for the creation of a joint steering committee to oversee all participation programs; a requirement for union approval of all design committees' final proposals; protection of seniority during every design process; protection of existing grievance and discipline practices; no loss of employment or pay through the actions of participatory teams; and the union's right to terminate the memorandum on 60 days' notice without penalty.

Mill managers were willing to press the parent corporation for the employment and wage guarantees and argued only mildly against the union's request that the language be framed in a Memorandum of Agreement, preferring to have the principles included in the new contract. The company argued successfully for exclusion of the union's seniority language, and the parties agreed to jointly written language recognizing the inevitability of change.

Many final economic proposals were negotiated in traditional fashion, with offer and counteroffer accompanied by many feints and threats. The International representative reminded company negotiators that package rejection would lead to a strike vote, which was only a reiteration of UPIU bylaws. The company negotiator declared that a strike vote would not affect the finality of the company's offered package, also a traditional remark. The union finally did accept a buyout of the Sunday premium, which consisted of a new continuous process allowance and lump-sum cash payments. The Sunday premium was, however, to be phased out with time and one-half pay for the first contract year (in addition to the buyout) and straight time thereafter. There were general increases over the second and third years of the contract, and increases in many benefits.

At the end of the following week, 80 percent of the members of the four UPIU and IBEW locals approved and ratified the contract signed by their committee. The contract signing ceremony was a businesslike affair, neither the bitter, defeated event of 1985 for unionists nor a hearty celebration of a renewed relationship. The UPIU International representative took the opportunity to denigrate the financial settlement in view of company profit levels, and to warn his members against taking consultants' and facilitators' rosy promises too seriously.

Over the next several years, management continued to make headway by negotiating employee commitment and union-management cooperation. Participation continued to broaden in scope and deepen its penetration into the management of operations. Union officials generally became more trusting of participation, in particular and mill management's intentions in general. The union officials who were entrenched in their opposition to participation activities became less active and more neutral in their positions. Performance of the mill continued to improve in ways that drew high praise from corporate executives.

Outcomes

By 1994, the substantive and relationship outcomes at Pensacola had been highly favorable. Perhaps the most significant outcome was a shift in the frames of reference of the parties.

Prior to the 1985 contract negotiations, both parties took their stable, accommodative relationship for granted. However, the erosion of the profitability of the mill's kraft paper products and the sale of the mill to Champion were critical events that portended major changes. Management indeed entered the 1985 negotiations with a new frame—that competitive conditions called for major substantive changes in terms of employment and would require a forcing strategy. The size of management's demands shocked the union negotiators. The union, for its part, did not see the need for the particular changes, but eventually accepted the power realities that enabled management to have its way. As a result, the accommodative relationship was soured.

In effect, management exploited their new-owner status and followed a forcing strategy that was significant in several respects: (1) controls over costs and labor deployment were negotiated (via hard bargaining) before constructive labor-management relationships had been established, and (2) all four union locals were established as signatories to a contract whose provisions became integral to subsequent fostering efforts. As a result, even overtly antiparticipation union officials became engaged in participatory processes as a part of their interest in effective contract administration.

The mindset that evolved for labor during the years between the 1985 and 1988 contract negotiations included an expectation that the gains from commitment and cooperation would be distributed equitably between labor and the company. This change in frame—toward a more participative workplace—counted on the cumulative effect of many activities, including the joint off-site meeting and the STS-related changes in the plant.

Management's choice of STS as the heart of its change processes made the company's simultaneous embrace of management-won flexibility and employee involvement intelligible: department groups would use the STS approach to *participate* in their departments' implementation of hard-bargained contractual changes, and they *might* benefit financially from that participation as well. For Pensacola, in the throes of complex technological change during much of the 1980s, STS also had the potential—not always realized—for engaging union members in their changing worklives in a proactive way.

Pensacola's story also demonstrates the myriad dilemmas and difficulties posed by the need for continuous, multilevel, negotiations. The process in the finishing and shipping departments, for example, ran aground on inadequate integrative bargaining and incomplete attention to intraorganizational consensus—between design teams and the rest of their department, and between local leadership (on both sides) and corporate negotiators.

Then, in 1988, when management adhered to the corporate multimill bargaining agenda to take away Sunday premium pay as such, union officials felt compelled to revise their approach—toward a more "realistic" notion of their relationship. Labor—as well as mill managers—were forced to recognize that both sides would not only cooperate to increase the size of the pie, but that each would compete to get favorable shares for their own constituents.

Other lessons emerge from the experience of the 1988 negotiations. Some issues were decided in small problem-solving groups, and management in particular attempted to positively influence union committee members through unprecedented information sharing. Although some management strategists had come to value consensus-seeking over power bargaining, it became clear that the intraorganizational consensus needs of elected union counterparts were sometimes best served by hard distributive bargaining. Specifically, the Sunday premium issue demonstrated the difficulties inherent in maintaining the pretense of integrative bargaining over an issue on which the parties' interests as well as positions were fundamentally different, and on which one or both teams were at risk politically.

Lessons Learned

In most respects, the Pensacola story appears to be an exemplar. Despite some similarities with the Bidwell situation (new ownership arrangements, use of outside consultants, and implementation of QWL-type programs), the results at Pensacola far exceeded the aborted change efforts at Bidwell.

In retrospect, it is clear that the parties would not have been able to agree on fundamental changes in the contract in 1985 via a fostering strategy. Management needed to employ the power inherent in its "new arrival" and the urgency inherent in forcing to secure changes necessary to justify its investment. In fact, it is interesting that the company did not make its purchase of the mill contingent on a revision of the contract, but elected to tackle this subject at the first negotiations after arriving on the scene. This willingness to work things out in the course of normal collective bargaining and to do so with key officials at the local level created a positive backdrop to the hard distributive bargaining that was necessary.

The question should be asked whether the local unions at Pensacola could have responded differently. They found themselves managing many dilemmas. Similar to the DeRidder situation, management at Pensacola moved aggressively to involve rank-and-file workers in a series of activities aimed at increasing commitment and motivation. But the unions at Pensacola were not held at arm's length—indeed they were afforded many opportunities to become co-sponsors of these programs. Local union leadership adopted, for the most part, a stance of supporting joint programs, but also bargained vigorously on behalf of member interests—short of taking strike action. As a result, they were able to share some of the credit with management for improvements associated with the work redesign. Equally, management indicated the important role of the union in its efforts to temper the impact of forcing during the 1988 round of collective bargaining.

In all, the Pensacola case points out the complex mix of negotiations associated with fundamental changes in a labor-management relationship. The parties' success reflects not only action taken, but also critical choices that prevented escalating conflict early on and that avoided a collapse in relations during hard bargaining after a period of fostering.

INTERWEAVING FORCING AND FOSTERING STRATEGIES

The Budd Company, the UAW, and the CAW

Over the past decade, labor-management relations between Budd and the UAW have moved toward social contracts based on worker commitment and union-management cooperation.[2] This case highlights plant-level forcing and fostering initiatives—primarily in Budd's Detroit, Michigan plant, as well as tracing key developments between the international union and the corporation.

Specifically, in the early and mid-1980s, Budd engaged in forcing, as was the pattern for many auto supply firms. As a result, it received a number of important economic concessions. As a backdrop for the concessionary pressure, the company had engaged in massive layoffs during the early 1980s—sometimes linking concessionary demands and threatened movement of work. Concurrently, Budd had initiated an employee involvement (EI) program modeled on initiatives begun at its automotive customers. This focused on shop-floor participation in decision making on issues of safety, work organization, and other matters. Unlike many of its competitors, however, Budd did not seek to escape from union representation on any large scale—even though the company did open a new nonunion facility in the late 1980s. The UAW worked closely with Budd management at plant and corporate levels, but an element of caution was always present, given the history of concessions and concerns over the nonunion facility.

At the level of national negotiations, the company attempted in 1987, to achieve concessions and mutually beneficial innovations by opening contract talks early and engaging in extensive communications. The first attempt failed, but a second attempt succeeded, and the parties signed a four-year agreement that set in motion a relationship characterized by quarterly meetings and continuous attention to common problems.

Significant Features

At the plant level, the Budd case illustrates several important dimensions:

* A long list of company demands departed from past practice and presented a "procedural" challenge to the union apart from their content.

* Union leaders who were persuaded of the company's need for concessions were rebuffed by members who were not persuaded. Subsequently, both management and union adjusted their tactics and embarked on a major communication effort prior to a subsequent round of negotiations.

* The negotiation of a hit-to-hit agreement for die transition teams at the Detroit plant involved a shift of negotiating power from industrial relations to manufacturing management.

* The juxtaposition of forcing (around the movement of work and layoffs) with fostering (around employee involvement and labor-management committees) helped to establish the importance of both the employee involvement and joint labor-management initiatives, and probably prevented even greater job losses.

At the national level, additional important dimensions include:

* Customers (especially the Big Three automakers) made demands on auto parts suppliers that the UAW found more credible than when the demands had originated solely with management.

- The parties created a quarterly forum to deal with "quality issues" that subsequently was used for potentially contentious issues— providing, in effect, a vehicle for continuous bargaining.

- Continued tensions were observable around the union's role in new production facilities located in "right-to-work" states.

The Budd case, then, is in many ways typical of mid-size firms facing considerable competitive pressures and saddled with histories of adversarial relations. While the parties at Budd generated many important joint innovations, they also experienced numerous difficult confrontations in which the outcomes were not always mutually beneficial. Ultimately, a complex mix of negotiations was required for the parties to make the substantial progress that they experienced in transforming their relationship.

Background

The Budd Company, a large independent auto supplier, was founded in 1912 by Edward G. Budd. The company has expanded steadily, with a worldwide workforce of 14,000 and sales of $1.3 billion as of the early 1990s. Budd was organized into three main divisions: stamping and frame; wheel and brake; and plastics. The majority of production operations were located in Michigan and Ohio, but the company also had facilities in Pennsylvania, Wisconsin, California, and Kentucky, as well as in Canada, Argentina, and Germany. The company was owned by the German conglomerate Thyssen AG at the time this case was written.

The UAW first organized workers at the Budd Company in the 1940s, and the majority of Budd manufacturing facilities remained unionized. In Canada, the Canadian Automobile Workers Union (CAW) represents Budd workers. Historically, labor relations have followed the pattern set by the UAW with the original equipment manufacturers (OEMs), including arm's length collective bargaining, high levels of wages and benefits, and very formal and adversarial contract administration.

Early Forcing and Fostering Initiatives at the Plant Level

The decade of the 1980s began with massive layoffs throughout the Budd Company. The Detroit plant was among the hardest hit, with union membership declining from 2,800 to 1,200 between 1979 and 1982. In this turbulent climate, the social contract between labor and management surfaced as a topic of negotiations.

Initial Concession Bargaining

Before the largest of the layoffs, which occurred in 1981, the company pressed for concessions. Many union leaders were persuaded that adjustments were needed and agreed to a mid-contract reopener. An agreement was reached, which involved significant wage and benefit concessions. This was presented to the membership, with the stated alternative being the loss of the plant's wheel and drum business, accounting for over half of the plant's workforce.

Although local union president, Norm Tunessi, recommended ratification, the membership was not convinced of the need for change. A 95 percent vote against the agreement devastated local union leaders, who had been persuaded that the company's situation was indeed serious. Following the rejection, jobs were indeed shifted out of the Detroit plant, resulting in a layoff of an additional 900 employees. As one union leader commented on the membership's vote against the concessions:

> We had a ferocious membership meeting. Talk about being scared, we had to be escorted out of the meeting ... They (the membership) never believed it until the machines were disassembled.

This early forcing (with limited fostering) ended up costly to both sides. The union and the membership suffered the loss of jobs, while the company incurred the costs associated with shutting down nearly 100,000 square feet of plant capacity.

The experience, which had parallels in other Budd facilities, illustrates the limiting effects of each side's frame of reference. Management assumed that its statements of the need for deep changes would be taken seriously since, from its perspective, the need was self-evident. For many in the union membership, however, there was no prior experience to suggest that management's statements were anything more than stronger versions of past rhetoric.

Following the layoffs, an increased willingness by union members to make informal accommodations was evidenced. As the local president recalls:

> We had 2,800 people in 1979, and 1,600 got laid off by 1981. One of the biggest problems was with the job classifications. Jobs were merged, and it became a problem for the bargaining committee.... We had to modify classifications, not by contract but by the bargaining committee and labor relations on a daily basis. You didn't know if the plant was going to survive, so the union was willing to move.

Employee Involvement and Statistical Process Control as Customer-Driven Changes

Beginning in 1982, the company and local unions in most Budd facilities agreed to establish employee involvement (EI) programs and statistical process control (SPC) programs. Both initiatives were dictated by the firm's customers, but in different ways. The adoption of the EI program was an example of the connection across companies in the auto industry; GM and Ford had pioneered quality of worklife (QWL) and EI programs, respectively, and Budd joined many other auto suppliers in adopting similar language in its collective bargaining agreements. In contrast, SPC represented one of the first domains where the OEMs insisted that their suppliers implement new work practices.

The structure of the EI and SPC efforts at Budd were patterned after the respective programs at Ford and GM. Union appointees and management designees served as staff coordinators. Also, the entire EI process was administered by a joint committee that made decisions on a consensus basis—a key shift in the norms of interaction.[3]

The most challenging negotiations associated with EI and SPC efforts, however, took place at the individual level. These involved negotiations over workers' voluntary participation and commitment to the new initiatives. As such, bargaining occurred between supervisors and employees, between QWL or SPC coordinators and employees, and among groups of workers. By the mid-1980s, the EI effort had expanded to include approximately one-quarter of the workforce in the Detroit plant, but very few other workers were interested in the process. This plateau in the number of volunteers occurred in other Budd locations and was typical of many EI initiatives (Cutcher-Gershenfeld, Kochan, and Verma 1991).

Many comfort and hygiene concerns of the workers were addressed via the EI process, along with some redesign of equipment and work operations aimed at greater efficiency. For example, an EI team improved quality and safety by developing a custom piece of sheet metal feeding equipment, dubbed the "Goesinta," since it takes metal from one press and helps as it "goes into" another. The SPC efforts also contributed to improved product quality. However, management was convinced that these joint efforts alone would not be sufficient to meet the competitive challenges in the auto supply sector—where customers had begun to pressure suppliers for annual price cuts of 1 to 3 percent.

For some union members and leaders, despite the history of layoffs and lost business, there was still considerable skepticism about the need for fundamental changes. For example, during the mid-1980s, the Budd Detroit plant was working high levels of overtime. As one union leader noted:

> It's hard to get the membership thinking long term, especially when the people are working all the overtime they want, actually more than they want to. It is hard to convince them their jobs are in jeopardy.

There were also institutional-level pressures on the union. For example, in the Detroit plant, the company repeatedly indicated its desire to cut back on the number of full-time paid union positions (which had remained constant despite reductions in the size of the workforce). Finally, here as in other locations, there were tensions regarding the ability of union leaders to engage in new forms of dialogue with management while still being seen as independent from management (Cutcher-Gershenfeld, McKersie, and Weaver 1988).

This role conflict experienced in the union was vividly illustrated by deliberations over the shape of the table in a special meeting room used by the union bargaining committee. The bargaining committee rejected a square table as lending itself to competing sides, but also rejected a round table as "going too far." The result was an oblong table with one end squared for the union and management co-chairs of the joint effort—illustrative of the parties's cautious commitment to a new social contract around commitment and cooperation.

Negotiating Flexibility and Autonomy in Detroit

In 1987, local negotiations began early at the Detroit facility paralleling early national negotiations (which are discussed below). The negotiations focused on a key aspect of economic performance in the stamping plant—the time required to change dies. This was a process by which large metal dies (some weighing as much as 50 tons) were removed from presses at the end of a production run and replaced with new dies for stamping a different part. Addressing the issue posed a dilemma, since it was not clear that a solution could be found via traditional collective bargaining.

The focus of the discussions centered on the establishment of a hit-to-hit, labor-management committee that would provide oversight to autonomous teams of approximately twenty craft employees responsible for changing dies. The goal for the die transition teams was to reduce the time between the last good stamping or "hit" in one production run and the first good "hit" in the next run.

In all, the local negotiations lasted about four months, with most of the time spent in discussions about the function of the hit-to-hit committee. Eventually the parties agreed to draft a letter of agreement that, in the words of the plant manager, required a new approach.

> We tried to do it the old way, but it didn't work. It could not be developed in traditional bargaining language. Thus, we got rid of the "mays," which has always been interpreted as something I don't have to do and the "shalls," which is something that I must do.

Yet drafting the letter proved difficult. The task initially fell on the plant's industrial relations department, but as the director of industrial relations commented:

> The die transition letter was important. We really struggled with that and modified our proposal three or four times. They didn't like it. We told them "You do it! If you don't like it then you write one up." . . . It was surprising, they came back with an almost perfect letter.

A UAW International representative recalled that the union was able to draft the letter on the basis of experiences in other locations:

> We put together language that was out of the norm for us. They acted like they won a million bucks. They called a caucus right away. We had a smooth flow after that point.

Critical to reaching agreement was a shift that occurred within the management team. It was the production manager (rather than the industrial relations manager) who took the lead. One union official characterized the role of local staff and line management in the bargaining as follows:

> In the local negotiations it was clear that local company IR guys were not running the show. The production manager had more clout than the local IR people. In the past there would be labor relations people and no one else in the room. Production people put positions across. This is still ongoing.

This tighter integration of line management into collective bargaining suggested some new requirements were being addressed for managing internal differences in the context of integrative negotiations.

Continued Complexities in the Management
of Internal Differences

The split between line and staff management that emerged in collective bargaining continued during the administration of the new contract language, with line management taking an activist role in the administration of the hit-to-hit committee. As one line manager commented:

> Certain groups are excluded from hit-to-hit. You are better off without their [industrial relations] involvement. It eliminates face-to-face discussions because for some groups it is best not to communicate. All people have labels in the company. IR does not do well in certain situations. A group will assume the personality of the individuals. When it gets down to the nitty-gritty, the key is partnership. The relationship has been building. The union has trust in [production management].
>
> We make sure that all the parties play by the initial rules created by the union and company in negotiations. We rule on particular areas. I guess it has taken over the traditional union-management role. During the meetings there are a lot of discus-

sions and negotiation. It's not really negotiations, it's mostly discussions. IR has no authority for hit-to-hit. What do you really need a labor relations department for in this setting?

The local union president echoed the manager's comments:

> When I'm in the plant, sometimes I go through the right channels and sometimes I go directly to managers. I know my job is to go through IR managers and not to the floor, but I have an advantage having worked with most of the people before.

In a conversation with the production manager, these relations were confirmed:

> I communicate with the union all of the time. I go with Herb (the local union president) to seminars and the union presidents in all three plants go to high-level quality and hit-to-hit meetings. It is difficult to get the okay for them to go. Vice-presidents and presidents don't understand why you would want to bring the union. I get them involved in everything I do...I don't ignore IR, but I look to do the job myself.

The forging of stronger links between line management and union leadership implicitly established a new norm regarding interactions, namely, solutions were driven more by functional needs than by formal protocols. Thus, when a bargaining issue related to production operations, line management pushed to take the lead in addressing the issue.

In practice, the die transition teams were a dramatic success. Instead of the traditional linear sequence of trades handling the removal, installation, and setting of dies, a cross-skilled team of about a dozen individuals descended on a production line, and an almost choreographed process followed. The bottom line result was a reduction in downtime by over 50 percent.

The broad implications of expanded interactions between line management and the union were severalfold. On the one hand, the organization was able to perform more effectively, since decision making increasingly involved key stakeholders. On the other hand, bargaining was multichanneled, which meant that there were increased opportunities for destabilization via "end runs." As well, certain roles had the potential for becoming rigid and isolated in problematic ways. For example, the industrial relations function had come to be defined more narrowly around bargaining over wage and benefit issues and the processing of formal grievances and discipline—all of which were issues that tended to be distributive. Thus, not only was management speaking with more than one voice, but the industrial relations function became constrained in its ability to generate joint gains with the union.

The new linkages also raised complex political pressures within the union. Like the splits within management, internal union tensions emerged around the role of staff appointees in programs such as EI and SPC and members serving on die transition teams. The threat posed by the EI, SPC, and die transition team programs lay in their creating channels of communications between management and labor that were separate from the grievance procedure and outside the formal management hierarchy. The very success of these initiatives depended on the new channels successfully tackling meaningful issues, yet the potential for success made them threatening to others in the union.

Shifting Patterns of Interaction at the Level of the Corporation and the International Union

While issues stemming from manufacturing operations were being more directly integrated into plant-level negotiations, a broader set of economic issues were being integrated into the national negotiations between the Budd Company and the UAW. The process began early in 1987, when Budd was pressured by customers who knew that the collective bargaining agreement was scheduled to expire. As one executive noted: "The customers became antsy and wanted a buildup of inventory." This buildup would have set in motion the traditional cycle whereby inventory is expanded before bargaining, making it possible for the company to contemplate taking a strike or ensuring layoffs if an agreement was reached on schedule. Either way, there would be substantial costs for both sides.

In order to avoid the inventory dilemma, Budd approached the union regarding early negotiations—indicating that an early agreement that avoided an inventory buildup might be sweetened with some of the resulting cost savings. This inducement to depart from arm's-length bargaining helped provide the union with an incentive and internal legitimacy for beginning discussions early. The union leadership was

also persuaded that the competitive pressures were real. As a local
UAW president commented:

> In March, 1987, the company notified us of a desire to negotiate
> early in order to be able to bid better on new work with better cost
> estimation. . . . We were told that this would help get the company
> into a more competitive position. The window would be open now
> on bids. We were persuaded that this was a legitimate situation.

As another local union official commented:

> In fact, part of what drove us to the table early was the fear of
> what would happen if Philadelphia lost 40 percent of their work—
> that's a lot of work. We have the same problem in Detroit. It's all
> vehicle-specific work. If that's pulled with a new model, we are in
> trouble. We don't want Budd to lose customers. Time forces you
> to do different things.

However, in reflecting on the experience, union leaders also expressed
some caution. As one senior UAW official commented:

> We had ongoing discussion to make Budd more ... I don't want to
> use the word "competitive," but there were competitive issues, and
> as a result, we were willing to look into the contract.

While the request was legitimate, framing the effort solely in competitive terms was uncomfortable for some union leaders.

Management Takes the Initiative

The bargaining process that followed was directly contrary to the
established practice where the union made most of the opening
demands in bargaining. Here, the company advanced a set of concrete
proposals designed to improve the company's competitive posture. The
shift was difficult for union leaders. One regional official in the UAW
described the 1987-1988 UAW-Budd national negotiations as follows:

> In the fall we started with local negotiations, which we couldn't
> resolve, then went to national negotiations. This was not tradi-
> tional negotiations. The whole process was different. I was
> shocked by their demands. . . . They came out demanding and I
> don't like bargaining this way. It was "this or else," with the
> demise of a couple of plants as a possibility held over our heads.
> We got to the point of no return. I told them to bag their ass.

In local negotiations, there was also a reversal of traditional patterns. As a personnel official in one of the Budd plants recalled:

> The local agreement was very different from what I'd seen before. We had eighteen items on the table and the union had only one.

The decision by management to come to the bargaining table early, with its own demands, clearly represented a pivotal event. Management's approach created a real dilemma for the union leadership. If the union engaged in negotiating the issues that management had initiated, it would be acknowledging the legitimacy of management taking similar initiatives in the future—i.e., establishing a new norm. If the union refused to work on the new issues, then the existing norms would be reinforced, but a deterioration in the relationship would most likely result.

Thus, the challenge was first whether to bargain early and then how to do so. The parties met the first challenge, but had difficulties with the second. As one local union leader commented on these negotiations:

> We need a capacity to communicate in a different way. You don't know if they are reading your signals and we aren't sure what they say. The union is reactionary, and it depends on what the company does.

The formal negotiations began in the fall. Although talks continued for three months, the union broke off bargaining in mid-December 1987. Even with the incentive of sharing the gains derived from not building inventory and the recognition of legitimate competitive pressures, the union was uncomfortable with the discussions—especially with the implied departure from an adversarial bargaining process. In retrospect, it is clear that the parties were attempting to make two potentially contradictory shifts in their pattern of interactions. First was the attempt to shift to a more integrated mode of interaction around what were acknowledged to be competitive pressures. Second, management's very efforts to enlarge the bargaining agenda carried distributive overtones. These complexities and dilemmas accounted for the union's withdrawal from early negotiations.

Information Sharing and New Norms of Interaction

Following the holidays, the company began a campaign to educate the union leadership and the workforce on the economic pressures it was facing. The information sharing was designed not just to shape union leader attitudes, but, based on the experiences of the early 1980s, the company started to educate the union membership directly. One senior executive described the process as follows:

> The communication process is the key element. One of our jobs is to meet the expectations of not only the UAW but also, for lack of a better word, the lowest member of the organization. We must communicate to individual workers, not just to Solidarity House. Our workers can't expect to get what Ford (workers) get and we have to communicate this.

As one union leader commented, the communications after the collapse of the first round of early negotiations represented a significant break from traditional practice:

> I was a bit surprised by the early negotiations, but more surprised by the company presentations. Roth and Harper [corporate and division executives] met with the hourly workers and let them know what was going on with the company. They were being honest and that was different.

A labor relations official in the Detroit plant also discussed these meetings:

> Roth met with groups of about 100 employees in Detroit and Philly. He talked to them face-to-face about the potential loss of business for the Lincoln and Econoline models. Something happened here, I saw a reaction and many scared people.

Another labor relations official noted that it was not just the information sharing, per se, but the fact that it was presented in a noncoercive way:

> Jim Roth's talks helped considerably. They (the workers) were getting the company message and it wasn't filtered. There was a better feeling of trust in this negotiation because we gave them the facts. It would not have worked if we had just held out the hammer.

In all, the communications process included the following elements: (1) initial management meetings with the union bargaining committee; (2) plant meetings where the division president spoke to all employees; (3) a shift in the content of the plant newsletter toward more business-oriented stories (and away from bowling scores); (4) Budd Bulletins issued at corporate level with further economic information; (5) UAW vice-president, Odessa Komer, spoke to management, helping to increase understanding regarding the UAW's interests; (6) state-of-the-plant meetings, and (7) additional meetings with high-level Budd labor relations staff and UAW-Budd department officers. One UAW International official concluded that:

> These were the most updated long-run forecasts that the company has ever given us. Everybody's eyes were wide open going in. It's not like they said "trust me." When the top guy in stamping comes in and says "I'm not going to bullshit you," we knew what he was going to say. It was a sellable approach.

The emphasis on education signaled a different tone from management, and brought the union back to the bargaining table. As one union leader on the national negotiations team commented:

> After Christmas, we started on national negotiations again. They were not as demanding. . . . Some of the locals, like Philly, moved to consider work practices.

In fact, the simultaneous local discussions (which were discussed in more detail earlier) also set these negotiations apart. One local UAW president stated:

> These were much different than in 1984. . . . This time there was no clear distinction between the national and local. It was a bundle of issues and one set of negotiations.

Elements of a New Contract

The parties settled in early 1988, over six months prior to the scheduled contract expiration. A key element of the agreement, beyond the early settlement, was the four-year term. As one union official explained:

> We went with a four-year agreement rather than three years because Budd has the ability to say we have a long-term contract.

Their ability to go in the market and bid for work is improved. A lot of their work was turning over. Work was especially being pulled out of Philly.

In fact, subsequent to the settlement, Budd was able to procure a long-term contract for business with Ford. Still, extending the length of the agreement raised a concern regarding bargaining issues that might arise during the term of the agreement. In response, the parties put in place a formal structure for quarterly meetings of the principals from both bargaining teams—a significant departure from the approach then extant among the major auto manufactures.

In other respects the parties also departed from the pattern of the OEMs. In fact, given that the settlement was early, only Ford had reached an agreement at that point, so the terms of all OEM settlements were not available for comparison (which would usually be the case). In the agreement, the union won wage increases but the increments for the second, third, and fourth years of the agreement were to be paid as lump sums (that would *not* be added to base wages). Also, while a holiday was added in the third year, there was a diversion of cost-of-living adjustment benefits and below-pattern settlements were reached on certain retiree benefits (reflecting the cost implications for a company with more retirees than active workers). These economic features of the settlement were designed to provide value to the membership while also enhancing the company's ability to bid on new business. The process also tightened the link between local and international negotiations. As one participant observed:

> For the first time, all local agreements were settled on the same day as the master agreement. Locals were present at the national table. We shortened the process.

One insight into the workers' perception of the 1987 Budd/UAW collective bargaining agreement can be seen in the ratification vote, which was 82 percent (even though the wage settlement was less than half that at Ford). The union was careful to not characterize the agreement as concessionary. As one union official commented:

> We sat down and structured an agreement. There were increases in wages and pensions, but it was subpattern. It was not reduced cost—it would be a mistake to call it that. But it did give Budd a better ability to project cost.

This individual also outlined the approach taken by the union leadership to the membership:

> External pressures force all parties to rise above the past and above internal politics. We told our people straight, we won't tell you that you can't get it, but look at the long-range liability. You better start looking at the year 2000 if you want work in old facilities.

A senior Budd executive commented on the same situation:

> There was no backwash after ratification. Both sides are happy. It's an economic settlement that you have to make politically acceptable. The union and Budd must cooperate to create realistic expectation levels in order for the company to survive.

The ratification was, in many ways, a ratification not just of substantive terms, but also of the new direction in relations. Traditionally, a large "yes" vote is seen as a victory for the union and a bare majority as a victory for management. In this case, both sides sought a large majority in favor of the agreement.

Thus, in the course of one round of national negotiations, the parties departed from their normal practice in terms of: the timing of bargaining, the length of the agreement, the substance of the settlement, the relationship between local and national negotiations, the approach toward ratification, and the structure of subsequent relations.

Movement Toward More Continuous Bargaining

The agreement between Budd and the UAW to hold quarterly meetings of the bargaining committees throughout the four-year contract was not part of the initial proposals from either side. Rather, the parties were caught in a distributive debate over wages that was resolved with a package proposal that established a new committee around quality issues. As Budd's vice-president for industrial relations recalled:

> The last thing on the table was another $.10 for the plants. The spontaneous solution to this was that we decided to give a lump-sum bonus of $150 if a supercommittee addressed quality improvement. It will meet quarterly and has potential for long-range communication for the life of the agreement.

These quarterly meetings of the labor-management committee were held on a regular basis. At the meetings, the parties used the forum not just for quality issues, but also for discussion of potentially contentious outsourcing issues and job security concerns. The broader scope of the quarterly meetings was reflected in the following description by a senior UAW official:

> At quarterly meetings we want to take a high-level look at problems—cost problems like insurance. We want to look at the long-range viability of the operation. Too often, neither side knows what to do with a problem. They haven't communicated the problem. You want to avoid the mentality that says, "Cross this line and I'll kick your ass." You want to avoid what might be a major stumbling block in upcoming negotiations.

Clearly, the function of the quarterly meetings was not just to foster discussion of issues of common concern—it was also a forum to surface potentially contentious issues that would only fester if left for the next formal contract negotiations. Further, so that the discussions at the quarterly meetings can be meaningful, both the company and union have assigned staff to work (independently and jointly) on issues that would be on the agenda for future meetings. Given the scope of issues addressed and the continuing nature of preparations to address these issues, the meetings represented a significant move toward more continuous collective bargaining.

The idea of continuous collective bargaining has been discussed by collective bargaining professionals for several decades, however the concept remains controversial. Both labor and management have been generally reluctant to see a signed agreement reopened during the life of the contract. In the case of Budd and the UAW, the parties were careful not to place the renegotiation of the economic package on the agenda for the quarterly meetings.

Still, the viability of this new forum underwent a severe test when a highly distributive issue entered the agenda. Specifically, when Budd opened a new facility in Shelbyville, Kentucky, the union status of the workforce in this facility came up for discussion at a quarterly meeting. Budd indicated that it was unwilling to grant to the union automatic recognition (with the same terms as other UAW contracts at Budd) since typical wages and benefits were so much lower in this area. The union was unwilling to accept any substandard agreement. Subsequently, a union recognition election was held in which local company officials campaigned strongly for a workforce vote against union representation. When a majority of the workforce did indeed vote "no," the leadership from the international union took personal offense at the perceived inconsistency between espoused values and behavior on the part of management. While hard feelings about the election persisted at the national level, the parties did not abandon the quarterly meetings. Joint discussions even tackled new subjects, such as health care cost containment.

Analysis

The Budd case features both substantive and relationship outcomes. The outcomes can be summarized in tabular form.

Significant Outcomes—The Budd Company

Substantice outcomes	Management-employee relationships	Management-union relationships	Other outcomes
Early economic concessions Work-rule flexibility Pilot work redesign initiatives	Some movement toward commitment under EI Sustained movement toward commitment within die transition teams	Movement toward more continuous bargaining and use of joint subcommittees Continuing tensions over union status in a new facility	Modest improvements in economic performance Massive layoffs in the late 1970s and early 1980s

Unlike many of the other large, independent auto suppliers, Budd has not systematically sold older unionized facilities and purchased or built newer nonunion facilities (i.e., the company has not engaged in wholesale escape from the union). Early on, it relied on a mix of forcing and escape as primary change strategies. While these options were operative in the early 1980s, the middle 1980s saw increasing reliance on a set of narrowly defined fostering initiatives around employee involvement, safety, and statistical process control. Consequently, the most important shifts in negotiations occurred at the plant level around issues of employee commitment and compliance, as well as instituting local union-management cooperation.

Both parties came to see the narrowly focused fostering efforts as inadequate to fully address their core interests, and consequently the locus of negotiations broadened. In both local and national negotiations, culminating in agreements in 1988, the parties joined a set of core issues around compensation, benefits, employment security, and flexibility. As a result, labor-management negotiations now occur on a more continuous basis, via multiple channels, raising a host of internal issues for both labor and management.

In the case of the Detroit plant before relations turned the corner there were rejected contracts and substantial cutbacks in employment. Even the employee involvement program did not serve as a sufficient catalyst for fundamental change. No one event or driving force can be identified as responsible for the shift in approach that emerged in the late 1980s and carried forward into the 1990s. The timing of the change can be associated with the shift in leadership for many agenda items from industrial relations to line management and by the breakthrough work of the hit-to-hit committee. It took a decade of mounting economic pressures and a trial-and-error approach to change before the conditions were right for a "sea change" in labor-management relations.

Similarly, at the national level it appeared that matters had to get worse before they could get better. While the company's initiative to open negotiations early failed at first, it set the stage for an extensive communication program and an eventual agreement that brought the parties together on a continuing basis to deal with a range of common concerns such as health care and pensions.

Could Budd and the UAW have reached an accommodation earlier in the decade? Possibly. Several factors might have made a difference. First, if the customers had exerted pressure earlier, change might have happened sooner. Second, if union leadership, both locally and nationally, had taken a stand with the membership calling for changes, then the revised contracts might have become a reality sooner. But this is not certain. The Budd story features a reappraisal process that slowly grows in intensity and it is not clear that the preparation phase would have been shortened by any of the above tactics.

Lessons Learned

To observe that it takes a decade of halting attempts before significant progress can be made does not alone make for a very noteworthy conclusion. Are there some aspects of the Budd story that stand out and that might have relevance in other situations? Several possibilities can be identified:

- Management's campaign to educate the membership helped union leadership in resolving internal differences.

- The addition of financial managers at the table enhanced the perception within management of the importance of the terms of the new agreement.

- The joint research conducted within the various subcommittees created a common information base and facilitated an attitudinal shift that important issues needed to be approached as problems to be solved.

- The active involvement of line management was instrumental in labor's willingness to go ahead with an open-ended experiment on new procedures for die transition.

- Continued competitive pressures provoked episodes of hard distributive bargaining within an ongoing fostering initiative.

Thus, the Budd case offers many tactical insights into the dynamics of strategic negotiations. Unresolved, however, are larger questions regarding alternative paths available to the parties. In many ways, the broad strategies of forcing and fostering were driven as much by market pressures and specific customer pressure for substantive gains as they were by the reinforcing evidence of relationship improvement.

CONSTRUCTING NEW SOCIAL CONTRACTS
The Case of Packard Electric and the IUE, Local 717

The Packard Electric division of General Motors produces the vast majority of wiring harnesses and related components used by GM. The home manufacturing facility is located in Warren, Ohio, where about half of the division's 25,000 employees work. All production workers in Warren are represented by the International Union of Electrical, Radio and Machine Workers (IUE), Local 717.

For many years, Packard Electric and the IUE had engaged in traditional arm's length labor relations, which had deteriorated steadily. Morale was low, absenteeism was high, and economic performance was declining. During the summer of 1977 alone, for example, there were three work stoppages. That same year, 97.9 grievances were filed for every 100 hourly employees. This statistic increased slightly in the next year, and then declined steadily thereafter, reflecting a shift in labor-management relations that began in the fall of 1977.

Indeed, as a result of a series of joint activities initiated in 1977, Packard Electric and the IUE moved to the forefront of U.S. employers and unions seeking a new social contract via a fostering strategy. The company and the union were among the early pioneers in the application of QWL principles in unionized locations in the United States. Like most QWL efforts, the initial focus was on shop-floor employee involvement, later expanding to include notable instances of work redesign, the joint design of new manufacturing facilities, and a dramatic *quid pro quo* linking a multitier wage system with unprecedented job security.

Significant Features

There are many significant dimensions to the Packard Electric case, including the following:

- The initial combination of forcing and fostering hinged on the credibility of management in arguing that cost competition was threatening the business. Ultimately, it took a loss of jobs before this message could be heard and affirmed.

- The education of the rank and file regarding the economic situation was critical to the union's handling of internal differences.

- The provision of employment security was an important *quid pro quo* to the creation of a multitier wage system.

• The union made strategic choices expressed in its willingness to let certain work go offshore in exchange for job security for the remaining, high-value-added work.

• The independence of the IUE from the UAW pattern created a considerable degree of freedom for the union leadership.

Among our cases, the Packard Electric case covers the longest time frame within which negotiations served as the vehicle for transforming the industrial relations system. Although it began with a fostering initiative, this quickly became a combined strategy as a result of the competitive pressures in the auto supply industry. Ultimately, a substantive accord addressing core economic concerns for both labor and management provided the turning point for a predominantly fostering strategy. Even within the fostering context, however, key distributive episodes created ongoing negotiating challenges. Ultimately, this transformation of a labor-management relationship turned on a combination of pivotal, high-profile negotiations, combined with a host of day-to-day negotiated exchanges.

A New Labor-Management Relationship—Initiation to Institutionalization

Packard Electric and the IUE first negotiated language on improving QWL in 1973, modeled on the pioneering letter of intent agreement signed by General Motors with the UAW in the same year. The initial efforts at Packard Electric emphasized easily identified areas of common concern, such as a toys-for-tots program, a joint safety communications program (featuring company and union logos), a joint United Way drive, voter registration, and credit counselling.

Broadening the Focus of the Cooperative Efforts

In 1978, the company established a management task force to increase productivity in the Warren operations. In response, the union leadership called for direct union involvement, which led to the formation of the Jobs Committee in May 1978—a pivotal event. The purpose of the committee was to "develop an ongoing union-management approach that will maintain job security and identify opportunities for hiring in the Warren operations." There were three ground rules: (1) Discussions regarding quality of worklife projects must be open and off-the-record; (2) No employee would lose employment as a direct result of a project; and (3) Bargaining must be reserved for the bargainers. As one of its first activities, the Jobs Committee jointly designed and administered a QWL survey in September, 1978—the first joint survey undertaken in a GM facility.

In February 1979, the Jobs Committee reached an agreement on a plan to hire 100 new employees—the first new hiring in the Warren plants of Packard since 1973. These employees, the first hires under the auspices of the Jobs Committee, demonstrated that jobs could be competitively placed at branch plants in Warren, Ohio rather than in company facilities in Mississippi or Juarez, Mexico. Under this agreement, the branch plants reduced job classifications, implemented job rotation, and introduced an emphasis on teamwork. At the union's urging, the facilities were located in the outlying communities to be more accessible to the residences of many employees.

Top union and management leaders spent many hours crafting the "operating philosophy" statement for the new Warren branch operations:

> We believe every business has a responsibility to its customers, its employees, and the community in which it exists, and shall strive to satisfy the needs and security of each.
>
> We share in the belief that a successful business provides and maintains an environment for change and is built on a foundation of trust, where every person is treated with respect and offered an opportunity to participate. We are totally committed to the patience, dedication, and cooperation necessary to build this foundation.
>
> We also believe that this can be accomplished through a functioning partnership built on the wisdom, the knowledge, and the understanding of the employees, the union, and management.

With this statement, the parties put into words their emerging social contract.

Following the establishment of the branch operations, the Jobs Committee addressed ways to retain the plastic molding business and a series of other related issues. Altogether, by June of 1981 the Jobs Committee had played a role in the addition of 850,000 square feet of floor space, $100,000,000 of new investment, and 379 new jobs. In the 1980 model year alone, Packard Electric distributed $454,000 in awards to Warren employees for suggestions that saved a total of $2.36 million.

A close look at the process by which these gains were achieved suggests that, in addition to extensive joint problem solving, several important distributive moves occurred. First, it took a union confrontation to establish the joint Jobs Committee as an alternative to a management-only effort. Then, at a number of critical junctures (such as the deployment of the Warren branch facilities), the union pressed for joint analysis and successfully halted management from implementing announced plans to locate work elsewhere. For its part, management pressed hard in the committees for flexibility and other changes bearing on cost competitiveness. Thus, interest-based confrontations by both sides played a key role in arriving at the "cooperative" gains.

Continued Competitive Pressures

Despite productivity gains achieved via the union-management efforts, it became clear to management in late 1981 that the Warren operations could not remain competitive in the face of declining auto sales and the cost advantage of doing business abroad—particularly in Mexico.[5] In the late 1970s, wages and benefits in Mexico were around $2.50 per hour, compared with over $19.00 an hour in Ohio, and this gap grew wider when the peso was devalued in the early 1980s.

In December of 1981, the company's executive committee and the union's bargaining committee met for a two-day, off-site session. This was a pivotal event in which management presented to the union a long-range analysis showing that, under current trends, only 64 percent of the business would remain cost-competitive within five years (leaving 3,800 jobs at risk). The result of the session was a jointly developed five-year business plan entitled the "Plan to Compete." It featured the twin goals of keeping jobs in the Warren area while being cost-competitive in all lines of work by 1986. Under the plan, the more labor-intensive final assembly work would be moved to low-wage-rate locations, while lead wire preparation would be brought back from Mexico to

Warren (with investments in new technology). In addition, early retirement options would be developed with an attrition goal of 1,650 direct labor jobs.

As the parties prepared for the 1982 collective bargaining negotiations, Richard Huber, then director of personnel and public relations, made the suggestion that the parties move the relationship to a new level. He suggested a problem-solving process be used in collective bargaining, wherein both sides would brainstorm options rather than resorting to the traditional exchange of demands. While some bargainers on both sides were skeptical, they agreed to try the new approach. Scott Copeland, manager of employee development, designed a training program for both sides and facilitated the new process.

In April 1982, negotiations over the national GM-IUE agreement concluded prior to the deadline with a number of cost-reducing changes, including cutting paid absence allowance (PAA) days from 14 to 5 and freezing the cost-of-living adjustment (COLA) until December 1983—paralleling changes in the national GM-UAW contract. Locally, for the Warren operations, the parties discussed a final assembly option (FAO), which would involve deep wage reductions (as large as $6.00 per hour) for new employees hired on any final assembly work that remained in Warren (in branch facilities). The FAO proposal was resisted by the union, and (on management's insistence) it was presented to the membership for a vote, where it was rejected by nearly a 3 to 1 majority. The rejection created dismay, not just within management but also within the local community. The Mahoning Valley was experiencing some of the highest unemployment in the nation at this time, and the Packard employees were criticized as "snobs" for rejecting an opportunity for expanded employment.

Consistent with the earlier "Plan to Compete," Packard continued to shift labor-intensive work from Mexico. However, it did not expand the number of jobs in Warren. In fact, by the end of 1982, about 2,400 employees were on permanent layoff and about as many were on temporary layoff. While all union leaders were critical of the layoffs, one zone committeeman, Nick Nichols, tackled the issue with a near religious fervor. He charged that the company was violating promises made back in 1977 that no one would lose their jobs as a result of work being shifted from the Warren operations or as a result of the use of new technology. It was based on such promises that he had become a leading advocate for QWL programs (abandoning what he termed the traditional "macho knight in shining armor role").

Nichols took the position that no work could be moved until all laid-off Warren employees were brought back to work. The company responded that there had not been any formal job loss—laid-off employees were still receiving supplementary benefits and maintained rehire rights with GM. Other union leaders backed away from Nichols' strong stance, reportedly because they judged it to be unfeasible, which created a split in the union.

In the fall of 1983, when local union elections occurred, the layoffs, the company's approach to QWL, and Nichols' insistence on the job security guarantees became the main issues. The outcome illustrated how pivotal intraorganizational developments could be: with the exception of Nick Nichols, all union officers and bargaining committee members were voted out of office. Many of the successful candidates ran on anti-QWL platforms. Nichols, was elected as chair of the bargaining committee.

A Crossroad in the Relationship

With 1984 negotiations on the horizon, management paid close attention as an internal debate unfolded among the newly elected union leaders. Many argued that the union should withdraw from all cooperative activities—feeling that there was not sufficient trust to sustain a social contract based on cooperation. Nichols, as chair of the bargaining committee, took a different stance. He indicated that he was still supportive of the idea of cooperation and that he recognized the company's concern with being competitive, but that the union was also concerned about job security. He further stated that, without attention to the union's concerns, "we were both headed for the ditch" (that is, a hard strike). In explaining the mixture of support for cooperation and the use of a strike threat, Nichols stated:

> There will be conflicts and you have to take them on the merits. It's like a marriage—two don't become one, you are still individuals—it's just that you are now both part of a family. It's a matter of learning how to deal with the conflict. You can't be caught half-stepping, but nor can you just roll over and play dead.

Following the union election, the personnel director invited Nichols to a private dinner to discuss the situation. A series of informal meetings followed, involving about a dozen top union and management leaders. They called themselves the Resource Group since they were exploring ways to address two core sets of interests—a union interest in job security and a management interest in flexibility and competitiveness.

While the actual 1984 negotiations were carried out in a traditional form (complete with opening positions and offers and counteroffers), a new spirit emerged from the Resource Group discussions and represented a dramatic departure from the concurrent 1984 negotiations occurring between the UAW and GM. Ultimately, the union agreed to a lower starting wage for new employees (at 55 percent of the base wage as well as 55 percent of COLA), which would increase over ten years to parity with the rest of the workforce. As a *quid pro quo*, the contract included a special section entitled the "Lifetime Job and Income Security Agreement for the Warren Operations," which featured the exact language that Nichols felt had been accepted back in 1977:

A. No employee will lose his/her job due to a shift of work from Warren operations to other locations or because of technological change.

B. The parties will manage the Warren operations workforce so that a layoff of protected employees for other than temporary reasons will not occur.

C. Opportunities to maximize employment for employees will be provided by training employees and reassigning employees and/or work with the Warren operations and pursuing new business so that income security will be provided.

The contract also included the phrase, "This agreement will remain in full force and effect forever." As such, the contract became one of the present era's earliest "living agreements."

Clearly, the 1984 negotiations represented a pivotal event. If the core issues of job security and compensation costs had not been addressed, the entire social contract would have been undermined. Once addressed, however, the parties in effect had fundamentally departed from the industry pattern (in which there was relatively little wage flexibility, with the compensating option to lay off workers).

The parties did not come to this unique combination of social and substantive contracts merely through an incremental set of cooperative adjustments, building on the QWL base. Each major advance in the scope of the social contract was preceded by a pivotal event where unilateral actions or past understandings were challenged. Expanded problem solving then followed. Critical to the success was the ability of the parties to engage in problem solving. Equally critical, however, was their willingness to utilize distributive tactics when necessary.

Emerging Challenges Around Temporary Workers

By the late 1980s, the union at Packard Electric proudly pointed to the fact that it's contract with multitier wages, the no-layoff pledge, and the joint approach to strategic planning had succeeded in bringing all workers back from layoff and on the job. This was in contrast with other GM divisions that were struggling with large numbers of employees either on layoff or in holding status under the JOBS bank provisions of the UAW contract. Still, the parties faced many challenges—as illustrated by their experience with temporary workers.

Among the *quid pro quos* for the no-layoff pledge was an arrangement that allowed management substantial flexibility in the use of short-term temporary workers. This was designed as a buffer to allow management to handle temporary increases in volume without hiring workers who would then make it hard to maintain the no-layoff pledge. The first group of temporary workers was brought in during February of 1985, and their departure surfaced tensions in the workforce with an intensity that surprised both union and management leadership. Essentially, many of the workers with the job security guarantees did not think it was fair to make these temporary workers leave.

Three years passed before management again attempted to utilize the flexibility available to it under the contract. By bringing in a group of temporary workers it would be possible to keep a partially utilized facility open—which was important to all parties. This time more comprehensive attempts were made to clarify expectations with the temporaries and with the regular workforce. Still, however, upon their departure there were the same difficulties. In reflecting on management's original request for this flexibility, one union leader commented, "there are certain things that you just shouldn't ask a friend to do, and this is one of them."

In the end, the union was far more divided internally on the issue of temporary workers than it expected. At the same time, management was less able to use the contractual flexibility that it negotiated. Thus, the many successes experienced by the IUE and Packard Electric management did not prevent the continued emergence of complicated and divisive issues as well.

Analysis

Subsequent to the signing of the 1984 contract, substantial reinvestment occurred in the Warren operations (totalling over $300 million). There also was extensive joint problem solving on the shop floor (via employee participation groups) and through higher-level union-management dialogue. Employees hired at the lower starting wage progressed toward parity and, as of the early 1990s, there were no longer any employees on layoff. It is interesting to note that the parties were aided by the increased use of electronics in automobiles, which assured an ever-rising volume of orders.

The following chart summarizes the main results of the Packard story.

Significant Outcomes—Packard Electric

Substantive outcomes	Management-employee relationships	Management-union relationships	Other outcomes
Multitier wage system	Movement toward commitment with temporary setback (after layoffs) and then sustained movement subsequently	Movement toward cooperation	Joint design of new work facilities
No-layoff guarantee		Early turnover of union leaders on cooperation issue	New tensions around the utilization of contract language on temporary workers
Work-rule flexibility			
Management ability to utilize a buffer of temporary workers		Sustained movement toward cooperation subsequently	
		Negotiations around business strategy	

In many ways, the Packard Electric case is unique. Massive capital investment was possible, and early workplace innovations (around QWL) were available—both as a result of the company being a division of General Motors. At the same time, it enjoyed more autonomy in labor relations than other parts of the corporation, since the IUE was not as bound by the UAW pattern and since it was in a line of business experiencing steady growth. Yet these circumstances alone did not account for the parties' success. Equally important were their responses to a series of critical events.

Early on, the parties tackled some easy-to-resolve subjects and created some win-win arrangements that expanded employment. However, the competitive situation continued to deteriorate, and the company attempted to bargain major changes in its labor costs. This effort failed, and the company commenced a partial escape strategy by moving work out of Ohio and laying off the affected workers. Here we observe a common sequence: limited fostering, the environment worsening, the company asking for big changes, and then the union and the workers saying "No, thank you." We observed this sequence in AP where at a similar juncture the parties plunged into a bitter confrontation.

In the case of Packard Electric, the response to the crisis was different. Early responses included the Jobs Committee and the opening of the branch plant operations. Ultimately, even these innovations were not able to satisfy the need that management felt to force reductions in labor costs. After a round of layoffs, the rank and file replaced the union leadership. While the new group came into office on a platform of stopping the outflow of jobs, the union leadership took a pragmatic approach and quickly joined the issue, leading to the innovative 1984 agreement.

In subsequent years, negotiations containing both forcing and fostering elements occurred not only in collective bargaining, but on a host of contract administration matters. Ultimately, the Packard Electric case provides insight into the complex array of negotiations associated with a set of change initiatives occurring over more than a decade and a half.

COMBINING FORCING AND FOSTERING
Mastering Complexity

The final three cases in this book have featured the most complex combinations of change strategies. They also embody some of the farthest-reaching change initiatives. To some extent, the complexity in these cases arises from external circumstances beyond the immediate control of union and management leaders at the plant level. Yet, the complexity also reflects conscious choices and artfully executed bargaining tactics that enabled the parties to combine what would otherwise be opposed strategies.

The complexity also mirrors the extended time periods under examination. Packard Electric, for example, was one of the early QWL initiators in North America—so a complex series of negotiations over a decade and a half around change issues is not surprising. However, in earlier chapters we examined cases that involved a single strategy over equally extended time periods. In particular, the Anderson Pattern case covers nearly a decade of sustained fostering. By contrast, we also have examined instances of fostering, such as Bidwell, where the initiative proved short-lived. So what accounts for these complex combined strategies?

In two of the cases—Budd and Packard Electric—a combined strategy in the early 1980s was responsive to the coincidence of external market pressures and customer insistence on evidence of labor-management cooperation. At Pensacola the use of a combined strategy was more internally driven. The forcing reflected pressure from the corporate parent and the intraorganizational realities within the union (it was politically better to be forced to agree to economic concessions), while at the same time Pensacola management was committed to reinforcing and sustaining its fostering initiatives. Thus, combined strategies may reflect the intentional juxtaposition of forcing and fostering, *or* the two change strategies may occur simultaneously as a result of different (but concurrent) driving forces. Either way, we are learning important lessons about this new phenomenon.

Significant Lessons

Many of the lessons identified in the analysis of sequential strategies in chapter 4 also apply to these more complex combinations of strategies. For example, key leaders from labor and management played important roles in these three cases, just as they did in the three cases featuring sequential strategies. Similarly, information sharing, persistence, and a learning orientation were also critical here. In addition to these lessons, further insights emerge from the analysis of the cases with combined strategies.

In all three cases, episodes of hard distributive bargaining occurred after sustained periods of fostering. Indeed, in the Pensacola case, the intensity and scope of the distributive bargaining around the Sunday premium led us to classify this phase as a combined forcing/fostering strategy. While a number of issues were also highly contentious at Packard Electric, they did not involve the sort of sustained pressure in the face of worker and union resistance that would constitute a forcing strategy. When management at Budd failed in their first bid to reopen the contract, they might have been expected to use force on the issue, but instead chose an educational path followed by a mixture of integrative and distributive bargaining.

Thus, forcing is not, in itself, inconsistent with concurrent or prior fostering, but many forcing tactics are. When distributive bargaining (or forcing) follows sustained fostering, the history of fostering leads to a tempering of hard bargaining tactics and to a focus on long-term objectives. For example, it would be inappropriate to undermine the credibility of the other side during forcing that is concurrent with fostering—even though this is a common tactic in a pure forcing strategy. Instead, the forcing must literally be justified to the party being forced. The party must be persuaded of the need, for example, for economic concessions and be disabused of any suspicion that management is just exploiting a power advantage.

A related lesson is that sometimes forcing is even desirable in a fostering context as a requirement for resolving intraorganizational differences. As we have already indicated, this was vividly illustrated by the Pensacola case, where the union could not politically agree to loss of the Sunday premium even if it granted the point that management had no alternative but to press the issue. In this situation it was politically better for the union to have been forced to accept the change.

The same is true when the union forces. For example, when the union at Packard Electric forced over the issue of job security, management was not pleased, but it did understand why the subject was of par- amount importance to the union. Local managers would have had a difficult time persuading corporate officials to endorse a lifetime job security guarantee, but they could make the case for the arrangement in the face of union insistence and especially when there were attractive *quids pro quo* in the offing (such as wage flexibility and use of tempo- rary workers).

Not only is forcing tempered by concurrent or prior fostering, but the fostering may actually be enhanced by the forcing. So long as the forcing is seen as legitimate and even as unavoidable, it signals core interests—i.e., issues on which they are willing to "go to the mat." If these issues are not surfaced explicitly, they will resurface ultimately in the form of hidden agendas. For example, when Budd initially began to use possible job loss as a threat in order to get wage concessions in the early 1980s, it did not coordinate this forcing with the concurrent EI efforts. As a result, it encountered disbelief on the part of the work- force, and the entire slate of union leaders was voted out of office. Later when Budd wanted to open the contract early, it learned the les- son: hard bargaining requires substantial and deep education on the underlying business circumstances giving rise to these issues. In this context a controversial issue such as health care costs could become the focus of a joint problem-solving task force. Thus, the forcing pro- vided an outlet and structure for engaging issues that might otherwise have undercut the fostering and even provided new direction and energy to the fostering initiatives.

A combination of forcing and fostering is thus likely where one or both parties is looking for major substantive changes and where one or both also value worker commitment and union-management coopera- tion. Where there is a well-established history of fostering, the hard issues are more likely to be raised in the context of distributive *epi- sodes* rather than a sustained forcing campaign. The one exception, of course, is where the hard issues are highly objectionable to the other party and only likely to be achieved via forcing. Either way, the analy- sis in this chapter suggests that it is accurate but incomplete to classify the three cases in this chapter as exemplary examples of labor-management cooperation. Ultimately, they should be viewed just as much as far-reaching examples of conflict resolution. It is in the throes of negotiations associated with transformation and change that we see an inevitable and critical interweaving of cooperation and conflict.

NOTES

1. Valuable research assistance was provided by Kathleen Rudd Scharf in the preparation of this case.

2. The majority of the material for the case study of the Budd Company, the UAW, and the CAW have been derived from field interviews. Also helpful were Herzenberg (1988) and Murphy (1988). Valuable research assistance was provided by Pat McHugh in the preparation of this case.

3. A vivid example of the consensus process arose when one of the authors of this volume initiated research in the facility in 1985. At that time, all but one of the twenty-member steering committee agreed to be part of the project. The individual (a shop steward) who had reservations about the research withheld approval for almost two hours, during which time he surfaced a number of important concerns about the parties being part of a research project. It was only after these issues were addressed that consensus was achieved and the research was able to begin.

4. The material presented in this case draws on "Packard Electric A and B," written by Elisabeth Ament Lipton under the supervision of D. Quinn Mills, Harvard Business School Case 9-484-109 (1984), other secondary materials, and our own interviews with current and former local union and management leaders. Valuable research assistance was provided by Pat McHugh in the preparation of this case.

5. The location of plants in the South no longer served as a lower-cost alternative since the IUE and the UAW had successfully challenged GM's "Southern strategy," namely, building new, nonunion facilities in the South. Attempts to organize these facilities, which featured autonomous work groups and other sociotechnical innovations, had not been successful and the UAW insisted that GM agree to a neutrality pledge in the late 1970s. This set the stage for the successful organization of most of these facilities—including several Packard Electric facilities in the deep South—and the achievement of wage parity.

6
Understanding the Context
and
Choices for Strategic Negotiations

What is the terrain on which strategic negotiations unfold? How do these contextual factors shape the negotiations? In addressing these questions, this chapter will focus on eight major topics: (1) the need for change, (2) the role of vision, (3) the role of leadership, (4) the role of third parties, (5) the requirements of internal alignment, (6) the opportunity for negotiations to engender a long-term learning process, (7) assessment of management's strategic alternatives, and (8) assessment of strategic alternatives for unions. We will also examine the strategic option of escape and its implications for strategies of forcing or fostering.

A Compelling Need for Change

Among labor and management practitioners, there is great debate over the relative importance of a crisis in motivating change. The social theorist Kurt Lewin (1951) highlighted the importance of "unfreezing" existing social relations as the first step in a change process. In today's parlance, this is referred to as a "significant emotional event." Simply put, the question arises as to whether a significant emotional event is a necessary prerequisite to fundamental change.

As we look across our cases, nearly all of them feature significant emotional events. For example, there were massive layoffs and movement of work out of factories in the Budd, Packard Electric, Adrian Fabricators, and AP Parts cases. Two of the firms we studied—Conrail and Adrian Fabricators—went into bankruptcy. Long and emotionally charged strikes occurred in nearly all of our forcing cases. Further, in some cases where there was no major significant emotional event—

such as Bidwell—the change efforts were easily stalled by disagreements around the pace and sequence of training activities. Thus, a superficial review of the cases would confirm the importance of significant emotional events as forces driving fundamental change.

A closer look at the cases, however, reveals that these significant emotional events were neither a necessary nor sufficient factor driving fundamental change. For example, in one case, Anderson Pattern, the company and the union engaged in a series of interactions that led to a gradually increasing acceptance of the need for fundamental change. There were some important learning events, such as a trip to a trade show by the majority of employees to take a closer look at proposed new technologies, but no single defining moment that accounted for what came to be a shared sense of a compelling need for change. In fact, perhaps the single most important driving force was the success that resulted from early pilot initiatives and the fact that each side generally lived up to promises made at each step of the way.

There are many reasons why the Anderson Pattern case may not be typical, however. It is a small, unionized firm with a highly skilled workforce and an owner who began his career as a skilled tradesman. It is also in an industry and a community where many other unionized firms have either gone out of business or the unions have been decertified. Still, the case suggests that a single defining emotional event is not a necessary requirement for the generation of a perceived need for deep change.

A closer look at the other cases supports this conclusion. While bankruptcy was certainly a key driving force for change in the case of Conrail, the same event did not mark a fundamental shift in the case of Adrian Fabricators. It was only after a strike and a change in management leadership that a shared perception of the need for change emerged at Adrian Fabricators.

Even where a crisis does trigger change initiatives, it is not always clear that such a crisis will continue to serve as a sustained driver for change. For example, prior to the acrimonious strike at AP Parts, there had been earlier rounds of concession bargaining. The concessions by labor were made in response to management concerns over competitive pressures. The concessions were not accompanied, however, by fundamental changes in the production process that led workers and union leaders to believe that management was itself changing in response to competitive pressures. Even though management was probably accurate in stating that competitive pressures were still present when they sought nearly $6.00 an hour in additional concessions in 1984, that argument in itself was not sufficient to sustain continued substantive change. In fact, with the lack of change in management itself and its continued requests for concessions, the deepening of the competitive crisis became a barrier rather than a motivator—workers felt that they had already given enough and resented management's demand for more.

In all the cases where fundamental change occurred, a perception developed on the part of one or both of the parties that there was a compelling need for change. In many cases, this perception was shaped by significant emotional events such as layoffs, lost work, and strikes. Even though our cases do, therefore, confirm that significant emotional events can be a compelling force for change, they also suggest that these emotional events will not necessarily produce change if they are not interpreted as providing compelling reinforcement of the need to change. Further, we see that change is possible even in the absence of such traumatic events—where a compelling need is appreciated through education or reinforced through restructuring of resources and rewards.

A Clear Vision of the Direction for Change

Given the turbulence confronting most labor and management leaders, as well as most employees (both exempt and nonexempt), a clear vision of the direction and goals of change represents one of the most elusive commodities in the present era. Since we only selected cases involving the potential for fundamental change, all of our cases feature at least one (or a few) individuals who possessed some degree of vision about the desired direction for change. A close look at the cases reveals, however, that in nearly all of the cases there were gaps in the initial visions that required learning and adjustment during the change process—which sometimes did and sometimes did not take place.

What constitutes a clear vision of the direction of change? In part, our cases suggest that a clear vision of the direction of change first requires a clear vision of the terrain over which the change process must travel. This terrain is composed of multiple stakeholder groups with a mixture of common and competing interests. Those change initiatives that more completely take into account the underlying interests look, in retrospect, to have been guided by a clearer vision. For example, the forcing at DeRidder centered on work rules, not wages. Indeed, the combining of classification resulted in substantial wage increases for nearly all employees. In this case management held a clear vision of its own interests (which centered on decreased grievance activity and increased equipment utilization rather than cutting labor costs) and an understanding of the interests of the workforce (which included both safety and continued economic stability and growth). As a result, just two years after the strike the plant was experiencing record levels of efficiency and profitability.

The union's interests in this instance (the DeRidder case) were compromised, however, by the forcing that occurred around work rules. In the short run, management had a relatively clear vision of how it wanted to align its interests with those of its employees. In pursuing this vision the union was marginalized, but not eliminated. Thus, at the time we concluded our case study, corporate management had decided to adjust the vision to address the union's interests for realizing institutional legitimacy and efficacy. It decided to work on union relations in all of its mills because in many of them it could only achieve employee commitment if it also worked toward institutional cooperation with the union.

A clearly stated position does not necessarily constitute a *viable* vision. If that position directly threatens the interests of one or more stakeholder, and if the change strategy does not fully anticipate the degree to which these interests are threatened, then we would argue that such a vision is not well formulated. For example, AP Parts took very clear positions in the negotiations, but it apparently underestimated the degree to which the union would interpret these positions as a threat to the local and international union (and even to other unions). It also apparently underestimated the degree to which its stance would polarize the community and surface concerns among its major customers. With a clearer understanding of this range of interests, it is possible that AP Parts might have modified its strategy in important ways.

In cases where multiple unions were involved, the task of constructing an effective vision for change proved enormously complex. In fact, disagreements among multiple unions at CSX and at Bidwell ultimately undermined management efforts to implement their respective change agendas. Instead, a more realistic vision might have called for joint interactions with some unions and scparate dialogue with the remaining unions, thereby getting underway with the change process rather than ending up in a stalemate.

Leadership Throughout the Change Process

In negotiations over fundamental change, leaders play pivotal roles. It is leaders who generally present (or fail to present) a clear vision of the direction of the change process, and it is leaders who generally have the primary role in articulating and gaining recognition for a compelling need for change. Yet, it is also leaders who are most at risk of becoming lightening rods for discontent during the change process.

The task of leadership is fundamentally different for union and management leaders. Union leaders are elected officials leading political organizations. Management leaders are appointed officials leading bureaucratic organizations. The dilemmas that each faces under forcing and fostering regimes reflect the different contexts in which each leads—a distinction that is central to understanding internal dynamics within labor and management.

Union leaders in the fostering context face a core dilemma that involves simultaneously maintaining their independence and working jointly with management. The dilemma is particularly acute given the political nature of unions—elected union leaders who work jointly with management are always vulnerable to the charge that they have moved too close to management and ignored union priorities. This is exactly what happened in union elections at Budd and Packard Electric where the entire slates of union officials were thrown out of office on the basis of the perception that the leaders had become too soft as a result of cooperative programs. Thus, in order to work effectively with union leaders, managers must educate themselves about the nature of these political dynamics.

Leaders on the management side in a fostering context face a somewhat different dilemma that involves ceding joint decision-making authority on matters for which they are still hierarchically accountable. The dilemma is particularly acute in that other management officials in the organization may not necessarily accept union input as legitimate, especially when it produces different results than would have occurred in the absence of such input. Yet the test of added value from union input must hinge on whether the process has raised new options and generated different decisions.

By the same token, union leaders must educate themselves about the nature of administrative processes (such as cost-benefit analysis and strategic planning) in order to work effectively with managers. While union input may differ from what managers unilaterally would implement, providing the input in a language familiar to managers avoids being rejected out of hand.

In the forcing case, both union and management leaders must struggle with the potential negative consequences of an escalating confrontation. The stakes are very different for the two sides, however. For management leaders, the core dilemma involves engaging in a strong enough confrontation to produce desired change without creating a legacy of resentment that precludes future movement toward employee commitment. This involves making critical and often subtle decisions about what is necessary change as compared to what is desirable change—with the former being much easier to defend as a legitimate change agenda.

For union leaders, the continued existence of the plant and the union local is very much at stake in such confrontations. Thus, union leaders in the early stages of a forcing campaign will be studying every move made by management in an effort to determine what are legitimate (albeit controversial) requests for concessions versus opening moves in a campaign to destroy the union. Once a union leader has reached a conclusion on this threshold issue, a fork in the road is at hand. Managers contemplating fundamental change need to be mindful of the pivotal importance of the responses that come from union leaders at this early stage of the change process.

Managers demonstrate leadership initially in the way they frame the debate. At least in the present era, it is primarily management who has the choice of defining the agenda as broad or narrow, and it is management who is or is not making a concerted effort to ensure that the agenda is seen as legitimate. Yet, union leaders have opportunities to frame the debate as well. Following the initial management request for change, union leaders can convert the issue into a larger contest over survival or keep it at the level of a problem-solving dialogue. Thus, a key function of leadership from both sides is in framing the debate relative to the interests at play. The way each side engages in this task will have important implications for the process of change.

The Role of Third Parties

While the leadership requirement for effective change is for the most part the responsibility of key management and labor officials, in certain crucial circumstances an important role can be exercised by third parties. In fact, the potential for third parties to play a constructive role was underrealized in several of our cases. While the two-party language of labor-management relations still captures most important interactions, a potential exists for additional parties, at least to some degree, to convert the bilateral interaction into a multilateral situation. Included among the additional parties are customers/suppliers, communities/governments, and third-party consultant/facilitators.

Current shifts in manufacturing operations toward just-in-time (JIT) delivery arrangements dramatically alter the links between a plant and its customers and suppliers. In a highly competitive industry such as auto supply, the impact of customers and suppliers on labor-management relations can be significant—for example, an increased emphasis on quality and flexibility. Customers shape the bargaining agenda by insisting on evidence of labor-management cooperation (prompting fostering initiatives), while at the same time insisting on price cuts (often prompting forcing strategies). Some of the customer-driven changes have the potential to radically rebalance the power equation. For example, just-in-time delivery arrangements imposed by customers can make management more vulnerable to various forms of collective action by unions.

Communities play particularly key roles in our forcing cases. As the forcing disputes worsened at International Paper and AP Parts, for example, community leaders became increasingly alarmed over the potential loss of jobs. Local officials often ended up taking sides and sometimes even supported partisan legislation, such as constraints being placed on replacement workers in Jay, Maine. Thus, in many cases, communities represent key stakeholders who become central to a full understanding of negotiations over fundamental change.

There is also some evidence regarding community and government roles in our fostering cases, such as the use of community training resources and multiemployer coordination at Anderson Pattern. Another example was Conrail, where the federal government played a central role in defining the framework for the entire fostering initiative. In most fostering cases, however, communities and governments were more notable by their absence.

It is clear that third-party consultants and facilitators are central to many of the fostering cases. These outside parties provide technical assistance via skills training, meeting facilitation, and organizational redesign, and by conferring legitimacy on what are highly ambiguous processes. Most labor and management practitioners in the United States look upon third-party assistance with great skepticism, however. Calling in a mediator during collective bargaining negotiation is generally considered a last resort prior to impasse.[1] As a result, most practitioners have not experienced the potential value that outside consultants and facilitators can provide in an ongoing relationship, nor are they skilled in managing the potential complexities in working with these outside third parties.

The Importance of Internal Alignment

Certainly, a need for change, an adequate vision, and effective leadership are key ingredients of a successful change effort. They clearly represent *necessary* conditions or prerequisites, but are they *sufficient*? In exceptional cases, the answer may be yes, but typically the answer would be that additional competencies must be present to deal with internal alignment.

It is often said in labor negotiations that it takes three agreements to get one—one agreement within labor, one within management, and one between the parties (Dunlop 1958). This internal or intraorganizational bargaining is often more difficult than the negotiations between the parties. In examining negotiations that occur at the cooperative and conflictual extremes, we find that internal dynamics are, if anything, further magnified.

In our cases, one of the greatest barriers to management effectiveness was fear, resistance, and contrasting priorities within its own ranks. The intraorganizational implications of fostering derive from the inherent challenge to the hierarchical structure. Most fostering initiatives create new channels for communications and problem solving, while pushing certain forms of decision making to lower levels of the organization. Such initiatives are not only threatening to middle managers and supervisors, but they can prompt a realignment of power relations across management functions. Moving too quickly with the change process, as occurred in the Bidwell case, for example, does not allow sufficient time for factions within management to sort out these implications. In the Budd case, the link between the union and line management—at the expense of the labor relations function—is another example of a shifting communications patterns creating tensions within management.

Similarly, as union leaders grappled with fundamental changes, one of the greatest barriers they faced was fear, resistance, and contrasting priorities within the ranks of union members. Union leaders were at risk both from being accused by members of working too closely with management *and* of not working closely enough to preserve jobs. For example, at the Budd Detroit plant, local union leadership became convinced of the competitive pressures facing their plants, but when they proposed a concessionary agreement to the membership, it was rejected by over 90 percent of the voting members, and the president of the local subsequently resigned.

The internal dynamics become even more complex where multiple unions are involved, such as in the railroad industry. In these cases, negotiations occurred within each union, across the different unions, and then between the unions and employer. Thus, the political nature of unions as organizations ensures that internal dynamics will be critical factors in the success or failure of change initiatives.

The internal dynamics were equally important in both forcing and fostering contexts, although they were played out in different ways.

A traditional distributive tactic involves building internal solidarity while looking to divide the other side (Walton and McKersie 1983). All of our forcing cases featured sustained efforts to maintain internal solidarity during the forcing campaigns. The cases differed sharply, however, in the degree to which efforts had the intent to divide-and-conquer the other side. In the cases that involved more restrained forms of forcing, the internal splits within the other side were not exploited to the fullest extent possible.

The approach to potential splits in the solidarity of the other party is very different in the unrestrained forcing contests. The forcing at AP Parts and at International Paper not only featured sustained efforts by labor and management to build internal solidarity, but both sides exploited every possible division they could find in the other side. Management sought to divide the unions in both cases with the threatened and then actual use of replacement workers. The unions sought to divide management with corporate campaigns, direct appeals to customers, and community pressure on local managers.

A clear lesson emerges from these cases. Neither managers nor union leaders will begrudge the necessity for the other side to build its own internal consensus. However, given the volatile context of industrial relations—where concerns about a company's financial stability and a union's institutional security are always just below the surface—each side is likely to react defensively and vigorously when its internal divisions are targeted by the other side. What starts as a traditional distributive bargaining tactic becomes a clear trigger point that distinguishes restrained forcing from unrestrained, escalating battles.

Internal alignment was also pivotal in the fostering cases, but in a very different way. The robust fostering cases all featured extensive educational campaigns to build shared understanding at all levels of labor and management about the importance of change. For example, at Anderson Pattern the education included fact-filled monthly newsletters, a pivotal trip to a trade show to learn more about proposed new technology, presentations at annual dinners and other events, and extensive training programs developed in conjunction with a local community college.

At the same time, initiatives that produced little change were characterized by inadequate efforts to address divisions within union and management ranks. For example, many managers and supervisors at Bidwell felt little ownership for the QWL initiative (they viewed it as a corporate agenda item), and there were splits among the unions regarding the wisdom of working jointly with management on this subject. These splits fed off each other—with each side's ambivalence providing justification for the other side to withdraw.

Interestingly, internal solidarity (achieved increasingly through education) represents the primary resolution to the classic dilemma that fostering poses for union leaders. So long as union members are divided in their views about change initiatives, a union leader who supports them will always be vulnerable to the charge that the union has grown too close with management. On the other hand, where there is a broad awareness and understanding of the competitive pressures and business requirements, the debate will focus on specific programs and decisions rather than on the merits of participating or not participating in the fostering initiatives.

Equally interesting are the implications of solidarity within the management ranks. As the DeRidder case demonstrates, if supervisors and middle managers have bought into the change agenda, they will behave in ways that reinforce the initiative. Alternatively, where there is internal disagreement within management ranks, workers and union leaders will observe this inconsistency—they will accuse management of "not walking the talk"—and lose faith in the initiative as a real vehicle for improving operations. It is therefore in the interest of each side for the other to have high levels of internal education and solidarity regarding the fostering initiatives.

Thus, internal dynamics within either side represent pivotal elements in the change process. When ineffectively managed, the internal dynamics can drive a forcing campaign out of control, and they can bring a fostering initiative to a halt. When skillfully managed, the forcing around fundamental changes can at least be acknowledged as legitimate and the fostering can generate high levels of enthusiasm and commitment.

Change as a Process of Continuous Learning, Marked by Pivotal Events

A key perspective for framing the context for change is the awareness that fundamental change usually does not occur in one programmatic burst but is more often a series of steps marked by pivotal events.

Viewed from a short-time perspective, the results of a particular change effort may not be impressive. However, from a longer-term point of view (one embracing a sequence of time periods and strategies), the results may be much more noteworthy. This perspective applies especially well to Pensacola and Budd. It was essential for the key leaders to take the long view, remaining steadfastly interested in both substantive and social contracts and not allowing the results of a particular time frame or phase to diminish the commitment to move forward with change programs.

The effectiveness of the step-by-step approach to change is illustrated by the progress that occurred at Adrian Fabricators. Ultimately, it was necessary for the union to see management as a partial ally and for the membership/owners to see management as concerned about their interests. Fortunately, there was time for these changes to take place. (If there had been a sharp downturn in the business, however, the past history may have been a blinder to the union and the membership for discovering this potential.)

The long-term view recognizes the potential for the parties to learn as they go. The journey is marked by what we have called "pivotal events." These are events or moments in which the very direction and tone of the relationship are, in effect, "on the table." They are truly pivotal in that there is more than one possible outcome and at least one of the alternatives represents a new direction for the relationship.

Returning for a moment to the example of Budd, when the parties shifted the bargaining process away from specifying the details around improving die changes, they had just completed a pivotal dialogue. By deciding instead to agree on the principle and leave the specifics to be worked out in a joint committee, the overall climate of labor-management cooperation was reinforced, line management took on a more central role in labor relations (at the expense of the personnel function), and a key aspect of business operations became a subject of shared oversight. It is clear that if they had not been able to find a way to jointly address the die transition issue, then the relationship could have shifted in an opposite direction.

We have discussed the strategies of forcing and fostering (as well as escape) and sequential and concurrent combinations of strategies as general characterizations of different paths down which negotiations might travel. In fact, progress along these paths is rarely smooth, continuous, or one-directional. If the events are consistently resolved in a certain way, then tactical moves take on a larger significance—they aggregate to become a strategy. For example, when the president of Anderson Pattern first approached the union about adding profit sharing to the compensation package, this tactical move did not yet constitute a fostering strategy. However, when the parties subsequently crafted an *ad hoc* agreement matching flexible work rules with the purchase of specified new technology (after extensive information sharing), a fostering strategy was beginning to fall into place. Later, this strategy took on clear form when a general agreement was reached allowing broad flexibility in exchange for certain job security and training guarantees. Subsequently, conflicts around the administration of training (which were also pivotal), were addressed in what had emerged as an explicitly fostering context.

We conclude that change is not a one-time event. Negotiated change then becomes a series of interactions in which the linkages across time are as important as the issues on the table at a given moment.

Assessment of Management's Strategic Alternatives

By this point, the advantages of a strategy that combines both restrained forcing and robust fostering should be apparent—especially when they are interwoven, as was illustrated in the three cases presented in the last chapter. To the extent that it is possible for the parties to wisely manage these sequences of pivotal events along lines illustrated in the Budd, Packard Electric, and Champion-Pensacola cases, then a superior strategic alternative is in place. However, in many instances such a combination is not feasible and other pathways must be chosen.

In this section, we examine three strategic options for parties initiating change—which in the present era is usually management. The three alternatives include: escape, forcing followed by fostering, and fostering followed by forcing. Note, however, that the lessons (especially on the later two alternatives) would apply equally to unions developing strategies to guide change initiatives.

Perspectives on the Strategy of Escape

In the next chapter we will summarize best practice regarding the primary change strategies of forcing and fostering, taken singly and in various combinations. At this point, there is one other threshold subject that merits consideration, namely, the strategy of escape.

While we certainly do not advocate a strategy of escape, it is important to consider the use of this strategy—if only as a tactic to enhance the effectiveness of forcing and fostering strategies. Several cases explicitly involved the escape strategy. Also, escape lurked in the background as an option in most of the other cases.

Escape strategies sometimes permit labor-management innovations that might not otherwise have emerged. However, they can also incur large social costs for individuals and communities.

The escape option was not equally available in the three industries we studied. Clearly, it was pursued much more readily in auto supply than in paper and railroads, where the heavy investment in infrastructure limited geographic movement. However, other forms of escape were available, as illustrated by IP's replacement of strikers with non-union workers in its Jay mill and Guilford's transfer of assets from one legal/financial entity to another.

Increasingly, key decision makers (e.g., managers, boards of directors and partners in joint ventures) are making proposed investments for modernization or new capacity contingent upon specified changes in work rules. Such *quid pro quos* were central to the innovative labor-management relations that emerged both at Anderson Pattern and Packard Electric. The linkage of a commitment to continue operations (and to reinvest capital) with changes in work rules and labor-management relations makes considerable sense. Thus, we conclude that when business conditions require consideration of options such as possibly closing a facility or contracting work out, labor and management should attempt to negotiate changes that would make such operations viable on a continuing basis.

Unfortunately, some companies often give up on securing changes within the existing relationship and resort prematurely to the escape strategy. In essence, this means that these firms have opted out of nego-tiations—forcing, fostering, or some combination of the two—and have decided to abandon the relationship (either by turning over the facilities to some other owner or by starting from scratch at a new loca-tion).

The auto supply industry is replete with examples where companies approached the union, received a negative answer, and then decided to move the facilities; or where companies did not even approach the union (assuming that the answer would be no) and made strategic deci-sions unilaterally to disinvest, closing down or selling existing facili-ties and starting anew at greenfield sites.

The effective use of escape as a strategy to set the stage for either a forcing or fostering strategy can be very demanding. First, the threat to escape cannot be a bluff. In other words, the alternative to continuing the relationship with the union *must* be available and creditable. Sec-ond, in underscoring the escape alternative, management must present the realities in a way that does not permanently sour the existing rela-tionship. The union will always feel threatened by any reference to escape. However, if it is done in a way that creates understanding (for example, by persuading labor that "You would do the same thing if you were in our shoes"), then it may be possible to prevent serious deterio-ration of the existing relationship. Third, the skillful use of escape requires considerable precision in proceeding step by step but ulti-mately avoiding a "point of no return" unless all else has failed. In the case of DeRidder, for example, management trained replacements but waited for the striking workers to reassess the situation before making any decision to bring the replacements on board. As a result, manage-ment was able to maximize the pressure on the union without turning its tactic into a strategy.

Forcing Followed by Fostering

A strong case can be made for launching a change effort by first confronting whatever painful bargaining work needs to be done and later proceeding to improve the relationship. Forcing, if successful, can produce more immediate and certain benefits, but the net advantage of starting a change effort with forcing depends upon how the forcing campaign affects negotiations in subsequent phases.

First, this sequence has particular attitudinal effects. Forcing will put pressure on existing accommodation between labor and management to the extent that management agendas and pressure tactics are viewed as more aggressive than past practice, a point underscored by several of our cases, especially Jay, Guilford, and AP Parts. However, this shock to established attitudes, if not too severe, can set the stage for a favorable response to subsequent fostering activities. This helps explain the improvement in attitudes after the strike at DeRidder.

Second, the sequence has potential educational benefits. Forcing substantive changes can dramatize competitive pressures, thereby setting the stage for a fostering approach to an array of other agenda items. This attention to economic imperatives may help labor resolve some of its internal differences. Moreover, the social contract may be redefined to incorporate competitiveness as a legitimate criteria for change.

Third, successful forcing can serve to confirm realities about the power equation. In many situations today management has gained a power advantage vis-a-vis trade unions, and organized labor finds itself in a position where its ability to serve its members depends more on its integrative bargaining skills than its distributive bargaining prowess. Thus, an initial forcing strategy can help labor adapt constructively to the new economic power realities sooner rather than later. Finally, of course, for management intent upon renegotiating the social contract, the ideal culmination of a forcing episode is contract language that either enables participation and cooperation (as happened in 1988 Pensacola contract negotiations), or provides for continued negotiation of flexible work practices (as illustrated by the pay-for-knowledge scheme won by DeRidder in its 1983 strike).

Thus, the initial forcing can be far-reaching when it occurs within a context characterized by an adversarial social contract (so there is not a violation of expectations). While subsequent fostering may be hampered by the adversarial aspects of forcing, the fostering that follows can be aided by the learning and the contrast that derive from the forcing experience.

Fostering Followed by Forcing.

Another option is for management to first attempt to elicit the voluntary cooperation of employees and their representatives and then subsequently reach agreement on substantive matters, e.g., reducing payroll costs and increasing contractual flexibility via distributive bargaining. It is possible that the fostering approach will be adequate, but the forcing alternative remains available if the need for substantive change becomes urgent. Management can explain the subsequent shift in strategy (if required) by stating, in effect, "We tried the persuasion approach first, and since that has not worked we have to insist on the changes."

What are the potential advantages of this sequence? Assuming they are implemented effectively, fostering activities, such as joint committees and communication programs, can provide labor with a better understanding of competitive realities, including the need to control payroll costs. Fostering activities can also produce attitudes that make it easier for the parties to develop integrative solutions to substantive issues. For example, the experience of jointly designing and administering QWL and EI programs can produce positive spill over effects, enhancing the parties' abilities to work together within the larger context of collective bargaining.

This attitudinal effect on subsequent contract negotiations is not assured, however. If the apparent motivation driving the subsequent forcing strategy is either not compelling to labor or is seen as inconsistent with the new social contract (and instead viewed, for example, as motivated strictly by superior bargaining power), then fostering followed by forcing can produce resentment and disillusionment. While not featured in our cases, this outcome characterizes the experiences of many companies in the paper industry during the mid-to late 1980s because management's case for work-rule changes and economic concessions had not been made credible to labor. Similarly, the use of mass layoffs at Packard Electric went far beyond the union's perception of the appropriate response to competitive pressures; as a result, the entire cooperative relationship was called into question.

After initial fostering has moved the relationship toward a new social contract, subsequent forcing may be required, but it can only be effective within the framework of a new social contract. Thus, while beginning with fostering does not preclude subsequent forcing, it does change its character. The changed nature of the process that follows intense fostering is illustrated by the handling of the Sunday premium issue at Pensacola. Management knew the issue was controversial and tried to utilize integrative bargaining to be consistent with the overall fostering strategy. For intraorganizational reasons, the union would not engage the issue on an integrative basis. Even though management then felt compelled to force the issue, it did so with restraint and accompanied its approach with explanations of the business rationale and a concurrent improvement in compensation via a 401k benefit plan. Labor did not like the change, but it did not allow the forcing to undermine the overall fostering momentum.

An important practical advantage of forcing within an overall context of fostering is that the drive to reach agreement on substance on a specific timetable allows the union leadership to characterize the proposed changes as a *fait accompli*. Thus fostering is used to communicate relevant information and to create as much understanding as possible, and then forcing is used to press for agreement.

Assessment of Strategic Alternatives for Unions

Today's union leaders find themselves on the receiving end of various corporate- and plant-level change initiatives. The following analysis is targeted for these union leaders, though many of the principles apply to any party confronted by a strategic change initiative.

For union leaders, the first and most basic point is that unions generally do not have any viable alternative to the existing relationship. The prior discussion of the option of escape underscored the possibility that in many circumstances management can shift (or at least threaten to move) to other locations. Such a scenario is only feasible for a handful of unions who are in a position (by virtue of stock ownership or other forms of strategic influence) to drive the sale of a company or the replacement of the management leadership team.

When we review the stance taken by unions in the cases where forcing was dominant, several conclusions are apparent. First, a strategy of mild resistance combined with flexibility appears to have been effective in several instances. For example, at Pensacola and Budd, where the unions accepted concessions, the strategy consisted of opposing the employees' proposals, but doing it in a way that preserved the relationship and enabled the leadership to deal with internal differences by, in effect, saying to the membership, "We did all we could to resist these demands of management. However, our only course of action is to accept some of the changes and to get on with preserving the business and our jobs." Specifically, during the 1985 negotiations at Pensacola, the UPIU attempted to avoid discussion of flexibility issues, and when the company's final proposal went to the membership, the leadership took a stance of "nonrecommendation."

Such a posture could be viewed as a very pragmatic response by unions to economic pressures. In the same vein, unions often advance their own agendas in order to achieve *quids pro quos* for the economic relief sought by management. In many of our cases, we saw the increased attention given to employment security and joint training programs, as well as the incorporation of unions into strategic levels of the business via various arrangements to facilitate consultation.

On the other hand, where unions exhibited strong resistance to a forcing initiative by management, the matter escalated rapidly. The response usually was triggered by a perceived threat to the integrity of the contract and the institutional security of the union. And internal solidarity within the union was usually enhanced as a result of the tough stance by the union, at least during the early phases of the confrontation. But ultimately the unions lost badly, as illustrated by the Jay, AP Parts, and Guilford stories.

Turning to the fostering strategy, most union leaders in our cases preferred to adopt a stance of cautious support for the initiatives. For political reasons (similar to the strategy of mild resistance), the safest approach for union leaders in terms of internal differences was to keep the fostering limited to a narrow agenda such as quality of worklife programs and to proceed on a step-by-step basis rather than embarking upon wide-ranging joint programs. The subject of new technology can serve as such an opportunity for the initiation of fostering; the step-by-step approach that the parties at Anderson took to this subject illustrates one very viable pathway for union leadership—where management is also proceeding on a step-by-step basis.

However fast or slow the management is fostering change, in time the initiative either fails or becomes robust. In the later case, the fostering typically becomes integral to the union's self-identity. Cases raising these issues include CSX and Packard Electric. The biggest challenge for union leadership in this context is to deal with internal differences, since it is likely that at least a few members will question the ability of the union to maintain its independence and to differ with management when the occasion requires such a stance. Thus, robust fostering is a viable strategy only when rank-and-file members are involved in various joint processes. Size then becomes a key correlate of the feasibility of this approach. Anderson, a small employer, possessed the ability to involve rank-and-file members much more easily than CSX, where intense fostering took place at the institutional level between company and union representatives but did not involve local union chairmen, let alone rank-and-file members—with the result that the recommended package was rejected.

Thus, the present era confronts union leaders with unprecedented challenges. Upon encountering a forcing strategy, union leaders must fashion a counterforcing approach that halts management's forcing without triggering an escalating "holy war." Upon encountering a fostering strategy, union leaders must embrace changes that protect and expand jobs—but at a pace and in a way that preserves their ability to serve as an independent check and balance in the system. Ultimately, the question not adequately answered by any of our cases concerns the ability of unions and their members to take the lead in fashioning their own effective change strategies.

Conclusion

This chapter has provided various perspectives on the terrain across which negotiated changes unfold. It is a terrain where small distinctions can make a great deal of difference. For example, progress along the journey is facilitated by a compelling need to change. Yet this compelling need does not have to be driven by a crisis. A clear vision for the direction of change provides guidance, but learning and adjustment along the way are perhaps more essential. The role of leadership is crucial, but the challenges are different within union and management organizations. Internal alignment is essential within both management and labor, but it is incredibly difficult to achieve and maintain. Ultimately, a continuous learning stance is clearly necessary—which is the only certain means for managing the many twists, turns, bumps, and barriers along the pathways of change.

NOTES

1. Personal conversation with Dale Brickner, East Lansing, Michigan, 1993.

7
Learning to be a Strategic Negotiator

What have we learned from a close look at highly cooperative and highly conflictual negotiations? Each of the cases in this volume represents a different path toward fundamental change in employment relations. All of the paths involved twists and turns. Ultimately, some led to dead ends or at least took the parties on nonproductive detours. Others represented highly viable avenues for change. All of the paths offer valuable insights into the process of negotiating over change.

Indeed, some of the cases stand as unique parables about change. The story that unfolded at the DeRidder plant of Boise Cascade, for example, could be a parable for managers desiring both rapid change and high levels of employee commitment. It is also a story that raises some challenging questions for union leaders. By contrast, Anderson Pattern could be a parable about transformed employment relations via a sequence of successively farther-reaching fostering initiatives. In the railroad industry, the Guilford story assumes parable status because the hard forcing stands in contrast to long-standing railroad traditions of incremental change coordinated across multiple unions. The International Paper strike in Jay, Maine and the AP Parts strike in Toledo, Ohio are similarly significant in their respective industries. They have literally become touchstones that executives use as object lessons with their management staffs and the union leaders interpret to their members—often drawing contrasting lessons from the stories.

We hope we have presented these stories in a way that facilitates learning from individual cases. As our discussion at the end of the cases suggest, we feel that each teaches many valuable lessons. Beyond the individual stories, however, there are also common lessons that cut across the cases.

Lessons from the Cases

The first set of lessons from the cases concerns the use of tactics within a given strategy. There are many tactics that can serve a particular strategy, and we highlight the constructive and destructive potential inherent in various choices. Next, we highlight lessons specific to the forcing path, followed by lessons specific to the fostering path and lessons inherent in various combinations of forcing and fostering. Finally, we present a set of guidelines designed to support strategic negotiations.

The Implications of Tactical Choices

The tactics deployed in support of a particular change strategy provide focus to the strategy. For example, tactics common to forcing involve making excessive opening demands, providing little supportive information, and threatening the institutional security of the other side. This set of tactics will typically engender a back-and-forth forcing contest where excessive demands are met with excessive counter proposals and institutional threats are met with counter threats. Similarly, a common set of fostering tactics involves the development of joint mission statements and ground rules that emphasize consensus decision making and formal problem solving. This set of tactics will typically focus attention on the cooperative and problem solving processes wherein mutual concerns are identified and addressed.

Inevitably, tactics are double-edged. At the same time that a set of tactics provides a particular focus and direction to a strategy, the tactics also divert attention from other possibilities. Too often in our cases we find evidence of tactics providing a misleading focus for a given strategy. The tactics are logical steps to take in service of the strategy, and they indeed often yield short-term advantages. In the long term, however, the strategies can be compromised by these tactics in fundamental ways.

In the forcing case, the tactical focus on winning the forcing contest risks winning the battle but losing the war. Some of the very tactics that are most helpful in winning a forcing contest—such as overstated positions, little supportive information, and institutional threats—can set in motion uncontrollable escalating conflict. Further, these tactics can compromise efforts to reestablish regular operations and relations after the forcing contest is over.

In this chapter we will challenge the conventional focus of forcing tactics. Instead of centering on the forcing contest, our research suggests that the most effective forcing tactics are focused on avoiding what we see as the two greatest risks along the forcing path. Attending to these "show stoppers" involves: (1) preventing uncontrollable escalation, and (2) ensuring the reestablishment of regular operations at the conclusion of the forcing contest. Winning the forcing contest is important, but attention to the risks or downside possibilities is even more important—which leads us to recommend a restrained form of forcing.

In the fostering case, the tactical focus on cooperative and problem solving processes may solve some immediate mutual problems, but may not build an enduring set of relationships. Indeed, some of the very tactics that are helpful in supporting cooperative and problem-solving processes—such as consensus decision making and formal problem-solving procedures—may constrain parties in surfacing controversial and potentially divisive issues. Further, the tactics may exacerbate tensions within each party.

In this chapter we will also challenge the conventional focus of fostering tactics. Instead of just focusing on cooperative and problem-solving processes, our research suggests that the most effective fostering anticipates two potential "show stoppers" by: (1) enhancing the capacity of both parties to address controversial and divisive issues, and (2) increasing the ability of each party to manage internal confusion and splits. Cooperative and problem-solving processes are important, but that alone will not generate a robust form of fostering.[1]

The table below summarizes the typical focus of tactics for forcing and fostering strategies. The table also lists what we term the show stoppers. These are the issues that we would argue should be the primary focus when implementing a given strategy.

Typical Focus and "Show Stoppers" that Should be the Focus

Strategy	Typical tactical focus	Focus on potential "show stoppers"
Forcing	The forcing contest	Preventing uncontrolled escalation
		Reestablishing regular relationships
Fostering	Cooperative, problem-solving processes	Anticipating divisive conflicts
		Managing internal differences

Lessons Along the Forcing Path

The first three cases presented in this book all began with forcing strategies by management. In each case—AP Parts, Jay, and Guilford—the forcing was marked by strong union responses, escalation, and strikes. While management prevailed in each case, the costs were substantial. Looking across these cases, there are a number of important lessons that emerge from travel along the forcing path. While other cases did not only involve forcing, nevertheless lessons about forcing can also be derived from the forcing periods contained in these additional cases.

Why would parties force change? Clearly they have concluded that their counterparts are unlikely to be receptive to the change. Yet, even where no alternative seems possible, the decision to force is never made lightly. Parties always explore to some degree what they see as the risks associated with forcing and the enactment of possible countermeasures on their part to minimize risks. For example, parties will often see a strike as a likely risk associated with forcing during collective bargaining, and strike contingency plans will be developed.

As we noted in discussion of the implications of tactical choices, however, parties are too often focused on preparing for and executing the forcing contest itself. They give much less attention to the process of setting the stage and framing the issues prior to forcing. Further, parties typically give even less attention to the process of recovery after forcing. Ignoring these pre- and postforcing time periods leaves parties inadequately prepared for life on the forcing path. Counterforcing and other forms of direct conflict are not the greatest dangers along the forcing path. As we have suggested, the real show stoppers are uncontrollable, escalating conflict, and an inability to not only reestablish but also upgrade ongoing operations following the forcing initiative.

The following lessons are not necessarily aimed at the back-and-forth struggles during a forcing contest. We will not, for example, offer guidance for managers as to how best to deploy replacement workers or for union leaders as to how best to conduct a corporate campaign. Indeed, the successful execution of these provocative tactics is likely to increase the risk of either of our two show stoppers. Our advice will instead point toward a set of restrained tactics in the service of an effective forcing strategy.

Forcing Lesson 1: Don't force without exploring other options.
Given the big risks associated with forcing, the best course of action is
not to force until the fostering options have been fully explored. If
change can be achieved via fostering, it has many advantages relative
to forcing when it comes to the generation of ideas and commitment to
implement new agreements. However, it is not only for these reasons
that we recommend exploring fostering options prior to the implementation of a forcing strategy. Even where a party has concluded that fostering is unlikely to yield results, it is important to precede forcing with
a good-faith exploration of fostering options. We make this recommendation for two reasons. First, it is possible that, upon investigation, fostering will prove more promising than it seems. Second, even if things
go as predicted, the initial attempt at fostering yields important divi-
dends during and after the forcing episodes.

Consider, for example, the comments of the UAW in the AP Parts
case. After the strike, union leaders stated that the company never had
made a genuine effort to work with the union in achieving flexible
work rules, benefit cost containment, or other apparent management
concerns. In this case there was a prior employee involvement effort,
though it was not targeted around the issues that management said
were its priorities going into the negotiations. We will never know if
the union would have been responsive to a well-designed fostering initiative. We will also never know if such an initiative would have been
more likely to achieve what the company gained at the end of the
strike. However, in the absence of a prior fostering, the union was able
to elevate the dispute into a moral contest of right versus wrong—
which constrained the company's success in its forcing strategy.

Forcing Lesson 2: Pick issues carefully—be clear about your aim.
That parties embarked upon forcing should pick their issues carefully
may seem obvious. If a party is forcing, after all, shouldn't it be motivated by particular issues to do so? The lesson, however, is that a forcing party typically contemplates forcing when it perceives itself as
having a power advantage.[2] In this situation, it is often tempting to use
the forcing occasion to accomplish multiple objectives. Or, more simply stated, parties sometimes get greedy.

When a party uses its power advantage to accomplish legitimate but
unpopular objectives, it will engender a measure of resistance and

resentment. But the level of resistance and resentment increases dramatically if the forcing party is seen as taking advantage of the moment and pushing for objectives that are not seen as legitimate. In such a case, the stage is set for an escalating conflict. Consider the contrast between the strike at the Jay, Maine papermill and the strike at the DeRidder, Louisiana papermill. In the case of the Jay strike, management was seen as pushing for economic concessions at a time of record profits. This context was not seen as a legitimate basis for the power tactics utilized. At DeRidder, on the other hand, management only focused on work rules directly tied to data on low productivity levels in the plant. The workers at DeRidder did not like giving up hard-won contractual rights, but they were able to reconcile the loss subsequently when the strike settlement included a generous wage increase and when they came to see the new team-based work system as a viable alternative to the narrow job classifications that they had relinquished.

A key point, then, is for the parties—especially management—to shape their agenda to what is reasonable. While management may feel its own needs for concessions are compelling and self-evident, labor will tend to focus on the way these concessions nullify decades of hard-won gains, threaten workers' standards of living, and undermine the union's strength and self-respect. Anticipating such reactions by the other party enables the negotiator to understand the hostility engendered and to take steps to avoid reciprocating it.

When management's demands are not carefully delimited, the union often misinterprets management's intentions, inferring that the demands for concessions are more than just a straightforward desire to improve productivity and reduce costs. Unions, for their part, often conclude—sometimes too quickly—that management has set out on a purposeful path designed to get rid of the union. While getting rid of the union may well be what many managers would prefer, this reality does not mean that their forcing actions are necessarily a prelude to such a plan.

Thus one guideline for management in this regard is to avoid hiring permanent replacement workers. Permanent replacements are usually seen by unions as moving matters beyond the point of no return, with an all-out battle inevitable. Further, management can help contain the conflict by finding credible ways to demonstrate its acceptance of the union as an institution (e.g., by offers to consult with the union on matters previously handled unilaterally by management).

So what are the criteria that will enable a forcing party to pick issues carefully and limit its objectives? Simply put, a forcing party should be able to construct a persuasive business or institutional rationale for its choice. It may seem ironic that a party about to use its power advantage to force a change should struggle with the construction of a persuasive rationale. Our point is that this is exactly when it is most important to be able to make a strong case for the proposed change—not because it is any more likely to make the other party agree, but because it reduces the odds of the kind of intense resentment that fuels escalation and because it increases the chances of being able to reestablish regular operations after the forcing initiative.

Forcing Lesson 3: Utilize forms of power that do not trigger escalation. When it comes to the forcing contest itself, parties invariably make estimates of their own power capabilities. These estimates begin during planning stages and are continually revised during the contest. For management, these estimates typically take into account the degree of shared commitment and resolve within the ranks of supervisors and managers; current inventory levels and the criticality of the operations in question; the legal levers available to management; the employer's vulnerability to external pressure from customers, suppliers or politicians; and other factors.

Sometimes the estimates of power capabilities are based on recent past experience. More often, however, the estimates are based on unchecked assumptions. It is these assumptions that can be dangerous in a forcing contest. For example, Guilford management embarked on the forcing path with certain assumptions about its rights under the Railway Labor Act and its vulnerability to decisions by arbitrators and courts. Given the way its efforts ultimately were stalled at so many critical junctures, it is quite likely that Guilford management was acting on the basis of overly optimistic assumptions. Also, given the history of labor relations in the railroad industry, it should have been possible—with full investigation—to check out assumptions about the potential actions of third parties that might impede the forcing efforts.

The type of power utilized also needs to be selected quite carefully. For example, too much reliance on attitudinal and intraorganizational tactics that seek to undermine the legitimacy of the other side may serve distributive bargaining well, but such tactics can so heighten the conflict associated with a forcing strategy that both sides end up in a prolonged battle that serves neither side's interests.

Hence our third lesson is for forcing parties to check out assumptions about their own power. Unrealistic assumptions may lead to overly aggressive forcing initiatives, which then set the stage for an escalating conflict and a dynamic where forcing takes on a life of its own, resulting in a legacy of bitterness and resentment.

Forcing Lesson 4: Check assumptions about your counterpart's power capabilities. This is the companion to Lesson 3, and it is as critical to learn about these assumptions as it is for each party to be clear about its own assumptions. For managers estimating labor's self-perception, for example, it is important to estimate labor's perceptions of its own internal solidarity; its capacity to disrupt business operations; its links to the local, regional and national labor movement; and available forms of legal leverage.

Failing to assess the other side's self-perceptions can severely constrain forcing efforts. For example, management at AP Parts did not anticipate that labor would interpret their hard line in negotiations as setting a precedent for concessions in their region. They were surprised, therefore, to find themselves the subject of a nationwide boycott, with food and financial support for strikers flowing in from across the nation. Similarly, they probably did not anticipate that the UAW vice-presidents negotiating with Ford and General Motors (two key customers of AP Parts) would break off national negotiations to join the UAW's picket line at AP Parts in Ohio. This is not to say that it would have been easy for management to predict labor's self-perception, but this is clearly a case were they were far off the mark.

Attention to Lesson 4 has an interactive effect with attention to Lesson 3. The worst-case scenario is one where the forcing party overestimates its own power capabilities and underestimates the self-perceptions of its counterpart(s). In these cases, an escalating conflict is virtually assured. Indeed, all four forcing lessons are interactive. Ignoring the first two lessons—no prior exploration of fostering options and overly aggressive aspirations—not only fuels escalation, but it also seriously hampers postforcing efforts to reestablish regular operations.

Forcing Lesson 5: Communicate regularly regarding the tenor of negotiations. Sometimes it is not possible to avoid the use of power with its potential for escalating tensions. In this situation, the best course of action is to limit the side effects and consequences of distributive bargaining.

When adequate communication takes place, differences over issues still remain but each side understands the reasons for these differences. Indeed, the parties may simply "agree to disagree." This is essentially what happened in the case of Pensacola where the union, strongly opposed to losing premium pay for work on Sunday, granted that it understood the reasons motivating management to insist upon this change. In turn, the company recognized how difficult, in a political sense, it was for the union to do anything other than to oppose the change, and consequently the company attempted to make the pay loss as palatable as possible.

Experienced negotiators (often on a trial-and-error basis) learn how to signal to one another what is important and what is not important in the lineup of respective agenda items. Such competency in communications can go a long way in minimizing some of the most serious side effects of distributive bargaining.

Attending to these lessons generally produces what we have termed restrained forcing. The forcing is restrained in its scope (to issues that are justifiable), is deployed with the appropriate intensity (based on realistic assessments of available power), and is openly acknowledged in the negotiations. The best guideline to bear in mind is the overall aim, which is to achieve forcing objectives without inadvertent escalation and with the capability for reestablishing regular operations after the forcing.

Lessons Along the Fostering Path

In contrast with forcing, the fostering path enjoys a certain moral legitimacy. In our society, it is considered highly appropriate for a party to reach out and work jointly with others in planning and implementing change. This does not, however, assure the success of fostering initiatives.

Ironically, fostering overtures are not typically welcomed with enthusiasm. Rather, they are most often greeted with caution and skepticism—by other parties and even by individuals within the party making the fostering initiative. Top management may announce a desire to foster employee involvement. This will be greeted with suspicion not just by the union, but also by first-line supervisors and middle managers.

The suspicions are rooted in a set of very real risks that lie along the fostering path. Most parties who travel down the fostering path concentrate their energy on cooperative processes. As a result, a great deal of time will be devoted to joint training in running effective meetings, making decisions by consensus, and utilizing problem-solving processes. While these activities are all important, our research suggests that inadequate cooperative processes do not represent the greatest threat to fostering initiatives. Instead, the greatest risks arise from two show stoppers: not anticipating episodes of conflict and forcing while traveling down the fostering path, and not addressing the internal splits that emerge along the way.

The following lessons, therefore, do not center on the details of cooperative processes. We are not offering yet another multistep problem-solving model or method for process improvement. Some lessons—such as our focus on making progress through small steps—are consistent with common understandings about cooperative processes, but we come to these lessons for different reasons. In other cases, such as our focus on conflict in the fostering context, the lessons could be seen as constraining or even undermining cooperative processes. However, all the lessons reflect a key insight guiding this book, which is that fostering initiatives involve negotiated change.

Fostering Lesson 1: Progress is built through small steps. It is conventional wisdom that parties engaged in fostering initially look for small successes before tackling larger, more contentious issues. This recommendation is based on the assumption that leaders need to build trust and learn to work together. We come to the same conclusion, but for different reasons.

The need for small steps may initially be driven by issues of trust and interactive skill. However, even where leaders do have some measure of trust and experience working together, it is still essential to proceed through small steps. This is because fostering does not just involve a restructuring of relations between parties—it also involves restructuring relations within each party.

Each cooperative success has a double-edged quality. It demonstrates the capacity to generate joint gain but it also raises questions about the independence of each party. For example, the die transition teams at Budd represented a cooperative success in the way they fostered cooperation among skilled trades, resulting in dramatic improvements in the time required to change the dies on a stamping line. At the same time, the operation of the teams raised difficult questions for union leaders and managers. Union leaders had to answer questions about whether relaxing job classification increased the risk of managerial abuse. Managers had to answer questions about whether the self-managing teams would be mature enough to wisely utilize their new autonomy.

Often the first small steps occur when the parties establish linkages across respective agendas. Consider several examples. The quest for greater flexibility in the development of the workforce (a management priority) usually can be constructively joined to enhanced employment security (a union priority). Similarly, the desire of the company to increase the union's sensitivity to competitive conditions can be realized by giving the union increased access to key managers and key business decisions.

The first issues addressed along the fostering path are therefore important, not just for their substance but also as test events within each party. Each event is interpreted both for the substantive gains or losses and the underlying significance for political or power relations. Many small steps allow for learning not just across but also within each party.

The substantive quality of each small step is equally important. The successful instances of fostering, especially Pensacola, CSX, and Packard Electric, all were characterized by a process that ensured that substantive agenda items would be considered. Negotiations did not concentrate on just quality of worklife subjects, the participants were not just industrial relations types, and the process was not allowed to drift. The general point is that when subjects important to both sides are discussed, when key management officials participate, when various levels of the union organization have input, and when deadlines are set, then the likelihood of the fostering strategy producing real movement increases substantially.

Fostering Lesson 2: Constituent education and awareness is crucial. Education and awareness are always cited as important in fostering initiatives. However, most of the education is focused on cooperative problem-solving skills and other specifics of the fostering effort. It is presented as a useful support activity. In our research, we find that internal education and awareness need to be seen as much more than a supportive activity. We find that a breakdown in communications with constituents can be a major show stopper.

Internal education is not a one-way communications process, nor is it limited to cooperative problem-solving skills. A typical threshold issue concerns a very basic question: "Why change?" Leaders from labor and management may be acutely aware of the need for new cooperative initiatives, but their constituents need to be exposed to sufficient data and experience for them to come to the same conclusions. As the fostering efforts unfold, continuing education and awareness are equally essential—especially as the consequences of fostering activities are not likely to be unambiguously positive for all concerned.

The collapse of the QWL effort in the Bidwell case can be directly traced to the parties' incomplete attention to constituent understanding. Management never fully brought its middle managers on board in recognizing either the importance of the initiative or the necessity of showing deference to union preferences for the timing of training. Consequently, there was no foundation of support for QWL to sustain it when a change in top corporate leadership occurred.

Similar dynamics can be found within labor, as is illustrated by the experiences at CSX. Here a sustained effort was made to attend to internal education and awareness. The company brought together the many unions representing its employees, and within each union efforts were made to educate middle-level union officials. This comprehensive effort still fell short. Splits across the unions and within one key union prevented a comprehensive fostering effort from moving forward.

Internal political fears and power dynamics could not be overcome and proved debilitating to the fostering strategy.

We conclude that internal education and awareness are critical, and that they are far more than a one-way communications process. They involve a process of intraorganizational negotiations in which the very fate of the fostering initiative hangs in the balance (Walton and McKersie 1993). Consequently, parties pursuing a fostering strategy must anticipate supporting this internal dialogue—within their own organization and within the other parties' organizations.

Fostering Lesson 3: Manage leadership turnover. Continuity of leadership is particularly important in a fostering initiative for three reasons. First, one of the jobs of a leader is to frame the issues. As such, union and management leaders provide the overall framework and logic that drives a fostering strategy—something that is not easily recreated when new leaders arrive. Second, another job of a leader is to provide the necessary resources (tools, information, and skills) for people to follow their lead. Fostering initiatives are particularly vulnerable in the absence of tangible support for suggestions and proposals that emerge from problem-solving efforts. Commitments of support and even ownership of the entire fostering initiative can be disrupted by the turnover of leaders. Third, many understandings reached among top leaders during fostering efforts are not recorded in contracts. Leadership turnover requires the remaining parties to reconstruct these many informal understandings with new leaders when they arrive—with the results often not fully apparent until a pivotal event emerges.

Even though leadership is central to fostering initiatives, our cases and other field experiences suggest that leadership turnover is a common and predictable event. Managers will often leave as a result of new assignments in the organization. Union leaders may turn over voluntarily through appointments to the international union or other positions at the local level. The turnover may also be involuntary as a result of local union elections.

The importance of leadership is well illustrated by many of our cases. The new plant manager at DeRidder was crucial to the realization of positive outcomes, and the president of Anderson Pattern demonstrated leadership in offering profit sharing without seeking anything in return—framing the fostering efforts around mutual interests. The continued tenure of this individual proved essential for the incremental change process that has unfolded for nearly a decade.

At Adrian Manufacturers, by contrast, fostering efforts were constrained by a president who had a nonparticipative, unilateral management style. It was only after this individual left the firm that a fostering strategy unfolded. This case illustrates that leadership turnover is not always negative in its implications.

Since it is rare within the time frame often required for a fostering effort not to encounter leadership turnover, the real challenge lies in managing the dynamics effectively. This means that critical decisions made in the fostering process need to be well documented. Transition procedures need to be developed to debrief departing leaders and to educate new leaders. Ultimately, however, increased ownership and leadership for the fostering process at multiple levels may be the best insurance against the disruption that arises with the inevitable turnover of key leaders.

Fostering Lesson 4: Anticipate forcing episodes. The emergence of divisive conflicts can be a major show stopper for a fostering initiative. Unfortunately, too many "experts" and leaders guiding fostering become preoccupied with joint activities. The focus is entirely on teamwork, cooperation and consensus. As a result, leaders are not adequately prepared to handle the divisive conflicts that inevitably emerge in the context of a fostering initiative.

It is important to distinguish between two types of divisive issues that may emerge in the same context with fostering. First, there are divisive issues that are unrelated to the issues around which fostering is occurring. Second, there are divisive issues that are directly interwoven with the fostering effort. Our recommendations are very different in these two contrasting situations.

The Pensacola case provides a good illustration of a divisive issue unrelated to the fostering initiative. In this case, corporate management mandated that local management bargain for the elimination of Sunday premium pay in local collective bargaining negotiations. The corporation wanted to present a united front across all its plants. Initially, local management attempted to pursue a fostering approach with the union on this issue, but was told by the union that there was no "nice" way for them to agree to such a concession. In the end, management forced the issue and the union said to its members, in effect, "We don't like it, but we don't have a choice." In retrospect, separating the issue from the fostering efforts proved most constructive for both parties. Both management and labor were under less pressure to reconcile the forcing incident with their ongoing fostering activities.

By contrast, the layoffs at Packard Electric set the stage for union forcing that was completely interwoven with the fostering efforts. The union, in effect held the QWL and other joint activities hostage over the layoff issue. In this case, the union argued that a no-layoff pledge had been given by management as a precondition for the union's partnership in the fostering, and this pledge was in the process of being broken. The confrontation had many ramifications involving internal turnover within the union and extensive side-bar meetings between labor and management. Ultimately, however, the parties did reach a landmark agreement providing lifetime job security in exchange for substantial management flexibility and a multitier wage scale. In this case, both parties' interests were best served by linking the divisive issue with the fostering initiative.

How do we make sense of these two contrasting incidents? The answer lies in the substance of the issues. Where the issues are largely unrelated, it will serve all parties to keep them separate. It is unrealistic for management to expect a joint problem-solving dialogue on a distributive issue, and it is inappropriate for the union to hold fostering efforts hostage. On the other hand, where divisive issues involve principles that are central to the fostering initiative it is appropriate and even essential to be explicit in attending to these linkages. In these cases, joint dialogue—even if contentious—must be undertaken. It would even be appropriate for either party, often labor, to hold joint activities hostage in order to compel such dialogue.

Unions must preserve their power to restrain work and their ability to force the resolution of issues when necessary. Concurrently, union leaders can derive influence from their participation in a fostering process, assuming there are positive benefits (especially if workers deliver more value as a result of problem solving and involvement). Or to make the point more concretely, the payoffs from the successful negotiation of commitment and cooperation in Champion Paper's Pensacola mill, Anderson Pattern, Packard Electric, and Conrail included not only increased competitiveness of the enterprise but also enhanced dignity and voice for labor. At the same time that unions draw strength from the process and results of fostering, they must also retain a degree of independence and freedom to challenge management on fundamental issues.

Lessons from Combinations of Forcing and Fostering

Inevitably, forcing and fostering strategies are combined. Sometimes they are concurrent, such as when Packard Electric pursued QWL activities concurrently with massive layoffs in the corporation. At other times the strategies are sequential, such as when Boise Cascade shifted from forcing to fostering in its DeRidder mill. Forcing and fostering are complex on their own, but infinitely more challenging when they are pursued in combination. As we have suggested above, the strategies invariably become intertwined, which presents a challenge for all to share and to solve. The following lessons focus on the combinations of the two strategies.

Combined Lesson 1: Actions speak louder than words—so be sure that consistent actions are taken and sustained. While actions always speak louder than words, this lesson is particularly important in making the transition from forcing to fostering. Even a restrained form of forcing will erode trust and raise larger questions about the other side's long-term commitment to the relationship. As a result, cooperative overtures following forcing will be treated with suspicion. A sustained pattern of actions that demonstrate a genuine concern for common interests will accomplish what words really cannot.

For example, in reestablishing relations after the strike at the DeRidder mill, the new management team concentrated for nearly a year on improving safety practices—including disciplining a supervisor guilty of driving unsafe practices. While safety is an issue of common interest, management helped shift from forcing to fostering by giving priority to safety over other issues, including managerial authority.

Combined Lesson 2: Roles become redefined—so anticipate a process to guide the redefinition. In the shifting from forcing to fostering, the roles of labor and management become redefined. This occurs on a daily basis with small interactions and to a larger degree as well. Union and management representatives commonly find themselves shifting from contentious to common concerns countless times in a given day. Over a longer time period, within the context of a restrained forcing initiative, each party will ultimately engage in some activities designed to support concurrent or future fostering. Similarly, within the context of a robust fostering initiative, each party will inevitably engage in some activities designed to support concurrent or future forcing.

At the Budd Company, such role complexity was evident in the ascendant influence of line management over industrial relations staff. The issue of die transitions involved a combination of forcing and fostering. On the one hand, management needed flexibility from the rigid lines of demarcation among skilled trades. On the other hand, employee commitment to any proposed solution was essential. Because line management was closer to the issues than the industrial relations staff, it was better able to target the forcing to just the level of flexibility it needed, and it was more willing to take the risk in trusting the employees to make the new arrangement work without detailed contractual rules. In the process, however, the roles of these departments within management shifted substantially.

Combined Lesson 3: Effective combinations of forcing and fostering transform the individual strategies—so build constituent expectations for a complex mix of forcing and fostering. Where forcing and fostering are effectively combined, each strategy becomes transformed—or it risks failure. Forcing needs to be restrained or it risks two show stoppers (escalating conflict and the inability to reestablish regular operations). Fostering needs to be robust or it risks two show stoppers (divisive conflicts and unmanageable internal differences). As each strategy attends to these interactions with the other strategy, it will change in form and focus.

For example, when the QWL effort at Packard Electric encountered the early test event of work being moved to Mexico, the joint steering committee proved an effective forum to discuss this divisive issue. The result was an agreement to build the branch plants, which had a different wage scale and flexible work rules. If the divisive issue had not been successfully handled it would have undermined the success of the QWL effort. Yet, in addressing the issue, the focus of the joint activities expanded well beyond the off-line, group problem solving that had been the primary feature of the initiative.

Combined Lesson 4: The successful juxtaposition of forcing and fostering drives changes in organizational structure and operations—so anticipate new organizational forms. Considering the various combinations of forcing and fostering that are possible, the most challenging task is to create approaches and structures that allow distributive activities to take place within a fostering regime.

The resolution of differences in the context of a fostering strategy occurs at both interpersonal and institutional levels. At the interpersonal level, it is important to facilitate the clarification of core interests and the surfacing of underlying feelings and values. In this way, conflict is seen as legitimately deriving from the exploration of interests and hence appropriate even in the midst of joint brainstorming and other collaborative activities.

At the institutional level, management and union leaders can make available multiple avenues for surfacing and addressing complaints. These can include formal grievance procedures, open-door policies to reach top executives, regular skip-level meetings, confidential suggestion/complaint boxes, and the offices of an ombudsperson. Within the union, the presence of a similar range of forums for meaningful debate among subgroups can be extremely important.

Combinations of forcing and fostering thus illustrate the dynamic nature of negotiated change. Not only are the negotiations over substantive change, but the process of discussing these issues also changes the relationship and the organizations involved. Ultimately, it is a challenge of never ending adaptation. Relations are either improved or compromised by the way the forcing and the fostering strategies are implemented—there is no middle ground.

Since both forcing and fostering strategies are usually necessary to achieve both substantive and relationship changes, it is essential for the parties, especially management, to anticipate—indeed plan for—an effective sequence or combination of the key strategies.

It is interesting to note that management's planning seldom looked beyond the extant strategy. Even in our three forcing-followed-by-fostering cases, at least two of them developed along these lines based on a perceived need for fostering that developed only after the forcing episode was completed.

Similarly, in the cases where management used fostering as the first major change initiative, management seemed to suspend any idea it would also have to engage in forcing.

Simple Reminders to Guide Strategic Negotiations

As forcing and fostering become intertwined, the guidance necessary for success becomes similar for each strategy. Certain tactics and behaviors turn out to be equally critical for both fostering and forcing. These insights are captured in the following table, which identifies helpful tactics and simple reminders for negotiators.

Useful Tactics and Simple Reminders

Useful tactics	Simple reminders
Data collection and analysis:	*Do your homework*
Interest-based assessment:	*Be realistic*
Targeting the issues:	*Don't be greedy—be constructive*
Bargaining over how to bargain:	*Negotiate the "rules of the game"*
Education within and across:	*Explain why*
Constancy of purpose:	*Don't give up on core values and principles*
Feedback and adjustment:	*Learn from experience and celebrate success*

To fully explain the logic underlying the recommendations in this table, each tactic and simple reminder is addressed below.

Data Collection and Analysis: Do your homework.

The first tactical move—prior to either forcing or fostering—is data collection and analysis. Initially, the data collection is wideranging so as to help guide the development of the change agenda. Here parties should refrain from just focusing on what they think are the issues, but instead develop many channels for input. This avoids centering forcing or fostering efforts on what may turn out to be symptoms, rather than root causes.

As a forcing or fostering initiative unfolds, additional data collection and analysis is required. In these cases, the data are more narrowly focused on the particular issues that have emerged. While the early data collection and analysis serves to prevent overly rapid narrowing of focus, later data collection and analysis serves to ensure that negotiations are not proceeding on unchecked assumptions.

Thus, our simple reminder is to "do your homework." We might also remind negotiators to "get your ducks in a row." The point seems obvious, but it is not possible to restrain forcing or to ensure robust forcing without adequate data collection and analysis.

Interest-Based Assessment: Be realistic.

Effective data collection and analysis begin to surface deeper understandings about priorities and those of the counterparts. We recommend pushing those understandings further into a formal interest-based assessment (Fisher and Ury 1991). That is, any party contemplating a forcing or fostering change initiative should fully examine its own interests and those of the parties with whom it is negotiating.

Examining interests results in the parties becoming less focused on positions. Becoming too focused on positions and being inattentive to the other side's interests can lead to uncontrolled forcing. Similarly, in fostering, becoming too focused on positions can create unrealistic or rigid expectations on the part of principals and constituents, while being inattentive to the other side's interests makes it much harder to anticipate divisive conflicts.

Our advice, then, is to "be realistic." An interest-based analysis can help guide the establishment of realistic aspirations for both forcing and fostering.

Targeting the Issues: Don't be greedy—be constructive.

Prior data collection and analysis, combined with interest-based analysis, offers an effective foundation for formulating the objectives of a forcing or fostering initiative. We urge parties to be clear in the way they express their objectives. Management may want to increase machine up-time, for example, but the message is lost if forcing is centered on working "bell-to-bell."

Targeting does not mean pressing a power advantage. Even if a forcing contest reveals the other side as weaker than anticipated, pushing for more than originally requested creates a legacy of bitterness and mistrust. In fostering, the targeting serves primarily to pace progress and for the lead negotiators to remain aligned with their constituents.

The simple reminder is, "don't be greedy—be constructive." If strategic negotiations go well, be satisfied.

Bargaining Over How to Bargain: Negotiate the "rules of the game."

Traditionally, the "rules of the game" in labor negotiations have been largely tacit. They would only be discussed in the context of perceived inappropriate behavior. By contrast, the pursuit of forcing, fostering, and combined strategies represents an intentional effort to change the way negotiations occur. Our recommendation is that such changes should not be made unilaterally. Instead, we urge parties to build their skills and capabilities to bargain effectively over how they want to bargain.

So much of our upbringing and early educational experiences teach the exact opposite message—to follow the rules of the game and not question authority. Even when faced with unconstructive rules, it is not always natural or instinctive for parties to focus on the renegotiation of these rules. Further, negotiating over the rules of the game is a high-stakes process, since these new rules then provide a framework for subsequent interactions. Difficult as it is, however, bargaining over how to bargain is preferable to the alternative—which is trying to achieve desired ends via a bargaining process that is limited in its scope, focus, or structure.

Education Within and Across: Explain why

Being able to explain the reasons for a strategic initiative is critical for forcing or fostering. It may seem ironic that a forcing party would have to explain itself, but we have seen that such justifications can temper an escalating conflict and aid the reestablishment of regular operations. Education in the fostering case is especially critical to help manage internal differences that might otherwise derail the initiative.

Remembering to "explain why" is the key. Other parties may disagree and oppose the proposals for change. However, the interaction may lead to reflection and adjustment. Even where adjustment is not required, however, explaining "why" helps to keep the forcing restrained, while ensuring that the fostering will be robust.

In several instances the prospect of losing a major chunk of business provided such a required justification. Merely promulgating information about what management perceives as compelling circumstances for change, however, does not guarantee that the recipients of this information will accept the proposed changes as justifiable. In some cases, rational arguments appeared to fall on deaf ears. For example, AP Parts attempted to use the leverage of a new contract with Ford to secure important changes in operating practices. The explanations have to be believed by the stakeholders.

Education also serves the purpose of achieving internal alignment. Negotiations, of any variety, do not occur unconnected to constituents, who have important stakes in the outcomes. Consequently, it is especially important to ensure that the internal negotiations are coordinated with developments at the institutional level. To the extent that the parties are able to reach agreement and bridge their respective interests, and possibly even enhance working relations as a result, then these accomplishments need to be shared with all concerned. Developing a track record wherein a combination of forcing and fostering strategies serves the needs of the parties for dealing with key agenda items can develop competencies and support for realizing change on a continuing basis.

Constancy of Purpose: Don't give up on core values and principles

Constancy of purpose has been highlighted by Dr. Deming (1986) in his recommendations for effective management. We extend this idea to the negotiations arena. Parties who are initiating either a forcing or a fostering campaign must be prepared to stay the course. It is essential, however, that the "course" be determined on the basis of data collection and analysis, interest-based assessment, targeted issues, and extensive education (within and across the organizations).

In the absence of a proper foundation, the forcing or fostering activities may be poorly focused. The change efforts may be centered on positions that address symptoms, rather than root causes. In such cases, constancy of purpose can turn into debilitating inflexibility. Constancy of purpose thus involves being clear and firm regarding core values and principles, but being flexible in their application.

Thus, a key recommendation to the strategic negotiator is, "Don't give up on core values and principles." Half-hearted support for the initiative or shifting objectives will undermine both forcing and fostering strategies. Our caution here, however, is to ensure that the constancy of purpose is centered on core values and principles, linked to a well-constructed strategy.

Feedback and Adjustment: Learn from experience and celebrate success

Even with the best preparations, unanticipated or pivotal events arise in the course of a change initiative. Consequently, an effective process includes mechanisms for ongoing feedback and adjustment.

When there are shifts in either forcing or fostering initiatives, they should be guided by all of the above recommendations. That is, a shift in approach should be driven by data collection and analysis, be guided by an interest-based assessment, involve a retargeting of the issues, be accompanied by extensive education (within and across), and represent true constancy of purpose (rather than inflexible adherence to an early stance).

Celebrating success is a critical form of feedback. Such celebrations send powerful signals about the aims and outcomes that are valued. This, in turn, enables others to learn from the experience.

Conclusion

Clearly, negotiated change is a dynamic process. We have found that forcing strategies are most effective when they are restrained—which requires constant attention and adjustment. We have also found that fostering strategies are most effective when they are robust—which also requires constant attention and learning. A strategic negotiator may not anticipate every event that arises along the path of change, but it is essential to anticipate the inevitable interweaving of forcing and fostering strategies. Remember: Do your homework. Be realistic. Don't be greedy—be constructive. Negotiate the "rules of the game." Explain why. Don't give up on core values and principles. Learn from experience and celebrate success.

NOTES

1.The concept of robust fostering is distinct from, but consistent with the Robust Unionism urged by Arthur Shostack.

2. Alternatively, a party will force when it sees itself as having no other alternative—though even here it is rare that forcing will be initiated by a party that expects to lose.

References

Cutcher-Gershenfeld, Joel E. 1988. "Tracing a Transformation in Industrial Relations: The Case of Xerox Corporation and ACTWU." Bureau of Labor-Management Relations Bulletin 138.

Cutcher-Gershenfeld, Joel E., Thomas Kochan, and Anil Verma. 1991. "Recent Developments in U.S. Employee Involvement Initiatives: Erosion or Diffusion?" In *Advances in Industrial and Labor Relations*, vol. 5, Donna Sockell, David Lewin, and David B. Lipsky, eds. Greenwich, CT: JAI Press.

Cutcher-Gershenfeld, Joel E., Robert B. McKersie, and Kirstin Weaver. 1988. "The Changing Role of Union Leaders." U.S. Department of Labor, BMLR 127.

Deming, W. Edwards. 1986. *Out of the Crisis.* Cambridge, MA: MIT Center for Advanced Engineering.

Dunlop, John. 1958. *Industrial Relations Systems.* New York: Henry Holt.

Fisher, Robert, and William Ury. 1991. *Getting to YES: Negotiation Without Giving In,* 2d ed. New York: Penguin.

Goldberg, Susan Galoway. 1990. "CSX and the Railway Unions: In Search of New Solutions." U.S. Department of Labor, Bureau of Labor-Management Relations and Cooperative Programs.

Herzenberg, Stephen (with Joel E. Cutcher-Gershenfeld and John Chalykoff). 1988. "Labor-Management Conflict and Cooperation: The Role of Shop Floor Leaders." U.S. Department of Labor, BLMR 131.

Ichniowski, Casey. 1986a. "The Effects of Grievance Activity on Productivity," *Industrial and Labor Relations Review* 40 (October).

_____ . 1986b. "The Impact of a Team Concept." Unpublished manuscript.

Kochan, Thomas. 1980. *Collective Bargaining and Industrial Relations.* Homewood, IL: Richard D. Irwin.

Kochan, Thomas, Saul Rubenstein, and Michael Bennett. 1994. "The Saturn Partnership: Co-Management and the Reinvention of the Local Union." In *Employee Representation: Alternatives and Future Directions,* Bruce Kaufman and Morris Kleiner, eds. Madison, WI: Industrial Relations Research Association.

Lewin, Kurt. 1951. *Field Theory in Social Science.* New York: Harper and Row.

McKersie, Robert B., and L.C. Hunter. 1973. *Pay, Productivity and Collective Bargaining.* London: Macmillan.

Mohrman, S.A. 1987. "A Case of Union-Management Cooperation: A Contextual Presentation," *Consultation* 6, 1 (Spring).

Murphy, Thomas P. 1988. "Partners in Progress: Employee Involvement Between the Budd Company and Local 757 and Local 813 of the United Auto Workers in Philadelphia." Pennsylvania Department of Labor and Industry, Harrisburg, PA.

Walton, Richard E., Joel E. Cutcher-Gershenfeld, and Robert B. McKersie. 1994. *Strategic Negotiations: A Theory and Change in Labor-Management Relations.* Boston: Harvard Business School Press.

Walton, Richard E., and Robert B. McKersie. 1993. *A Behavioral Theory of Labor Negotiations,* 2d ed. Ithaca, NY: ILR Press.

INDEX

About the Institute

The W.E. Upjohn Institute for Employment Research is a nonprofit research organization devoted to finding and promoting solutions to employment-related problems at the national, state, and local level. It is an activity of the W.E. Upjohn Unemployment Trustee Corporation, which was established in 1932 to administer a fund set aside by the late Dr. W.E. Upjohn, founder of The Upjohn Company, to seek ways to counteract the loss of employment income during economic downturns.

The Institute is funded largely by income from the W.E. Upjohn Unemployment Trust, supplemented by outside grants, contracts, and sales of publications. Activities of the Institute are comprised of the following elements: (1) a research program conducted by a resident staff of professional social scientists; (2) a competitive grant program, which expands and complements the internal research program by providing financial support to researchers outside the Institute; (3) a publications program, which provides the major vehicle for the dissemination of research by staff and grantees, as well as other selected work in the field; and (4) an Employment Management Services division, which manages most of the publicly funded employment and training programs in the local area.

The broad objectives of the Institute's research, grant, and publication programs are to: (1) promote scholarship and experimentation on issues of public and private employment and unemployment policy; and (2) make knowledge and scholarship relevant and useful to policymakers in their pursuit of solutions to employment and unemployment problems.

Current areas of concentration for these programs include: causes, consequences, and measures to alleviate unemployment; social insurance and income maintenance programs; compensation; workforce quality; work arrangements; family labor issues; labor-management relations; and regional economic development and local labor markets.